D0942581

Sports Psychology in Performance

Sports Psychology in Performance

Edited by:

Richard J. Butler

PhD, MSc, BSc, AFBPsS, CPsychol

Consultant Clinical Psychologist, Leeds Community and Mental Health Services (NHS) Trust; Honorary Lecturer, University of Leeds; Visiting Research Fellow in Sports Science, Chichester Institute of Higher Education, UK

Butterworth-Heinemann
Linacre House, Jordan Hill, Oxford OX2 8DP
225 Wildwood Avenue, Woburn, MA 01801-2041
A division of Reed Educational and Professional Publishing Ltd

☁ A member of the Reed Elsevier plc group

OXFORD   BOSTON   JOHANNESBURG
MELBOURNE   NEW DELHI   SINGAPORE

First published 1997
Reprinted 1998

© Reed Educational and Professional Publishing Ltd 1997

All rights reserved. No part of this publication may be reproduced in
any aterial form (including photocopying or storing in any medium by
electronic means and whether or not transiently or incidentally to some
other use of this publication) without the written permission of the
copyright holder except in accordance with the provisions of the Copyright,
Designs and Patents Act 1988 or under the terms of a licence issued by the
Copyright Licensing Agency Ltd, 90 Tottenham Court Road, London,
England W1P 9HE. Application for the copyright holder's written
permission to reproduce any part of this publication should be addressed
to the publishers

British Library Cataloguing in Publication Data
Sports psychology in performance
   1. Sports - Great Britain - Psychological aspects
   I. Butler, Richard J. (Richard Joseph)
   796'.01'0941

ISBN 0 7506 2437 X

Library of Congress Cataloguing in Publication Data
Sports psychology in performance/edited by Richard J. Butler
   p. cm.
   Includes bibliographical references and index.
   ISBn 0 7506 2437 X
   1. Sports - Psychological aspects.   I. Butler, Richard J.
   GV706.4.S6816   96-51509
   796'.01-dc21   CIP

Origination by David Gregson Associates, Beccles, Suffolk
Printed and bound in Great Britain by Biddles Ltd, Guildford and King's Lynn

What deeply affects every aspect of a man's experience of the world is his perception that things could be otherwise.

Michael Frayn

Contents

Part Four

Contributors

Stephen J. Bull, BEd, MA, PhD is a Principal Lecturer and Course Leader for sport and exercise science at the University of Brighton. He was Headquarters Psychologist for the Great Britain Team at the 1994 Winter Olympic Games in Lillehammer and is a member of the British Olympic Association (BOA) Psychology Advisory Group. He is a qualified Senior Coach with the National Cricket Association and is consultant to the England Women's Cricket Team and the British Ski Team. He is co-author of *Play Better Cricket* and *The Mental Game Plan* and editor of *Sport Psychology: A self-help guide.*

Richard J. Butler, PhD, MSc, BSc, AFBPsS, C.Psychol is a Consultant Clinical Psychologist with the Leeds Community and Mental Health Services (NHS) Trust, Honorary Lecturer at the University of Leeds, and Visiting Research Fellow in Sports Science at the Chichester Institute of Higher Education. He has conducted extensive research into the cognitive effects of amateur boxing, and since 1987 has been the psychologist to the Amateur Boxing Association. He is a founder member of the BOA's Psychology Steering Group and Psychology Advisory Group. Richard was HQ psychologist for the Great Britain Team at the 1992 Summer Olympics in Barcelona. He is the author of the recent book *Sports Psychology in Action* and is proud to support his boyhood football team Huddersfield Town.

Richard Cox, MEd, PhD, C.Psychol, AFBPsS is Lecturer in Psychology at Moray House Institute, Heriot Watt University, Edinburgh and staff tutor for the National Coaching Foundation. He is a consultant in sports psychology to three governing bodies of sport in Scotland and member of the BOA Psychology Advisory Group. Richard has written widely on the subject of psychological preparation for competition and is currently a member of the Editorial Board for the International Journal of Sport Psychology. He attended the 1992 Summer Olympics in Barcelona as psychologist to the Great Britain Swimming Team.

Peter Galvin, BA, PGCE, MEd(Psychology), MSc is an Educational Psychologist. For the last ten years he has been involved in research and development in schools in the area of discipline and behaviour.

He has been particularly concerned with looking at how schools develop an ethos which underpins a whole school approach to discipline and behaviour. He has applied his findings about how schools operate as organizations and the effects the organization has on behaviour to amateur sports clubs. He is author of a number of articles, chapters and books in the area of behaviour and discipline including *Building a Better Behaved School* published in 1991. He is currently working in New Zealand.

Tim Holder, BSc(Hons) studied Human Movement Studies at St Mary's College, Strawberry Hill, and since graduating in 1989 has been the psychological advisor to the English Table Tennis Association. He is currently studying for a PhD at the Chichester Institute of Higher Education where he is a postgraduate demonstrator working on the Sports Studies degree programme.

John Kremer, BSc, PhD, AFBPsS is a Reader in Social Psychology at The Queen's University of Belfast where he has taught since 1980. His research interests have ranged across applied social psychology, including group dynamics, leadership and the relationship between gender, exercise and psychological well-being. Over recent years John has developed a number of sport consultancies with a range of sports including athletics, golf, rugby, hockey, weightlifting and soccer.

Ian Maynard, BEd, MA, PhD is Senior Lecturer in Sport Psychology and Physical Education at the Chichester Institute of Higher Education. Previously a teacher of physical education, Ian studied at the University of Victoria in British Columbia. He played rugby union, soccer and cricket to county level and currently coaches the Sussex County Senior Rugby Union Team. He is Consultant Sport Psychologist to the Royal Yachting Association, English Table Tennis Association and the All England Women's Lacrosse Association and Richmond Rugby Football Club. Ian is a member of the BOA Psychology Advisory Group and attended the 1992 Summer Olympics in Barcelona as psychologist to the Royal Yachting Association.

Brian P. Miller, BEd, MA is currently the Consultant Sports Psychologist to the BOA. From 1984 to 1988 he was an applied sport psychologist at the Australian Institute of Sport in Canberra. Brian has worked as a team psychologist at four Olympic Games, two

Commonwealth Games and three World Student Games. In a career spanning 16 years he has worked with Olympic gold medallists from four sports and medallists from a further three sports. Brian is currently Team Psychologist with the British Rowing Team.

Sheellagh Rodgers, BSc, MSc works as a Consultant Clinical Psychologist in York. She previously worked with the Department of Health and Social Security and was a police inspector with the Royal Hong Kong Police Force. Although she has worked with other athletes, since 1990 she has primarily worked with the British Ice Figure Skating Squad. A badminton and squash player to county standard, Sheelagh is a runner, preferring distances longer than the marathon, and once held the record for the world's highest and lowest marathon. She is also a member of the BOA's Psychology Advisory Group.

Denis Salter, BSc, MSc is a Consultant Clinical Psychologist and Honorary Clinical Research Fellow at the University of Leicester. Previously he carried out clinical research with the Medical Research Council at the University of Edinburgh, and became interested in the psychological aspects of sport whilst a Fellow in Therapeutic Psychology. His work with athletes includes members of the British Orienteering Squad, track and field athletes, golfers, tennis players and competitive rock climbers. He is currently investigating psychological factors in the rehabilitation of elite athletes with physical injuries. Denis has represented various universities in cross country running and currently orienteers, plays basketball and badminton at club level while pursuing the ultimate backhand in tennis.

Deirdre Scully, BEd(Hons), MSc, PhD is a Lecturer in the Department of Sport and Leisure Studies at the University of Ulster at Jordanstown. She obtained her first degree in Physical Education and her MSc and PhD in Sport Psychology from the University of Illinois. Her research interests span a variety of areas including motor development, skill acquisition and applied sport psychology. An accredited sport psychology consultant, Deirdre has gained considerable practical experience across a range of sports including golf, gymnastics, swimming, basketball, athletics and netball.

Carole Seheult is an Accredited Sports Psychologist and Chartered Clinical Psychologist who lives and works in the north east of

England. She is a member of the BOA's Psychology Advisory Group and provides support to the Amateur Fencing Association, the Great Britain Shooting and Field Archery Squads. She previously worked as Senior Lecturer in Sport Psychology at the University of Sunderland but now divides her time between independent practice in clinical sport psychology and working as a Consultant Clinical Psychologist in the NHS. Her current research interests focus on the role of personality and its influence on performance. She is a keen runner and as a result of her research interests has recently taken up fencing.

Peter Terry, BA(Hons), PGCE, MA, PhD is Senior Lecturer in Sport Psychology at Brunel University. He has provided psychological support to the British Olympic Association, Lawn Tennis Association, British Canoe Union, British Bobsleigh Association, Jockey Club, Royal Ballet School and the England Cricket Team. As a consultant he has attended four Olympic Games, eight World Championships and thirteen World Cup events, helping more than 1,000 international and professional performers. A former chairman of the British Association of Sports and Exercise Sciences Sport Psychology section, he is author of over 40 journal articles, books and professional papers. Peter lives in Twickenham with his wife, Sue and son, Dominic.

Acknowledgements

This project has been both inspirational and taxing. The spark of an idea – to compile an account of how psychological theories variously apply and ultimately stand up to the rigours of top level sport – was nurtured and so positively directed by my editor Susan Devlin. Without her encouragement I would metaphorically still be loosening up before the starting blocks.

I am indebted to my colleagues who eagerly agreed to contribute their thoughts and experiences to this volume; and from whose writings I have discovered much to enhance my own sports psychology practice. Myriam Brearley deserves particular mention for coordinating and shaping the manuscript which must at times have seemed distinctly disorganized.

Finally I must thank my wife Sue and three sons Joe, Gregory and Luke who encouraged me, in their different ways, to persist with the venture in the belief that on completion I could free up more time to be with them.

Foreword

Kevin Hickey

Whilst no-one could question the vital role psychology plays in elite performance, the acceptance of the sport psychologist is not as automatic. Not only do some sports argue against the use of sport psychologists, others have contrasting views as to how the psychologist should be used. For a long time it was held by some national coaches that psychology was their exclusive territory. Perhaps they felt that their role was being threatened. Some would refer to statements by world famous athletes, confirming that they never had the need for a sport psychologist.

One would support the statement that, where possible, the psychologist should work through the coach. Indeed, most of the governing body coach education programmes embody an understanding of some of the basic concepts from psychology. Athletic performance at world level is, however, a different matter. The coach must recognize that there are areas of specialism, especially in sports science, which will undoubtedly aid the performer in the world arenas. S/he cannot have sufficient knowledge in all of those areas. To some extent, the coach becomes the filter through which those services are delivered by a specialist. Psychology is arguably the central pillar to these services. The coach-psychologist has to develop a clear understanding of their respective roles and the extent of their responsibilities. An understanding based on mutual respect and confidence should exist in providing a service which is athlete centred and delivered in a sport-specific context.

I met Richard Butler in 1987. I was then preparing the British team for the Seoul Olympic Games, my fifth as a coach. Whilst I had previous positive experience with sports psychology, Richard showed me that there was much more to the science than handling the crisis situation. As our relationship developed, so did his services to the squad and individual boxers. I think that we learnt together the areas that were appropriate for his skills. There is no doubt that he made a significant contribution to the boxers' programme of preparation as well as my development as a coach. Gradually he brought the sport of boxing into many of the areas of psychological support upon which this book is based.

The British Olympic Association (BOA) is arguably the lead body in providing an elite support programme for Olympic athletes. Since the inception of the Psychology Steering Group in 1988, the BOA has shown a recognition of the role of the sport psychologist. Its Psychology Advisory Group runs workshops attended by BOA registered members. Olympic training camps are staffed by psychologists, and the pattern is established for psychologists to attend Olympic Games as HQ staff members. One must also give acknowledgement to the professional underpinning of sport psychology given by the British Association of Sports and Exercise Sciences (BASES), the body which deals with the professional accreditation of sports psychologists. All of the BOA's registered psychologists are BASES accredited.

The exciting part of the future is the unknown. We know that records will continue to be broken; that human performance will achieve new horizons. The question will be whether British athletes are given the opportunity to keep up with the rest of the world. It will require a coordination of all the resources available to British sport. Something that perhaps we have not done well in the past. We have the talent in Britain, but not yet a support structure which reflects a British philosophy and of which success can be expected as a matter of course. Whatever the shape of this model might be, it is certain that sport psychology must play a leading part. The seeds of this future are given within the chapters of this book. They give the experience of some of the leading practitioners in sports psychology in Britain. I would ask all readers to read them with an open mind.

Introduction

'The most important thing of all is your mind set.
Success is not a one-day phenomenon. It is a
conscious effort to pursue excellence all the time.'

Wes Hall

Athletes,* coaches and other individuals with a committed investment
in improving their sporting performances recognize intuitively and
experientially the important role psychology has to play in this
venture. Psychologists, from sometimes remote and uninvolved positions, have sought to understand the psychological determinants of
successful performances. For many years these two perspectives – one
framed as a request for serious involvement, and the other a stance of
scientific respectability – ran like tramlines, in parallel, and with only
a hope of meeting on the horizon.

Recently, over the last decade or so, the two perspectives have
meshed. Psychologists tentatively stepped into the sporting arena,
with their bag of 'mental training' techniques, apprehension about
acceptance, and hesitant questions concerning their role. Athletes and
coaches, many of whom were initially quizzical or openly scathing of
'shrinks' in white coats who were set on disrupting training and
offering analysis of the psyche, discovered with delight that psychological approaches could be successfully applied to improve their
performances.

Applied sports psychology was on its way. The last few years has
seen a dramatic increase in the number of psychologists practising
their wares within sport, a growth well documented in Peter Terry's
chapter.

Sports performance may be conceptualized in terms of six global
yet inter-related factors (Butler, 1996). Figure F.1 illustrates how the
factors – physical, character, psychological, strategy, technical and coordination – fuse together. It also presents some of the attributes
which compose each factor.

Different sports and events vary in the emphasis given to any factor.
English football, for example, has repeatedly been described as relying
on the physical attribute of strength and determination of character.

---

*Athlete is used generically to represent participants across all fields of sport.

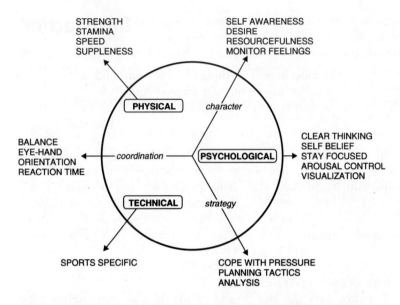

Figure F.1 *A model of attributes necessary for successful performance*

In contrast, football the Ajax way is reliant on technique, intelligence, personality and speed. Individuals will, of course, develop attributes that best serve them within their chosen sport.

Sports psychology has sometimes been viewed synonymously with mental skills training. This is illustrated in the figure with positive 'clear' thinking, self belief (confidence), staying focused, arousal control and visualization being categorized as psychological. These attributes might be construed as the core of sports psychology. The incorporation of such mental skills training into sports psychology practice is described in the chapters by Stephen J. Bull, Richard Cox, Deirdre Scully and John Kremer.

However, psychological processes might be considered to play an influential part in the acquisition of all attributes necessary for successful performance. Thus technique might be enhanced through the employment of visualization, reaction time through biofeedback and knowledge of results, and stamina through goal setting. Sports psychology can thus play a fundamental part in all aspects of performance enhancement.

This book is concerned with how psychology might be employed to enhance sporting performance. Psychology is a broad discipline. It houses many theories and models designed to facilitate a greater understanding of the nature of human actions. Sports psychology equally, and perhaps expectedly, has a broad front. A major theme in collating the chapters for this book has been to capture the varied approaches sports psychologists have adopted, and how they have sought to apply their theoretical standpoints and models to assist athletes in their search for success.

Richard Cox, Deirdre Scully and John Kremer grapple with behavioural and cognitive-behavioural principles wherein behaviour is conceptualized as a product of the environmental experiences impinging upon the person. Help for the athlete emanates from the identification and manipulation of effective reinforcers. Carole Seheult describes a psychodynamic approach, describing subconscious defence mechanisms which are activated when the individual is confronted by situations perceived as anxiety provoking. I adopt some principles embraced by personal construct theory in describing performance profiling. Such a stance proposes that individuals interpret and construe the world in very unique ways, and an understanding of them is best achieved through eliciting how they make sense of events that confront them.

Other guiding and significant psychological models which have been embraced by sport psychologists include attribution theory from which Tim Holder draws widely, Bandura's model of self efficacy which Sheelagh Rodgers incorporates into an understanding of confidence building, and the social psychological principles of group cohesion to which Brian Miller and Stephen J. Bull allude in their chapters.

Whilst models and principles drawn from general psychological theory have proved fertile ground for sport psychologists, Denis Salter cogently argues that the sporting context is unique, and as such sports psychology needs to innovate using this context rather than 'ride on the coat tails of mainstream empirical psychology'. Intriguingly sports psychology is beginning to evolve models from within, models representative of the way individuals act in a sporting environment. The chapters by Ian Maynard and Stephen J. Bull which engage Nideffer's model of attentional style, and Sheelagh Rodgers' incorporation of Butler's model of confidence are examples of this.

Sports psychology is a most compelling applied discipline. The broad front of sports psychology is again evident in the range of applied models which have proved influential in its development. Commercial and industrial psychology have offered an understanding of team effectiveness, which Brian Miller describes in his chapter on team cohesion; clinical psychology has advanced mental skills training, psychometric assessment and mood profiling; educational psychology has seized organizational models to enhance the effectiveness of those working within hierarchical structures, a thesis elaborated in Peter Galvin's chapter.

A leading theme in this book is an exploration of how psychological theories, models and concepts, from wherever they were hatched, projected and developed, are applied in practice. The authors in this book describe, in the main, work undertaken with athletes at the top of their sport. In choosing the elite level the sternest test is provided for the psychological approach. Not only are elite athletes and coaches individuals of a discerning nature, they will, through having to perform regularly in situations of extreme pressure, only accept approaches which serve their purposes effectively.

Each chapter characteristically focuses on how a psychological approach has been applied to one or a selected number of sports. This invites a detailed exposition of the approach, and offers the possibility, with amendments and appropriate adaptations, of evolving the approach to meet the demands of other sports. In this sense the sport is the backcloth on which the applied psychological approach is examined. The sports discussed range across a wide spectrum of individual, team, combat and artistic events. They include amateur boxing, bobsleigh, cricket, cycling, fencing, golf, hockey, ice skating, rowing and table tennis.

The book is divided into four sections.

- Section one covers a range of methods designed to understand the athlete and performance. Peter Terry and Ian Maynard, respectively, describe methods for detecting mood change and attentional shift. I report on how performance profiling – a method by which the athlete's perspective on performance is elicited – is adapted to meet the changing demands of a sport. Finally Tim Holder describes a way, through performance evaluation, of encouraging athletes to monitor their performance.
- Section two is given over to a consideration of specific psychological interventions. Sheelagh Rodgers examines processes which can help facilitate confidence. Brian Miller draws on his experience of three Olympics in analysing the appropriate psychological input for a team.
- Section three depicts different styles of service delivery. Richard Cox illuminates the practice of individual consultation where problem solving strategies come to the fore. Deirdre Scully and

John Kremer describe an educational approach where athletes were exposed to psychological methods over a two day intensive course. Stephen J. Bull outlines the immersion approach where the psychologist lives through training and competition as an integral part of the team. Finally, in this section, Peter Galvin describes a need to work with all aspects of the sports organization – the athlete, coach, support staff and governing body – as the culture of an organization has a powerful effect on the performance of all those working within the organization.

- In section four, there are two contributions which might loosely be construed as more radical. Carole Seheult provides an overview of how particular defence mechanisms might be manifested behaviourally in both adaptive and maladaptive ways. Finally Denis Salter argues the importance of constructing a psychology of sport by valuing our own personal experiences.

Several themes arise repeatedly throughout the chapters. As these surface independently, originate from the application of different psychological models and have been examined under the rigour of high level competition, it suggests these common findings lay the foundations of good practice in applied sports psychology.

Some of the common themes are as follows:

- A move towards tailoring work to individual needs. Deirdre Scully and John Kremer found a request for more individual work following an evaluation of their programme, and Brian Miller, even within the context of teamwork, highlighted the importance of individual performance by commenting that 'when individual efforts are lost in the crowd performances decrease', and he consequently suggests that each member of the team has acknowledged responsibilities.
- Uncertainty over the usefulness of psychometric assessment. During the 1966 World Cup in England it was reported that the Brazilian team's psychologist had all the players draw a figure, and suggested the balance of the team should be determined by these drawings. As Pele and Garrincha's drawings were so poor, the psychologist further suggested these two, indisputably amongst the best players in the world, should not be in the team. Thankfully the psychologist was ignored. Hopefully the employment of psychometric instruments has moved on some way. Peter Terry discusses how one measure, mood profiling, can be helpfully enlisted. In contrast Deirdre Scully and John Kremer make the point that all

the psychometric measures they employed proved to be no more use than individual interviews, an impression echoed by Ian Maynard who feels psychometric assessment can be useful as a starting point in developing rapport with athletes. Richard Cox is categorical in asserting that questionnaires fail to assist the psychologist to understand the athlete's problem, and Stephen J. Bull queries the appropriateness of using assessments in his style of working with teams. What emerges with clarity, however, from the debate is the inappropriateness of advocating the results of any psychological assessment for the purpose of selection.

- The need to integrate psychological approaches into an already full training schedule, so that they are not perceived by the athlete and coach as threatening but as ways of facilitating performance enhancement.
- The desirability of becoming a member of the team. This enhances rapport and credibility, enables on site evaluation of any interventions that have been developed or suggested, and hopefully invalidates any mystique that can accompany the profession. Fascinatingly, becoming a member of the team can mean 'mucking in' and taking on tasks perhaps not at first considered part of psychological practice. Both Stephen J. Bull in undertaking video tasks and Richard Cox becoming the caddie for the golfer he worked with, admirably reflect this aspect of applied sports psychology which is now accepted as part of what is required to be successful.

Applying psychological principles and theories to the sporting context has come a long way. There is a general acceptance now that psychological approaches can make a positive contribution to performance enhancement and the credibility 'hurdle' has largely been overcome. Many of the chapters in this book emphatically assert this position. What is equally exciting is the growing interest in enlisting psychology as a vehicle for addressing a vast array of other issues pertinent to sport. The contributions in this book hint at the directions and potential psychology has to offer sport. The success of the book lies in inviting the reader to consider fresh and invigorating ideas to apply to their sport.

Richard Butler

Reference

Butler, R.J. (1996) *Sports Psychology in Action*, Oxford: Butterworth-Heinemann.

Part One

1

The application of mood profiling with elite sports performers

Peter Terry

Sports: Tennis, Bobsleigh, Canoeing, Cricket

Introduction

Sports psychology in Great Britain has enjoyed a boom period over the past decade. The 1980s witnessed almost linear growth in the use of sports psychology consultants by National Governing Bodies (Figure 1.1), while literature on the subject has expanded many-fold.

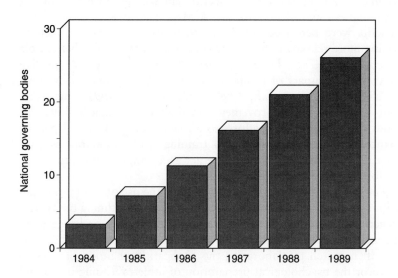

Figure 1.1 *Growth of National Governing Bodies utilizing psychological support 1984–1989 (Terry and Harrold, 1990)*

Hardly a week goes by without some newspaper report appearing in which sports psychology is credited with helping, or in some cases failing to help, a prominent performer to sporting achievement. The vast majority of literature on mental training supports its efficacy, but too often such judgments emanate from sport psychologists who present minimal empirical support, or are based upon anecdotal evidence from athletes and coaches. Conceptual models for the delivery, and particularly the evaluation, of mental training programmes have been largely overlooked in the rush to claim a bit of reflected glory.

Despite the bias inherent in subjective self-assessments of mental training effectiveness, there does appear to be a growing body of empirical evidence to support its use. Objective evaluations of mental training have demonstrated its effectiveness in lowering anxiety amongst elite junior skiers (Hellstedt, 1987) and collegiate gymnasts (Elko and Ostrow, 1991), enhancing imagery ability in figure skaters (Rodgers *et al.*, 1991), advancing imagery ability, relaxation, and attentional control in young tennis players (Terry, 1995a), and improving table tennis performance in 7–10 year olds (Li-Wei *et al.*, 1992).

By contrast, the addition of mental training to the usual regime of technical training did not significantly enhance performance among adult equestrian riders (Fitzpatrick, 1993) although several other benefits were perceived by the participants in this study, such as feeling more relaxed in life, more organized in their jobs, better able to concentrate, and better able to prepare for events. A positive motivational impact of mental training has been proposed by some practitioners (Cohn *et al.*, 1990; Rodgers *et al.*, 1991) suggesting that if athletes see improvements in their psychological skills this tends to encourage their efforts to achieve improved overall performance. A programme of mental training which monitors psychological development may therefore act as an important precursor to performance enhancement.

The purpose of this chapter is to first set the use of mental training with elite performers into an overall framework, outlining the typical structure and content of mental training programmes, and suggesting a general model for interacting with athletes and coaches. The focus will then switch to elaborating the application of mood profiles to monitor the psychological preparation of athletes leading up to and during major international competition.

General strategy for mental training

A programme of mental training should be guided by some underlying structure. Most proposed structures include formal or informal
assessment, a period of education during which psychological skills
are developed, and strategies for implementing psychological skills
during competition. To direct my work with performers, a five phase
model for mental training is utilized, including assessment, education,
implementation, problem solving, and evaluation (Figure 1.2).

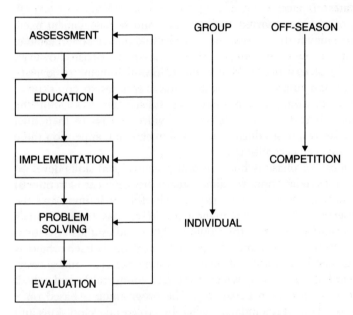

Figure 1.2   *General strategy for mental training programmes*

Inherent in this model is a general tendency away from group
strategies and towards individualization as the programme
progresses. Similarly, the programme tends to focus on implementation and problem solving during competition periods, whereas assessment and education tend to take place during periods of little
competitive activity. It could be said, therefore, that the model
proposes a periodized structure whereby mental training parallels and
becomes integrated with an athlete's physical and technical preparation schedule.

The assessment phase may include psychometric testing, semi-structured interviews, self-assessment and performance observation. Psychometric testing, the justification for which is an enduring point of contention among applied sport psychologists, is employed primarily to individualize the programme towards specific needs rather than to make predictions about performance. It has been argued that the lack of reliable relationships between trait measures and athletic performance effectively negates their use in applied settings. However, tests which provide a simple but often revealing 'snapshot' of an individual help to identify areas where education may have greatest impact.

This process is supported by interviews and self-assessment exercises which may further reveal the attitudes and mindset of an athlete. The most revealing component of the assessment phase, however, tends to be observation during competition. This helps to identify productive and unproductive behavioural responses to competitive situations, providing key pointers for subsequent phases of the programme. If a performer sits through video replays of their own unproductive responses during critical moments in competition there is often enhanced commitment to change.

The education phase is built around psychological skills development such as relaxation training, stress management, attentional control training, motivation strategies, self-efficacy training and the use of imagery. These may be taught in group sessions, but individuals are encouraged to monitor their own progress and establish personal objectives for the development of psychological skills. Each athlete is usually exposed to a range of mental training exercises and encouraged to utilize those with which they feel comfortable and which prove effective for them personally. The programme is based on a principle of planned redundancy, whereby athletes develop skills and knowledge which facilitate independence from the sport psychologist.

Although the education phase equips athletes with practical techniques to, for instance, maintain calm or energize or mentally rehearse, it is not seen as the central thrust of the programme. In isolation, knowledge of psychological skills may serve to confuse rather than clarify, and experience suggests that the key phase involves helping athletes to implement this knowledge effectively in practice or competition.

The implementation phase revolves around the integration of learned mental skills into routines for pre-competition preparation and other situations which have a critical impact upon performance.

It is common for the robustness of these routines to be put to the test in various simulation exercises. For example, biofeedback techniques may be utilized to assess relaxation ability when time stressors are imposed, such as 'You have 20 seconds to lower your arousal level (galvanic skin response) by 50 points (scale 0–1000)'. This exercise simulates the task of regaining composure after a frustrating incident. It also develops greater self-awareness of emotional arousal. Simulation exercises follow the overload principle, in that an athlete's capacity to produce an effective response is developed by being exposed to progressively more demanding situations.

The problem solving phase is based around individual counselling sessions. Every athlete involved is encouraged to be proactive in dealing with performance-related issues and to initiate one-to-one sessions to prevent rather than to cure problems. When a problem is identified, an athlete is guided towards a solution which is implemented during practice or competition and its effectiveness evaluated at the next meeting. Support at major competitions is provided to contribute to last minute 'fine tuning' and occasionally to intervene during crises of confidence.

The evaluation phase should actually be more of an ongoing process than a phase. At any stage in the programme, ongoing evaluation may dictate that additional assessment of a psychological characteristic is necessary, or that learning a new technique would be beneficial, or that developing a novel way to implement an existing psychological skill is required. When it comes down to more formal evaluation of a mental training programme, it is recommended that at least four sources of feedback are utilized: objective data, athlete feedback, coach feedback, and feedback from a sport psychologist (not necessarily the one delivering the programme).

Interaction models for dealing with elite performers

The success or failure of psychological interventions with sports performers depends greatly upon the interaction style adopted by the sport psychologist. Athletes and coaches are usually pragmatic, and occasionally cynical, in their approach to innovation. They do not respond enthusiastically for any length of time to an approach which relies heavily on 'this is a scientifically proven fact' or 'this is the way it should be done'. Hence, if a sport psychologist sets himself or herself up as some sort of guru passing down tablets of wisdom they

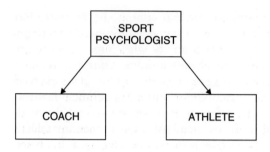

Figure 1.3 *Interaction model 'Mount Sinai'*

will lose credibility as soon as an ineffective piece of advice reveals their fallibility. This 'Mount Sinai' approach (Figure 1.3) may be especially tempting on those occasions when the client's opening line is, 'I need you to tell me what to do'. A response along the lines of, 'I can't teach you anything about your sport, I can only help you learn how to get the best out of yourself' helps to establish a more realistic set of expectations from the outset.

It is not uncommon in elite sport for coaches to zealously guard direct contact between sport psychologist and performers, preferring instead to 'filter' advice and pass on what they consider appropriate (Figure 1.4). Sometimes this is a wise precaution, especially where the coach has been successful with a particular performer. After all, why should a coach share his or her influence with an outsider, particularly one whose opening gambit may be to initiate change? A valuable principle to bear in mind is the need to work *with* the coach and *through* the coach. Fears of their position being undermined may perhaps be seen as paranoia on the part of the coach, but it is indicative of the need to develop trust between coach and sport psychologist.

Figure 1.4 *Interaction model 'Psst! pass it on'*

Often many aspects of mental training, such as simple relaxation exercises or imagery training, can be delivered effectively (perhaps *more* effectively) via the coach, and certainly it is advantageous to get the coach involved. However, coaches should be educated to the fact that it is not possible to condense the expertise gained over years of training to become a sport psychologist into a few self-help lessons, and there are times when 'hands on' rather than 'arms length' involvement is necessary. Also, there are many occasions when an athlete welcomes the opportunity to discuss issues, problems as they see them, which pertain directly to their relationship with the coach.

Such occasions sometimes place the sport psychologist in the position of 'go between' (Figure 1.5) expected on one side to 'find out' things for the coach and on the other to 'negotiate' with the coach on behalf of the athlete. This position clearly throws up ethical considerations, not only in terms of confidentiality but also about who exactly is the client, the athlete or the one paying the fee (usually the governing body). A solution to this dilemma, which happens more frequently that one would hope despite efforts to avoid it, is to withdraw to the position of 'facilitator' (Figure 1.6) setting up situations where issues of potential conflict between coach(es) and athlete(s) can be resolved amicably, or hopefully prevented through regular constructive dialogue. Establishing the ground rules for such discussions is a very common function for the sports psychology practitioner.

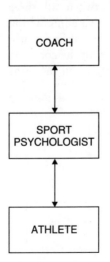

Figure 1.5 *Interaction model 'The go between'*

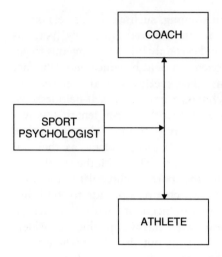

Figure 1.6   *Interaction model 'The facilitator'*

The most desirable position to establish for interacting with athletes and coaches is the model of equal expertise (Butler, 1989) (Figure 1.7) where the sport psychologist provides a support service, ensuring that the athlete feels independent and the coach's sense of primacy remains secure. Two-way interaction between all three parties is essential, with the coach supportive that private interaction between sport psychologist and athlete is both beneficial and confidential. In effect, the sport psychologist becomes part of the coaching team, a development which is signified most directly when the same

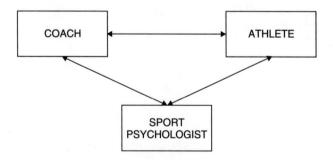

Figure 1.7   *Interaction model 'Equal expertise'*

uniform is worn, the same activities shared, the same sacrifices made. One of the most effective means of becoming part of the team is to show willingness to perform menial tasks around the training environment. This never goes unnoticed and usually enhances the closeness of working relationships.

Funding for a sports psychology programme tends to be provided either by the governing body of a sport or requires governing body approval if funding comes from an outside agency. Therefore, the relationship between sport psychologist and governing body is an important issue in the delivery of mental training. The interaction model presented in Figure 1.8 illustrates the need for a sport psychologist to understand the requirements of the organization for which they are working. This involves taking the time to understand the structure and function of the governing body, and its relationship with coaches and athletes in the sport. It usually involves keeping the governing body informed about the progress of the psychological programme via regular reports and recommendations. Often the sport psychologist is valued for their position of informed objectivity, and functions not unlike a management consultant, advising on procedures, on education programmes, or on team-building activities.

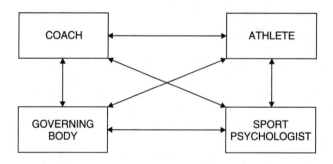

Figure 1.8   *Interaction model 'The complete picture'*

Overall, the sport psychologist's role should be seen as one of broad involvement, where commitment to the sport and the individuals concerned is demonstrated by perhaps being available over and above the time contracted, and by being proactive in presenting ideas for improvement. To gain the trust and respect of athletes their interests should always be put first, with the most basic indicator of whether a sport psychologist is doing a good job being if they are perceived as being a 'good person to have around'. This means that in the competition environment, the sport psychologist must provide the coolest head and be positive and enthusiastic in dealing with problems.

The general strategy for mental training which has been presented has emphasized that psychometric testing has a part to play. Many sport psychologists find that as their experience grows they rely less on a full range of formal tests and adopt a more intuitive approach supported by perhaps one or two psychometric tests which they find especially useful. My own experiences, working with more than 1000 international performers in nearly 30 sports, has drawn me progressively towards mood profiling as a worthwhile application.

Review of literature on mood profiling in sport

The link between mood and sport performance has a strong intuitive appeal among both athletes and researchers. It is common for athletes to attribute poor performance to their failure to 'get in the right mood', while researchers in sports psychology have strived to unravel the complexities of mood–performance relationships. The use of mood profiling in sport was pioneered by William Morgan and a number of associates (Nagle *et al.*, 1975; Morgan and Pollock, 1977; Morgan and Johnson, 1978). To assess mood state among athletes, Morgan utilized the Profile of Mood States (POMS) (McNair *et al.*, 1971) a 65-item questionnaire which summarizes mood on the subscales of tension, depression, anger, vigour, fatigue, and confusion. Morgan proposed the desirability of the 'Iceberg' profile, combining above average vigour with below average scores on the other five mood scales and popularized such a profile as the 'Test of Champions' (Morgan, 1980).

A recent scientific review (Renger, 1993) is critical of Morgan's work on methodological grounds and highlights the confusion surrounding the use of POMS in sport. Renger maintains that mood profile research has focused on two central issues, differentiation between athletes of varying achievement levels and differentiation of the athlete from the non-athlete. In respect of the first issue, studies in basketball (Craighead *et al.*, 1986), football (Daiss *et al.*, 1986) and marathon running (Durtschi and Weiss, 1986; Frazier, 1988) provide compelling evidence that POMS does not differentiate between elite and non-elite performers on the basis of cross-sectional comparisons.

This would appear to be the case regardless of how the construct of 'elite performer' is operationalized.

It is reasonable to assume that variations in physical functioning, such as skill and fitness levels, will contribute more to sporting achievement than will variations in mood, and from the work of Silva *et al.* (1981) it is apparent that physiological measures have greater discriminatory power than psychological profiles even among physiologically homogeneous samples. Hence, where physical variations are substantial, it is entirely unreasonable to expect mood to predict achievement.

As far as discriminating between athlete and non-athlete is concerned, variations in physical functioning will be even greater and hence the same argument would tend to apply. However, it is well established that many types of physical activity have mood-enhancing effects (Berger *et al.*, 1993) and therefore, if this is the more powerful moderating variable, differential mood profiles could be anticipated between active and inactive populations. Significant mood differences between active and sedentary samples were demonstrated by Cockerill *et al.* (1990) and indeed a substantial number of the athletic samples reviewed by LeUnes, *et al.* (1988) displayed 'Iceberg' profiles. By definition such profiles represent variations from tables of normative data, which are derived from the general, largely non-athletic, population (McNair *et al.*, 1971).

While the balance of evidence may point to athletic populations showing more positive mood profiles, a research paradigm which searches for cross-sectional differences in state measures between groups without setting the state measurement in some situational context, such as prior to a sport contest or a business presentation, is effectively treating the construct as though it were a stable disposition. It could be argued that both research issues identified by Renger (1993) may be tainted by the tendency of researchers to treat mood as a stable disposition and to assume that high performance athletes somehow have a monopoly on positive moods. More pertinent research issues may be to assess the discriminatory power of POMS within homogenous groups and to investigate how *intra-individual* mood fluctuations are related to fluctuations in individual performance.

In those studies which have investigated the predictive capability of mood profiles among athletic samples which were homogeneous in skill level and physical conditioning, there has been greater success in differentiating between successful and unsuccessful performances.

This is particularly true where successful performance has been operationalized as one which leads to selection for a national team. Several studies have revealed differential POMS profiles between selected and unselected Olympic triallists in the sports of lightweight rowing (Morgan and Johnson, 1978) and wrestling (Nagle *et al.*, 1975; Silva *et al.*, 1985). Similar results were found by Silva *et al.* (1981) with Junior World Wrestling Championship qualifiers and non-qualifiers. In each study, differences were in the direction predicted by Morgan's model.

A point of confusion in the mood–performance literature revolves around the definition of success in sport. Renger (1993) rightly points out that it is misguided to classify an elite performer who fails to be selected for a major championship as an *unsuccessful athlete*. However, it may be justified to operationalize their performance during the trials as an *unsuccessful performance* because the immediate outcome goal was not achieved. Even acknowledging the methodological question marks raised by Renger (1993) the balance of evidence suggests that POMS has significant predictive capability amongst athletes at the elite level. By contrast, Miller and Miller (1985) found no significant differences in pre-trial mood between selected and unselected World Netball Championship triallists, suggesting that the nature of the sport may also mediate the predictive capability of POMS.

Performance success has sometimes been operationalized in absolute terms using time, finish position or some other continuous scale, and attempts made to predict performance from pre-performance mood using multiple regression models. Generally, this approach has facilitated significant predictions where samples were selected from within relatively narrow ability bands. For example, Cockerill *et al.* (1991) demonstrated that tension, depression and anger could collectively predict finish time in cross country running, while Friend and LeUnes (1990) identified anger and vigour as significant predictors of a range of performance indicators in baseball. Mahoney, M. (1989), using a battery of psychological tests to predict weightlifting performance, found depression and anger scores to be significant predictors.

Recent studies (Terry, 1993; Hall and Terry, 1995; Terry, 1995b,c) have dichotomized performance on the basis of post-event self-ratings by athletes according to whether they perceived themselves to have 'performed to (their own) expectations' or to have 'underperformed'. Performance categorized on a relative rather than an absolute basis in this self-referenced manner provides a more sensitive indicator of performance outcome than simple finish position. Using this method it proved possible to correctly classify 70.9 per cent of performances at World and Olympic level on the basis of pre-performance mood profiles in the sports of rowing and bobsleigh (Terry, 1993) (Figure 1.9). Hall and Terry (1995) replicated this strategy during the 1993 World Rowing Championships with 100 per cent discriminatory success (Figure 1.10) albeit with a smaller sample group. A further replication during the 1993–1994 Bobsleigh World Cup event in Winterberg, Germany (Terry, 1995b) revealed a similar pattern of profiles (Figure 1.11). Performances were classified to 64.7 per cent accuracy, even though the discriminant function was not significant.

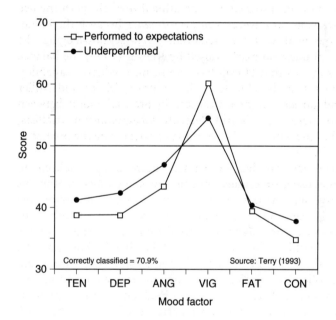

Figure 1.9 *Comparison of mood profiles for GB rowers and bobsleighers performing to expectations (n=42) and underperforming (n=37) during World and Olympic competitions*

Contrastingly, pre-game mood profiling showed no discriminatory capability among the England Cricket Team during three matches against Australia (Terry, 1994) (Figure 1.12) with only 48.5 per cent

16   *Sports Psychology in Performance*

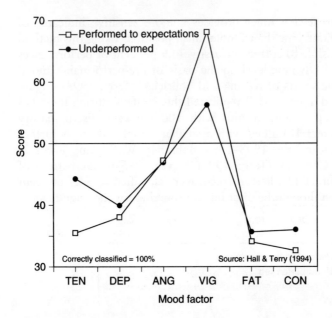

Figure 1.10 *Comparison of mood profiles for GB rowers performing to expectations (n=6) and underperforming (n=6) during the 1993 World Championships*

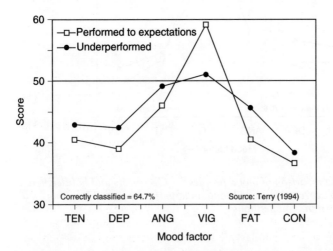

Figure 1.11 *Comparison of mood profiles for GB and Canadian bob-sleighers performing to expectations (n=8) and underperforming (n=9) during the 1993 World Cup (Winterberg)*

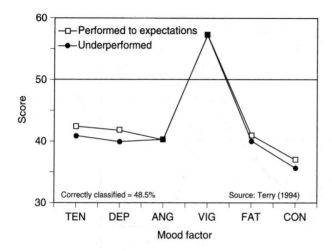

Figure 1.12 *Comparison of mood profiles for England cricketers performing to expectations* (n=18) *and underperforming* (n=15) *in three Ashes test matches during 1993*

of performances correctly classified, less than by chance. This contrast offers weight to the argument that the characteristics of the sport mediate the impact of pre-performance mood. Sports such as wrestling, rowing and bobsleigh are of short duration (less than 10 minutes) whereas netball lasts 60 minutes and a cricket test match lasts five days. It is suggested, therefore, that because the potential for mood fluctuations *during* performance increases with performance duration, the predictive capability of pre-performance mood will decrease accordingly.

It is also possible to conclude from a review of the literature that the presence of an 'Iceberg' profile *per se* contributes little to the prediction of athletic performance, for two main reasons. Firstly, there appears to be substantial variation between sports in terms of the desirability of specific mood factors. For instance, success in karate (Terry and Slade, 1995) and perhaps surprisingly, cross country running (Cockerill *et al.*, 1991) appears to be associated with above average anger scores. Similarly, high levels of tension have occasionally been shown to be facilitative to performance rather than debilitative (Cockerill *et al.*, 1991).

Secondly, as with most state measures, individual differences are great, and it is not uncommon for athletes to perform well despite having theoretically 'negative' profiles. Terry (1993) showed that 73.8 per cent of successful performances were associated with pre-performance 'Icebergs', indicating that more than a quarter were not. Conversely, 54.1 per cent of unsuccessful performers exhibited 'Icebergs'. Therefore fluctuations around intra-individual norms may prove more sensitive indicators of performance, and indeed such a strategy has shown its effectiveness in longitudinal projects (Morgan *et al.*, 1987; Terry, 1992; Mahoney and Kremer, 1993).

This review suggests that when certain conditions are met, pre-performance mood profiles predict a greater proportion of performance variation. Viewed in this light, previous literature is generally consistent in showing significant relationships between pre-performance mood and performance outcome. The proposed conditions (Table 1.1) should be considered in future research utilizing mood state profiles.

Table 1.1   *Proposed conditions which increase the predictive capability of pre-performance mood profiling*

Homogeneity of physical conditioning
Homogeneity of skill level
Short duration (< 10 minutes) events
Self-referenced performance criterion

Measurement issues in mood state profiling of athletes

For mood profiling to be a worthwhile exercise with elite sports performers, a range of measurement issues needs to be addressed. Perhaps the most critical of considerations is the means by which mood is evaluated. Although the original 65-item version of POMS has dominated the literature, there is a growing list of alternative measures (Table 1.2). Two shortened versions (Shacham, 1983; Grove and Prapavessis, 1992) have been developed to cater for situations where time is of the essence, reducing administration time from 3–7 minutes down to 2–5 minutes.

Concern has been expressed that, with five negative mood factors and one positive factor (two in the shortened version by Grove and Prapavessis, 1992), the unipolar versions of POMS have an excessively negative orientation. From the viewpoint of the sports psychology practitioner responsible for maximizing performance, this

Table 1.2 *Versions of the Profile of Mood States*

Authors	No. of items	Subscales	Type
McNair *et al.* (1971)	65	Tension Depression Anger Vigour Fatigue Confusion	Unipolar
Lorr and McNair (1988)	76	Composed–Anxious Agreeable–Hostile Elated–Depressed Confident–Unsure Energetic–Tired Clearheaded–Confused	Bipolar
Shacham (1983)	37	Tension Depression Anger Vigour Fatigue Confusion	Unipolar
Grove and Prapavessis (1992)	40	Fatigue Anger Vigour Tension Esteem Confusion Depression	Unipolar

may well be a strength rather than a weakness. There is compelling research evidence from many areas of the literature that negative affect inhibits sports performance, whereas the notion that positive affect enhances performance is less strongly supported. Hence, the original POMS may provide the most thorough indicator of performance-threatening moods.

The exact nature of moods is the subject of continuing debate (Nowlis and Nowlis, 1956; Mahoney, C., 1989). An issue of persistant interest has been whether semantically contrasting mood states, such as happy and sad or vigorous and fatigued, can truly co-exist or belong at opposite extremes of a bipolar continuum. Advocates of the bipolar theory may be drawn towards mood profiling using the bipolar version of POMS (Lorr and McNair, 1988) which quantifies mood along six affective continua (Composed–Anxious, Agreeable–Hostile, Elated–Depressed, Confident–Unsure, Energetic–Tired and Clearheaded–Confused). POMS-BI has been used productively in exercise (Cogan and Parfitt, 1994; Daley and Parfitt, 1994) and injury rehabilitation (Pearson and Jones, 1992) environments. However, there is tentative evidence that the original POMS may be more sensitive in assessing mood changes than POMS-BI. Turner (1993) randomly assigned participants in an exercise class to pre- and post-exercise mood assessments using either POMS or POMS-BI. Significant mood enhancements emerged for participants profiled using the original POMS whereas no mood changes were evident for the POMS-BI group, even though the exercise activity met the mood-enhancing criteria proposed by Berger *et al.* (1993).

Temporal considerations are also important both in terms of the instructions to subjects and the administration of the questionnaire. Instructions to subjects on the original POMS request a description of 'How you have been feeling *during the past week including today*'. The transient nature of moods can make such a description problematic for athletes, and the impact of prior moods upon current performance is questionable. Hence, where mood-performance links are being investigated, there is a strong case for using 'How are you feeling *right now*' instructions to athletes.

The timescale between mood profiling and performance is also an issue related to the transient nature of moods. Logically, a greater proportion of performance variation could be accounted for by a mood profile taken one hour prior to performance rather than one day. However, in Olympic or World Championship environments it is generally considered too intrusive to take psychometric measurements on competition day, and therefore administration on the eve of competition often proves the best compromise. Indeed from the sports psychology consultant's perspective, eve of competition profiles may be superior. Such profiles have been shown (Silva *et al.*, 1985; Terry, 1993; Hall and Terry, 1995) to have similar predictive capability to 'one hour' profiles (Cockerill *et al.*, 1991) but have the advantage of allowing time for intervention by the sport psychologist should the profile indicate this. It is clear from the results of Miller and Edgington (1984) that response distortion can occur if athletes suspect that the profiles are to be used for selection purposes. Hence, the post-selection period on the eve of competition may provide the optimum time for profiling elite athletes.

Another measurement issue concerns the comprehension of items by subjects. Grove and Prapavessis (1992) have pointed out the ambiguity of some items, and experience suggests that 'listless', 'deceived' and 'full of pep' often require explanation, while 'ready to fight', which as part of the anger dimension should be taken literally, is often interpreted as a metaphor for 'ready to compete'. Furthermore, words such as 'blue' and 'bushed' may be better established in the North American culture than elsewhere, while 'grovely' (Shacham, 1983) may not be universally understood as part of the anger dimension. To minimize misunderstandings, subjects should be supplied with a culturally appropriate alternative word list such as that developed by Albrecht and Ewing (1988). The age of subjects may also moderate their comprehension of items and there is a need for a POMS version designed specifically for younger athletes. Such an instrument is presently in the final stages of validation (Terry *et al.*, 1996).

Uses of mood profiling in elite sport

There are a number of distinct uses for mood profiling available to the sports psychology practitioner working with elite athletes (Table 1.3) although in many instances a single profile may facilitate more than one objective. The primary function of profiling is as a general indicator of athlete mindset. Explaining an athlete's profile to him or her acts as an effective catalyst for discussion during one-to-one-sessions, perhaps guiding questions towards the *reasons* tension is higher than usual and what the outcome of increased tension is likely to be. Once athletes understand the principles underlying POMS, their profile serves almost as an intervention in its own right, for example, helping them to restructure tension into excitement or anger into determination.

Once built into the preparation routine of athletes at major international competitions, profiling helps in the early identification of problematic issues, such as interpersonal conflict, confusion over managerial decisions, acute self-doubt, or fatigue caused by over-training. A mood profile will often reveal changes in mindset before they show themselves in behavioural terms, effectively nipping them in the bud before energy is wasted on unproductive courses of action or misdirected towards uncontrollable variables.

The Olympic Games generates many hassles not always encoun-

Table 1.3 *Proposed uses of mood profiling in elite sport*

General monitoring of athletes' mindset
Catalyst for discussion during one-to-one sessions
As an intervention in its own right
Early identification of problem areas
Monitoring mood of team officials and support staff
Monitoring training load
Identifying overtrained athletes
Monitoring rehabilitation from overtraining
Monitoring emotional responses to injury
Prediction of performance
Contributing to the individualization of mental training

tered before, such as strict accreditation procedures, frequent queueing, problems getting tickets for family and friends, increased media intrusion and, perhaps surprisingly, boredom waiting for competition to start. In the emotional melting pot of an Olympic environment, there is a strong case for extending mood profiling to include team officials, coaches and support staff, who often bear the brunt of athlete frustration and whose resultant mood disturbance can in turn further threaten the mood stability of performers. Figure 1.13 shows a pattern of mood change for a group of British team officials at the 1992 Olympic Winter Games in Albertville, France. The profiles on day two of the Games prompted a decision to allow each team official a daily period of 'personal time' away from the seemingly endless list of problems which occurred. By day four group mood had returned to a desirable 'Iceberg' profile.

Another potential use of mood profiling concerns the systematic monitoring of training load. This is particularly true in sports such as rowing, swimming and distance running where athletes often function on the edge of a precarious balance between effective training and overtraining. Mood disturbance usually accompanies, and frequently precedes, the negative physiological effects of overtraining. Indeed, an 'Inverse Iceberg' POMS profile, incorporating low vigour with high fatigue, tension, anger, depression and confusion, is regarded as an important diagnostic indicator of the overtraining syndrome by staff at the British Olympic Medical Centre. The process of rehabilitating athletes from an overtrained state (which usually necessitates a complete cessation of physical training) back to full training involves a step by step introduction of progressively more demanding training

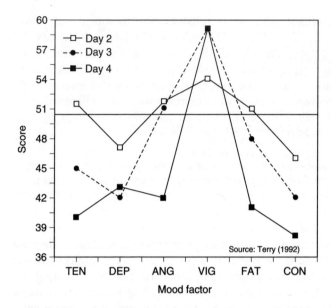

Figure 1.13   *Comparison of mood profiles for British team officials (n=5) on days two to four of the 1992 Olympic Winter Games*

loads. During this process, mood profiles provide an indicator of the athlete's adaptation to these training load increases, with mood disturbance suggesting a delay in increasing training load or even a temporary reduction of load.

There is also scope for including mood profiling as a regular feature of training with any athlete, even those without a history of over-training, to raise awareness of mood fluctuations and their possible impact upon performance. This is a strategy I have recently used with marathon canoeists preparing for the World Championships, which they won, and with a professional steeplechase jockey in his successful attempt to retain the Champion Jockey title and ride the winner of the Grand National. The link between mood fluctuations and physiological fluctuations was investigated by Mahoney and colleagues (Mahoney and Kremer, 1993) who made small adjustments to the training intensity of elite swimmers on the basis of mood profiling, building on the strategies developed by Morgan *et al.* (1987).

An injured athlete undergoing rehabilitation treatment may also benefit from mood profiling. The emotional response to injury is often extremely acute, not unlike the classic five-stage grief response of denial, anger, depression, acceptance, hope. POMS provides both a general measure of the emotional response and also an indicator of the response 'stage'. This is very useful when counselling injured athletes, and may even serve to speed the athlete through to the hope stage, which is associated with a more motivated approach to rehabilitation.

Perhaps the most salient use of mood profiling with elite performers is to predict forthcoming performance. Using an intra-individual approach and a self-referenced performance criterion, the 'ideal' profile for a particular athlete may be identified within six to eight performances. Thereafter, a pre-performance profile which is substantially less positive than the ideal suggests that performance is threatened and that intervention may be advantageous. The subjectivity of this process is freely acknowledged, reflecting perhaps that applied sports psychology sometimes shifts from a science to an art.

Clearly such a process is both individual- and sport-dependent. However, having adopted this approach with hundreds of international performers, it is notable that almost all perform best when their profile is iceberg shaped. Superior performance is almost always associated with high vigour scores, occasionally with above average levels of tension or anger, but rarely with above average depression, fatigue or confusion. On those few occasions when athletes have performed well with high depression, fatigue or confusion scores, they invariably conclude that they succeeded despite their mood and not because of it. There are many occasions when athletes perform below expectations even though they exhibit an 'Iceberg' profile. This renders as misleading any claim that mood profiling is the 'Test of Champions' (Morgan, 1980) and emphasizes the benefit of POMS tables (see Terry and Hall, 1996) of normative data relating specifically to elite athletes. An 'Iceberg' profile plotted against athletic norms should prove more predictive of athletic performance than one plotted against student or psychiatric outpatient norms.

Perhaps the best single indicator of superior performance is what could be termed an 'Everest' profile (Terry, 1995c) (Figure 1.14), with vigour at least one standard deviation above average (i.e. a T-score of 60 or more) and the remaining factors at least one standard deviation below average (i.e. a T-score of 40 or less). When such a profile is evident underperformance is rare, and it is even rarer for an

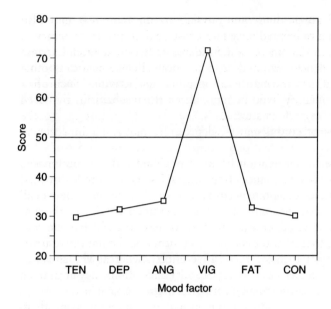

Figure 1.14   *Example of an 'Everest' profile*

athlete showing a pre-performance 'Everest' profile to attribute underperformance to mood-related factors. In deciding whether intervention is required, more weight should be given to the vigour, depression, fatigue and confusion scores than to the tension and anger scores where a wider range of scores are associated with good performance.

At the intervention stage, mood state profiles may contribute to the individualization of mental training as advocated by Power (1986). For example, an athlete who characteristically shows high anger may benefit from strategies aimed at transferring anger into vigour, or one who shows low vigour might work at developing activation skills.

Factors for consideration in cross-sectional comparisons

It would appear that the prime consideration in cross-sectional comparisons is the control of possible confounding variables. It has already been argued that the selection of a sample group homogeneous in terms of ability and physical conditioning is essential for mood profiling to be predictive of performance. It is further proposed that the task environment be considered carefully. It would appear from the evidence reviewed that pre-performance mood is more closely related to performance in short duration activities. Such a link may be explained by hypothesizing about the mechanisms by which mood influences performance.

High levels of confusion and depression may result in difficulty maintaining correct attentional control, and certainly no study has shown a positive correlation between either of these mood components and sport performance. Tension may lead to loss of fine muscle control and hence debilitate performance, or alternatively it may facilitate performance for the under-aroused athlete, which may help to explain the equivocal findings related to this subscale. Fatigue may reduce both physical capacity and self efficacy, and from the research evidence appears to have no positive effects, whereas vigour which enhances both perceived physical capacity and self-efficacy appears to be closely associated with superior performance. Anger, being perhaps the most powerful mood component, may act either to divert attentional focus or to enhance determination. Its link with increases in adrenaline, an established agent in pain tolerance, may explain its association with superior performance in contact sports such as karate.

The pre-performance mindset of athletes may be highly influential upon performance but if their mindset changes *during* performance then the influence is reduced. Logically therefore, duration of event will be an important moderating variable. Investigation of the impact of *mid*-performance mood profiles upon athletic performance may help to clarify the moderating effects of performance duration. There may appear to be inconsistency in the argument that short duration events facilitate the predictive power of mood profiling due to the transient nature of moods and yet eve of performance is the optimum time for profiling. It has been shown (Cratty *et al.*, 1984) that performance related thoughts dominate athletes' thinking for some time prior to performance. The emotional response to pre-performance mental rehearsal will be less intense than the response to actual events once performance has commenced, and hence it is proposed that mood will tend to fluctuate more dramatically during performance than in the day leading up to it.

Another area of consideration is the impact of task variability upon the predictive capability of mood profiling. There is an argument that the fewer external influences upon performance the more athlete mindset will determine outcome. This would suggest that reduced task variability in the form of self-paced, relatively closed skills offers increased prediction. This argument is supported by the significant findings from sports such as rowing (Morgan and Johnson, 1978; Hall and Terry, 1995), weightlifting (Mahoney, M., 1989), cross country running (Cockerill *et al.*, 1991) and bobsleigh (Terry, 1993). Interactive, open-skilled sports on the other hand may reduce predictive capability, explaining findings in sports such as netball (Miller and Miller, 1985), hockey (Terry and Youngs, 1996) and cricket (Terry, 1994). Significant predictions found in wrestling (Nagle *et al.*, 1975; Silva *et al.*, 1985) and karate (Terry and Slade, 1995) suggest that the individual nature of a sport may be the stronger moderating variable than task variability.

Factors for consideration in intra-individual comparisons

By the very nature of intra-individual comparisons it is difficult to generalize. The key issue is, however, that the predictive capability of individual profiles tends to be enhanced the longer the profiling process continues. Once an individualized database of mood profiles is generated through regular profiling then variations from an athlete's normative profile may suggest performance fluctuations. It should be emphasized that individual differences are large and therefore a single profile may tell little about forthcoming competition prospects. For example, Figure 1.15 shows profiles for two athletes prior to World Cup medal winning performances. Although the profiles are very different from one another they both represent profiles typically associated with good performance *for those individuals*.

There is some evidence that good performance is associated with mood stability during the pre-performance period. Mood profiles taken daily during World Cup and Olympic competition (Terry, 1992) revealed a pattern of significantly fluctuating moods for an underperforming four-man bobsleigh crew and mood stability from competition to competition for the top performing crew. Similarly, World Championship rowers who performed to expectations tended to show a steady *downward trend* in tension, depression, anger, fatigue and confusion as competition approached, whereas their underperforming colleagues showed increasing tension and fluctuating anger and confusion during the same period (Hall and Terry, 1995). While it is easy to accept that an athlete whose mood becomes progressively

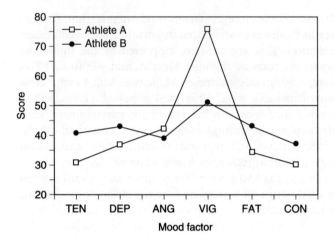

Figure 1.15   *Comparison of mood profiles for two athletes prior to World Cup winning performances*

more positive is likely to perform well, there is a clear need for further research aimed at understanding the impact of pre-performance mood fluctuations upon performance outcome. An intra-individual approach may prove a productive strategy in gaining insight in this area.

An important issue in intra-individual mood comparisons is the frequency of profiling. In situations where mood profiles have been linked to training load, as a psychological monitor of staleness and overtraining (Morgan *et al.*, 1987; Mahoney and Kremer, 1993) POMS is sometimes completed before and after each training session, but for most purposes this is excessive. There is a need to strike a balance between building up an individual database while not exhausting the cooperation of athletes. In my work as a sports psychology consultant, frequency of profiling varies from three times a week when on the road with squads, to once a week or once a fortnight with athletes communicating by fax.

Conclusions

From the evidence reviewed it can be concluded that mood profiling has little utility in differentiating between sporting groups of hetero-geneous ability and only a limited capacity to distinguish the athlete from the non-athlete. It is also possible to conclude that, in certain specific elite sport environments, pre-performance mood profiling has been shown to significantly discriminate between successful and unsuccessful performances with some consistency. Clearly, further research is needed to fully understand how intra-individual mood fluctuations influence athletic performance, and to understand the impact of pre-performance and intra-performance mood trends upon performance. Until greater clarity is achieved in this research area, this chapter has attempted to offer the student or practitioner of applied sports psychology both an overall framework within which to present a mental training programme, and specific guidelines regarding the application of mood profiling with elite performers.

References

Albrecht, R.R. and Ewing, S.J. (1988) Development of alternative word lists: A procedure for standardizing the administration of the Profile of Mood States (POMS). Paper presented at the annual meeting of the North American Society for the Psychology of Sport and Physical Activity, Knoxville, TN, June 1988.

Berger, B., Owen, D.R. and Man, F. (1993) A brief review of literature and examination of acute mood benefits of exercise in Czech and United States swimmers. *International Journal of Sport Psychology*, 24, 130–150.

Butler, R.J. (1989) 'Psychological preparation of Olympic boxers. In *The Psychology of Sport: Theory and Practice* (J. Kremer and W. Crawford, eds.). Leicester, UK: British Psychological Society pp. 74–84.

Cockerill, I.M., Nevill, A.M. and Byrne, N.C. (1990) Mood, mileage and the menstrual cycle. Paper presented at the Hellenic Society for Sport Psychology, Athens, May 1990.

Cockerill, I.M., Nevill, A.M. and Lyons, N. (1991) Modelling mood states in athletic performance. *Journal of Sports Sciences*, 9, 205–212.

Cogan, H.M. and Parfitt, G. (1994) The relationship between intensity of running (mph) and psychological mood state in female runners. *Journal of Sports Sciences*, 12(6), 88.

Cohn, P.J., Rotella, R.J. and Lloyd, J.W. (1990) Effects of a cognitive-behavioural intervention on the pre-shot routine and performance in golf. *The Sport Psychologist*, 4, 33–47.

Craighead, D.J., Privette, G., Vallianos, F. and Byrkit, D. (1986) Personality characteristics of basketball players, starters, and non-starters. *International Journal of Sport Psychology*, 17, 110–119.

Cratty, B.J., Lange, C. and O'Neill, M.R. (1984) Mental activity in individual sport athletes. *Sportwissenschaft*, 14(1), 50–59.

Daiss, S., LeUnes, A. and Nation, J. (1986) Mood and locus of control of a sample of college and professional football players. *Perceptual and Motor Skills*, 63(2), 733–734.

Daley, A.J. and Parfitt, G. (1994) Physical fitness, levels of physical activity and mood state in members and non-members of a corporate health and fitness club. *Journal of Sports Sciences*, 12(6), 190–191.

Durtschi, S. and Weiss, M. (1986) Psychological characteristics of elite and non-elite marathon runners. In *Sport and Elite Performers* (D. Landers, ed.). Champaign, IL: Human Kinetics pp. 73–80.

Elko, P.K. and Ostrow, A.C. (1991) Effects of a rational-emotive education program on heightened anxiety levels of female collegiate gymnasts. *The Sport Psychologist*, 5, 235–255.

Fitzpatrick, N. (1993) Development and evaluation of a mental training programme for equestrian riders. MSc Thesis (unpublished), West London Institute/United States Sports Academy.

Frazier, S.E. (1988) Mood state profiles of chronic exercisers with differing abilities. *International Journal of Sport Psychology*, 19, 65–71.

Friend, J. and LeUnes, A. (1990) Predicting baseball player performance. *Journal of Sport Behavior*, 13(2), 73–86.

Grove, J.R. and Prapavessis, H. (1992) Preliminary evidence for the reliability and validity of an abbreviated Profile of Mood States. *International Journal of Sport Psychology*, 23, 93–109.

Hall, A. and Terry, P.C. (1995) Trends in mood profiles in the preparation phase and racing phase of the 1993 World Rowing Championships, Roundnice, the Czech Republic. *Journal of Sports Sciences*, 13(1), 56–57.

Hellstedt, J.C. (1987) Sport psychology at a ski academy: Teaching mental skills to young athletes. *The Sport Psychologist*, 1, 56–68.

LeUnes, A., Hayward, S.A. and Daiss, S. (1988) Annotated bibliography on the Profile of Mood States in sport, 1975–1988. *Journal of Sport Behavior*, 11(3), 213–240.

Li-Wei, Z., Qi-Wei, M., Orlick T. and Zitzelsberger, L. (1992) The effect of mental-imagery training on performance enhancement with 7 to 10 year old children. *The Sport Psychologist*, 6, 230–241.

Lorr, M. and McNair, D.M (1988) *Manual for the Profile of Mood States – Bipolar Form*. San Diego, CA: Educational and Industrial Testing Service.

McNair, D.M., Lorr, M. and Droppleman, L. (1971) *Manual for the Profile of Mood States*. San Diego, CA: Educational and Industrial Testing Service.

Mahoney, C. (1989) Mood state and performance in sport. In *The Psychology of Sport: Theory and Practice* (J. Kremer and W. Crawford, eds.). Leicester, UK: British Psychological Society, pp. 54–59.

Mahoney, C. and Kremer, J. (1993) Mood state variation during anaerobic training of an elite swimmer. In *Proceedings of the VIIIth ISSP World Congress of Sport Psychology* (S. Serpa, J. Alves, V. Ferreira and A. Paulo-Brito, eds.) pp. 256–259. Lisbon, June 1993.

Mahoney, M.J. (1989) Psychological predictors of elite and non-elite performance in Olympic weightlifting. *International Journal of Sport Psychology*, 20, 1–12.

Miller, B.P. and Edgington, G.P. (1984) Psychological mood state distortion in a sporting context. *Journal of Sport Behavior*, 7(3), 91–94.

Miller, B.P. and Miller, A.J. (1985) Psychological correlates of success in elite sportswomen. *International Journal of Sport Psychology*, 16, 289–295.

Morgan, W.P. (1980) Test of champions. *Psychology Today*, July, 92–99.

Morgan, W.P., Brown, D.R., Raglin, J.S., O'Connor, P.J. and Ellickson, K.A. (1987) Psychological monitoring of overtraining and staleness. *British Journal of Sports Medicine*, 21, 107–114.

Morgan, W.P. and Pollock, M.L. (1977) Psychologic characterization of the elite runner. *Annals of the New York Academy of Sciences*, 301, 382–403.

Morgan, W.P. and Johnson, R. (1978) Personality characteristics of successful and unsuccessful oarsmen. *International Journal of Sport Psychology*, 9, 119–133.

Nagle, F., Morgan, W.P., Hellickson, R., Serfass, R. and Alexander, J. (1975) Spotting success traits in Olympic contenders. *Physician and Sports Medicine*, 3(12), 31–34, 84.

Nowlis, V. and Nowlis, H.H. (1956) The description and analysis of mood. *Annals of the New York Academy of Sciences*, 65, 345–355.

Pearson, L. and Jones, J.G. (1992) Emotional effects of sports injuries: Implications for physiotherapists. *Physiotherapy*, 78(10), 762–770.

Power, S. (1986) Psychological assessment procedures at a track and field national event squad training weekend. In *Sports Science* (J. Watkins, T. Reilly and L. Burwitz, eds.). New York: E. and F. Spon pp. 181–186.

Renger, R. (1993) A review of the Profile of Mood States (POMS) in the prediction of athletic success. *Journal of Applied Sport Psychology*, 5, 78–84.

Rodgers, W., Hall, C. and Buckolz, E. (1991) The effect of an imagery training program on imagery ability, imagery use, and figure skating performance. *Journal of Applied Sport Psychology*, 3, 109–125.

Shacham, S. (1983) A shortened version of the Profile of Mood States. *Journal of Personality Assessment*, 47, 305–306.

Silva, J.M., Schultz, B.B., Haslam, R.W. and Murray, D.F. (1981) A psychophysiological assessment of elite wrestlers. *Research Quarterly for Exercise and Sport*, 52, 348–358.

Silva, J.M., Schultz, B.B., Haslam, R.W., Martin, M.P. and Murray, D.F. (1985) Discriminating characteristics of contestants at the United States Olympic wrestling trials. *International Journal of Sport Psychology*, 16, 79–102.

Terry, P.C. (1992) Mental training and psychological support for the British Bobsleigh team, 1989–1994. Presented at the Olympic Scientific Congress, Malaga, Spain, July 1992.

Terry, P.C. (1993) Mood state profiles as indicators of performance among Olympic and World Championship athletes. In *Proceedings of the VIIIth ISSP World Congress of Sport Psychology* (S. Serpa, J. Alves, V. Ferreira and A. Paulo-Brito, eds.) pp. 963–967. Lisbon, June 1993.

Terry, P.C. (1994) Pre-performance mood profiles of the England cricket team during the 1993 "Ashes" series. Presented at the Xth Commonwealth and International Scientific Congress 'Access to Active Living', Victoria, BC, Canada, August 1994.

Terry, P.C. (1995a) Mental training for elite junior tennis players: Issues of delivery and evaluation. In *Science and Racket Sports* (T. Reilly, M. Hughes and A. Lees eds), pp. 212–220. London: E. & F. Spon.

Terry, P.C. (1995b) Discriminant capability of pre-performance mood state profiles during the 1993–94 World Cup Bobsleigh. *Journal of Sports Sciences*, **13**(1), 77–78.

Terry, P.C. (1995c) The efficacy of mood state profiling among elite performers. *The Sport Psychologist*, **9**(3), 309–324.

Terry, P.C. and Hall, A. (1966) Development of normative data for the Profile of Mood States for use with athletic samples. *Journal of Sports Sciences*, **14**(1), 47–48.

Terry, P.C. and Harrold, F. (1990) Development of sport psychology in Britain. Presented at *Centre of Excellence Seminar 'Sport Science in Action'*, West London Institute, July 1990.

Terry, P.C. and Slade, A. (1995) Discriminant effectiveness of psychological state measures in predicting performance outcome in karate competition. *Perceptual and Motor Skills*, **81**, 275–286.

Terry, P.C. and Youngs, E. (1996) Discriminant effectiveness of psychological state measures in predicting performance outcome in field hockey trialists. *Perceptual and Motor Skills*, **82**, 371–377.

Terry, P.C., Keohane, L. and Lane, H. (1996) Development and validation of a shortened version of the Profile of Mood States suitable for use with young athletes. *Journal of Sports Sciences*, **14**(1), 49.

Turner, J. (1993) A comparison of two versions of the Profile of Mood States in monitoring mood change after exercise. MSc Thesis (unpublished), West London Institute.

Author note

This chapter is based on two articles published previously by the author (see Terry, 1995a, 1995c).

2

Performance Profiling: assessing the way forward

Richard Butler

Sport: Amateur boxing

The relationship between coach and athlete is crucial to the achievement of successful performance. The same might also be said of the relationship between the sport psychologist and athlete. It might range from a close, symbiotic and protective relationship to a more distant advisory role which is largely dependent on how the coach or psychologist assesses the demands of the situation and the needs of the athlete.

In practice the working style adopted by coaches and psychologists is traditionally conceptualized as similar to a teacher–pupil relationship. The coach assesses the needs of the athlete in relation to the demands of the competition and designs a training programme to best meet these needs. The psychologist typically undertakes a similar exercise in analysing how the athlete's performance might be enhanced by applying psychological approaches and then, with the athlete's agreement, seeks to discover how they can best be taught and employed by the athlete (Boutcher and Rotella, 1987; Gordon, 1990). Whilst these time honoured traditions can prove effective they place the athlete in the position of a passive recipient – someone with little say in how training (physical, technical and psychological) can serve their particular needs.

The effectiveness of a training programme thus becomes dependent on the athlete's perception of how relevant the coach or psychologist's assessment and interventions are in meeting their requirements and overcoming performance issues unique to them. Consequently this will effect the athlete's commitment to the training schedule, their engagement in any educational package and adhesion to any programmes they are expected to undertake in the absence of their coach/psychologist (Bull, 1991).

An alternative metaphor for the coach/psychologist–athlete relationship is that contained in the supervisor–PhD student relationship where both are recognized as experts in their particular fields (the supervisor/coach/psychologist being conversant with the broader aspects and demands of the field of study whilst the student/athlete is an expert in their particular piece of research/performance), and where progress is made through the sharing of information, ideas and theories and a negotiation about the way forward. This type of relationship acknowledges contributions from both participants – coach/psychologist and athlete – as important. Of value in the sports setting is the opportunity to access different perspectives on the athlete's performance. The coach/psychologist can make astute observations about the athlete's performance from, as it were, 'outside', whereas the athlete is the only one who can comment on the performance from 'inside' (Butler, 1995). The athlete's assertions, discriminations and insights are not only valid but valuable. They can make a significant contribution to the development of an effective training programme.

Such ideas have given rise to Performance Profiling (Butler, 1989; Butler and Hardy, 1992; Butler *et al.*, 1993), a process which facilitates the athlete's self-awareness with regard to performance coupled with enhancement of the coach and psychologist's understanding of the athlete's perspective. The Performance Profile thus encourages not an understanding of the athlete (which is the 'outsiders' impression) but an understanding of the athlete's own understanding. In its most usual format a Performance Profile consists of a 'visual display of those areas perceived by the athlete to be important in achieving a top performance, on to which the athlete's current assessment of self is mapped' (Butler *et al.*, 1993).

Figures 2.1 and 2.2 depict Performance Profiles of two amateur boxers in preparation for the World Championships. As typical examples they will be used to illustrate the important theoretical notions that underlie the procedure. The basic methodology of Performance Profiling is described elsewhere (e.g. Butler and Hardy, 1992; Butler *et al.*, 1993) and is beyond the scope of this chapter.

Initially the process begins by inviting the athlete to reflect on what qualities are commonly expressed by those performers who excel at their particular sport. The athlete might be prompted to think of one elite performer or a composite 'ideal' performer, and to consider qualities which relate to their own 'style', performance needs and over which they can assume some control. This might encompass qualities of performance in the physical, technical, psychological and attitudinal arena (Butler, 1995).

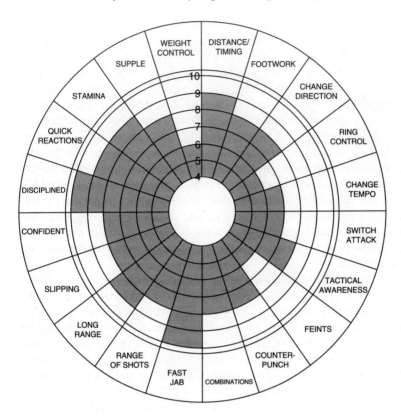

Figure 2.1   *The performance profile of amateur boxer, Andy*

Figure 2.1 illustrates Andy, a boxer whose style is based on sound technique. The majority of qualities ($n = 14$) are concerned with technical aspects (e.g. ring control, change tempo, counterpunch, switch attack) with minor emphasis on physical, attitudinal and psychological attributes. In contrast, Figure 2.2 depicts Paul, a boxer with what might be described as a 'fighter' style, where more emphasis is given to physical and attitudinal qualities and the technical attributes describe power and the ability to box at close range (i.e. working inside). Through inviting the athlete to describe such qualities we are essentially eliciting a series of constructs, which when coupled together, provides a vision of the athlete's ideal perceived performance.

Theoretically Performance Profiling is embedded within the frame-

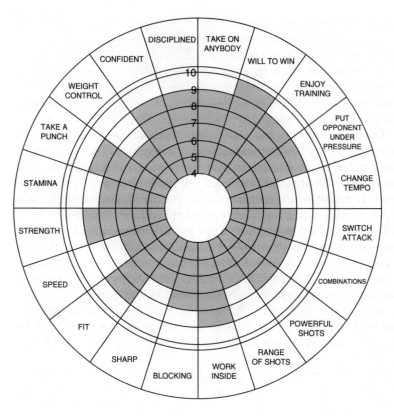

Figure 2.2 *The performance profile of amateur boxer, Paul*

work of Personal Construct Theory (Kelly, 1955; Bannister and Fransella, 1986). The theory proposes that individual's seek to construct meaning by searching for repeated themes in the events before them. Kelly (1977) suggested that our only access to events is through the psychological devices we create for looking at them. These 'psychological devices' he called constructs. Thus it is the way we construe events which gives then personal meaning, and as such, an individual's understanding is anchored essentially in their assumptions, not in the bedrock of truth itself.

The uniqueness of each individual's construing is thus celebrated within Personal Construct Theory. Such a fundamental notion is often overlooked by coaches and psychologists who assess the situation and deliver a programme to meet what they perceive to be the athlete's needs. The problem is that they might miss the point entirely. If the programme fails to meet what the athlete considers is important, the likelihood of success is minimized. Athletes differ in their interpretation of situations, how they construe themselves and their ability to perform; where they feel this is not addressed by those responsible for their training, it is unlikely they will fully engage in the training programme.

The discriminations that individuals make in attempting to understand the events before them are called constructs. These by nature are bipolar. Many constructs have verbal labels (e.g. Healthy – Ill, Awkward – Rhythmic, Determined – Casual, Creative – Orthodox), but it is important to recognize that a construct is the discrimination a person makes, not the label that is applied to it (Bannister, 1983). All constructs imply contrast. Thus by perceiving oneself as strong there is an implicit denial of weakness, cowardliness or frailty; by recognizing tiredness there is an implied lack of freshness, alertness or energy. Although Performance Profiles describe only one end of a construct (what might be considered the emerged end in response to what qualities the athlete thinks are important), this does not deny the contrast end, which could be elicited by asking the athlete to describe what someone would be like who did not possess the quality in question.

Usually the contrast pole of a construct defines its meaning. Thus weight control, an important quality in amateur boxing, might be contrasted with indulgence for one boxer, but contrasted with less control for another boxer. The implications for the two boxers are palpably different. For one the implication is that weight control is achieved by restrictions in diet; for the other boxer the implication surrounds a greater focus on maintaining some control when out of training. Only by gaining insight into both poles of a construct can the personal meaning be elucidated (Fransella and Dalton, 1990).

However Performance Profiling rarely advocates the elicitation of a contrast. It thus becomes imperative to seek a clarification of precisely what the athlete means for each quality suggested as important (Jones, 1993). Usually asking for a description of what is meant highlights any differences in interpretation. This might easily be overlooked by assuming a common terminology means the same thing to both athlete and coach. Thus 'range of shots', a quality elicited by both boxers whose profiles are illustrated in Figures 2.1 and 2.2, meant the ability to accurately and efficiently throw a variety of punches (e.g. hooks, uppercuts, jabs), yet might easily, without clarification, have been construed by their coach as the ability to be within range (distance from their opponent) before throwing a punch. Seeking clarification is a central tenet of Personal Construct Theory as its demonstrates the coach's and psychologist's wish to understand the experience from the athlete's perspective.

Having obtained the athlete's vision of important qualities and invited an assessment of their current attributes on these qualities through the process of rating (where a rating of ten suggests a perfect or near perfect evaluation), a Performance Profile has taken shape. The visual display readily describes how the athlete is evaluating their current performance, what they consider their strengths and where they assess their weaknesses. Andy, in Figure 2.1, construes his strengths as being disciplined, having a fast jab, stamina, quick reactions and boxing from a long range. He perceives his weakest areas in weight control, ring control and feinting an opponent. Paul (Figure 2.2) also regards weight control as one of his weakest areas along with changing tempo, ability to use a range of shots, sharpness and speed, whilst it is apparent from the profile that he regards his strengths in the areas of attitude (e.g. will to win, being disciplined, put opponent under pressure) and psychological preparation (confidence).

Interestingly the process of eliciting and evaluating self on the basis of personal qualities can prove enlightening for some athletes. They become more consciously aware of what they construe as important and how their own performance matches what they expect. This is in perfect accord with the predictions of Personal Construct Theory, as Ravenette (1977) suggested a person's system of constructs is created, developed and maintained at a low level of awareness. Thus in endeavouring to discover something about how an athlete construes his performance we are inviting him to explore and communicate that which he is at the moment taking for granted. Thus exploring the athlete's perspective in this way, leads to an enhanced self awareness concerning performance issues. The emergence of self awareness has been described by Ravizza (1986, 1989) as an important first step in the development of self control over performance.

Crucially the Performance Profile enables the coach or psychologist to discern something of the athlete's perspective (Butler and Hardy, 1992). Given such knowledge, future decisions the coach or psychologist make regarding the design of training programmes should be palpably more relevant to the athlete's needs. This notion is made explicit in Personal Construct Theory in what Kelly (1995) described as a sociality corollary. This essentially suggests that for a person to effectively relate to another person, they have to begin to construe, or understand, something of the way the other person makes sense of events which impinge on him. As Winter (1992) suggests, the attempt to view the world through the athlete's eyes lays the foundation for a 'constructive social interaction'.

A further issue raised through the Performance Profile concerns the degree to which any two athletes might be considered similar. Much training from both a coaching and a psychological perspective is directed to groups of athletes. There is an assumption that all athletes will benefit from a session devoted to footwork or a group session on relaxation, for example. However, the individual within the group will benefit only to the extent that he feels the training will serve his needs. From a Personal Construct Theory perspective athletes are not alike because they are observed to be similar, but alike only to the extent that they employ similar ways of construing their experiences (Button, 1985). Thus a coach may observe that two athletes need to improve their ring control, for example, but for any intervention to be effective the coach would have to assess the degree to which both athletes considered it to be important for them. With the boxer illustrated in Figure 2.2, ring control is not considered to be an important quality and therefore the coach would need to explain his reasons for thinking the athlete required work on ring control before embarking on a programme to improve it.

Performance Profiles may be employed in a variety of ways. Butler *et al.* (1993) and Jones (1993) describe the following:

- To highlight areas of perceived weakness, so training can be tailored to the athlete's needs, a process which commits the athlete to training.
- To monitor change, and assess whether the training is achieving the desired effect.
- To detect mis-match between the athlete and coach or psychologist's rating of performance.
- To assess the athlete's view of what might realistically be expected through obtaining an evaluation of a top performance along the various qualities.
- To help in the de-briefing process where the athlete (and coach/psychologist) rates his performance on each quality.

Figures 2.1 and 2.2 illustrate two contrasting styles. Until very recently both types of boxer would stand a fairly equal chance of winning a bout because the winner was determined by judges making a comparative assessment of which boxer demonstrated the better attack and defence. Style was only influential in terms of enabling the individual boxer to increase his effectiveness in attack and defence. By itself, the boxer's style made little difference to the result. The Performance Profile served this situation well because it focused on those qualities the athlete thought were necessary to produce a top performance.

However in 1989 the ruling bodies of amateur boxing introduced a revolutionary form of scoring bouts. Gone were the judges subjective impressions of a boxer's performance. Computerized scoring was introduced. This relied on five ringside judges each recording a scoring punch by pressing an appropriate button (red for the boxer from the red corner and blue for the boxer from the blue corner) immediately the punch was thrown. Each judge was therefore required to assess the quality of every punch, for both boxers, to determine if it hit the target with sufficient power and press the appropriate button within a very short time span. A punch was only recorded by the computer if three judges pressed within one second of each other. Thus each scoring punch should be independent of what has happened before in the bout. The winner is the boxer with the greatest number of scoring punches (points) at the end of three rounds.

The impact of this change of scoring has been dramatic. Whilst the methodology is continually being developed and refined, the concept appears to be here to stay. Since 1989 all major championships have relied on computerized scoring. Cursory examination of some early bouts employing the scoring machine suggested some boxing styles suited the demands of the system better than others. It appeared the demands of judging, which is after all, a fast flowing activity, led to some punches being more likely to score than others. The implications of this were profound. It suggested that boxers at the elite level could no longer seek to perfect a particular style and hope necessarily to be effective.

Coaching had inexorably to gear itself to developing a style which maximized the boxer's chance of succeeding when performing with computerized scoring in operation. In addressing this issue the possibility of a Scoring Machine Profile evolved. This would be a profile depicting the qualities a boxer required to advance their chances of succeeding. It is important to note that this profile was developed in addition to the Performance Profile, not as a substitute for it.

Where the Scoring Machine Profile differed theoretically from the Performance Profile was in the identification of necessary qualities. The Performance Profile invites the athlete to generate the qualities they consider important, a process compatible with the notion of individuality within Personal Construct Theory. However the Scoring Machine Profile reflects more of a notion of group consensus because it is developed from the ideas, opinions and viewpoints of a team of boxers, coaches and sport scientists. However, it remains compatible with the central tenets of Personal Construct Theory through the compilation of a vision of the idealized style which taps the 'expertise' of individuals who have experienced the computerized scoring machine. In addition the construction of such a profile sits comfortably with a recent corollary proposed by Thomas (1979), that of complimentality. This corollary suggests that where individuals face a common series of events, but by virtue of their position sample the events differently, their constructions of experience will develop to complement each other. It is proposed that such complementation will produce a construction which exhibits greater complexity and stability than what exists in the construction of any individual contributing to it.

The process of constructing a Scoring Machine Profile began by inviting a group of elite boxers to comment on their experiences of competing where the scoring machine was in operation. They were then asked to define what the important qualities were. Two coaches and an exercise physiologist, all of whom had encountered the scoring machine at a major championship, were subsequently and independently asked to describe what attributes they considered essential. Finally cognizance was given to the findings of a study analysing the outcome of every bout at the 1992 Olympic Games (Butler, 1993). Discussion with all three parties led to the following qualities being accepted as important:

- Fast start. Of the 12 Olympic boxing finals, all of which were decided on points, NO boxer behind on points after round one went on to win. As scores were made public after each round it is possible the judges were vulnerable to a 'halo' effect whereby their observations of the second and third rounds were influenced by their expectations of a boxer who was ahead after the first round. Other factors must also come in to play, not least the way a boxer might tactically defend an early lead. An effective start to the bout, whatever the reason, seems to place the boxer at an advantage.

- Positive/dominate. The boxer moving forward, trying to capture the initiative, and seeking to gain control of the ring seemed eminently more likely to find favour with the judges, as if such prominent actions raised their profile in the judges' perception of the contest.
- Avoid warnings. Alongside the red and blue button, each judge has a white button to acknowledge a warning the referee might give to a boxer for contravening the rules. A warning incurs the loss of three points. Clearly the lower the scoring of a bout the more influential a warning becomes in determining the result. At the 1992 Olympics the average number of points per contest was 18.1 (only six points per round) and 16 per cent of bouts were decided by a margin of three points or less. This suggests a warning can have an inordinate impact on the result.
- Boxing distance. This refers to keeping within range of the opponent so that the probability of punches landing is increased, whilst not moving into a range too close to the opponent which results in punches not being registered by the judges because they become more difficult to distinguish.
- Clear shots. A clean accurate punch delivered from an appropriate distance improves the chance of each judge differentiating it from the hectic milieu.
- Powerful jab. The leading punch, often used as a 'feeler', has to be delivered with some force if the judge is to register it as a scoring shot.
- Quick rear hand/powerful rear hand. The rear hand delivers the usual scoring shot (hooks, straight, uppercuts) and with the scoring machine, needs to be executed with speed and power, given the few shots that judges record.
- Fast doubles (combinations). Landing a combination of two punches increases the likelihood of a judge recording a punch.
- Phases of attack. A concerted attack consisting of a flurry of punches is unlikely to score more than one point because the judges have difficulty in distinguishing between them. Thus attacks consisting of phases – moving in and out with single shots or two punch combinations – increase the chance of more than one shot counting.
- Body shots. Most scoring punches seem to be those that land on the head. Shots to the body were included to add variety and surprise in addition to intimidating the opponent to drop his guard.
- Work for opening. Encouraging the boxer to employ various

tactical approaches to increase their opponent's vulnerability, particularly during the later stages of the contest, has the advantage of conserving energy, maintaining control and scoring with more calculated punches.

- Catch them coming on. Often the punch which catches the attention of the judge is the one which lands as the opponent moves into attack, as it stops them in their tracks.
- Use of feet. The ability to move in all directions is imperative in defence and launching effective attacks.
- Come back with last punch. Often the final shot landed in a cross-fire of punches is the one that will be scored by the judge.
- Tight guard. Effective defence is always essential and having a tight guard seems the most appropriate way of preventing an otherwise scoring punch landing.

Figure 2.3 illustrates a Scoring Machine Profile for a boxer in preparation for the European championships. This profile has a different structure to the Performance Profile in order to make the distinction clear. Apart from it being constructed from a consensus of views it meets, in general, all the theoretical assumptions that underlie the Performance Profile. The process of completing the Scoring Machine Profile is also similar with the boxer being clear as to the meaning of each quality, rating himself out of ten on each quality and presenting the rating visually on the profile.

A profile like the one illustrated in Figure 2.3 can influence the training programme quite markedly. It indicates the boxer's perceived strengths (clear shots, powerful jab) and perceived weaknesses (phases of attack, footwork). Strengths might become the focus during the taper towards competition as a means of emphasizing the boxer's confidence (Butler *et al.*, 1993). Weaknesses call for intervention.

Traditionally goal setting has been advocated as a means of enabling athletes to structure a direction, delineate necessary tasks to achieve a goal and help sustain their efforts whilst working on the tasks. There is much to be said for integrating a goal setting approach with that of profiling in order to help the athlete improve in areas in which they consider themselves weak. However goal setting has its theoretical roots in industry and management (Ravey and Scully, 1989), and therefore integrating such diverse theoretical notions can only be undertaken with some caution.

Weinberg's notion of goal setting is useful here. He defines a goal

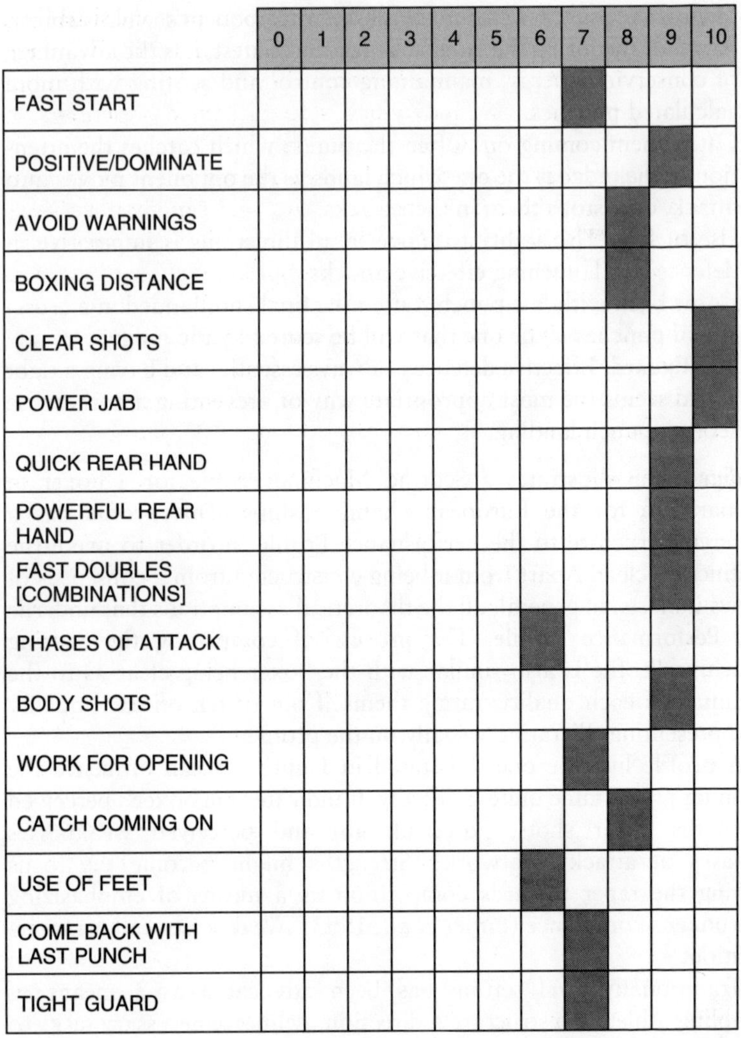

	0	1	2	3	4	5	6	7	8	9	10
FAST START								■			
POSITIVE/DOMINATE										■	
AVOID WARNINGS									■		
BOXING DISTANCE									■		
CLEAR SHOTS											■
POWER JAB											■
QUICK REAR HAND										■	
POWERFUL REAR HAND										■	
FAST DOUBLES [COMBINATIONS]										■	
PHASES OF ATTACK							■				
BODY SHOTS										■	
WORK FOR OPENING									■		
CATCH COMING ON									■		
USE OF FEET							■				
COME BACK WITH LAST PUNCH								■			
TIGHT GUARD								■			

Figure 2.3   *Scoring machine profile*

simply as 'what the individual is consciously trying to do' (Weinberg, 1994). This stance predicts an athlete is likely to define goals for himself following a perception of weakness in any area, if he considers it to be of any importance. Indeed Weinberg and his colleagues found that the majority of athletes set their own goals even in situations where they are specifically asked just to 'do your best' (Weinberg *et al.*, 1985). This collates with a Personal Construct Theory notion of choice which suggests that individuals select a course of action that will best validate their view of events. Thus athletes, by their very nature, will elect to act in ways which they consider will improve their performance. The problem may be that their choices might not always be the most appropriate ones. The coach and psychologist's responsibility is to guide the athlete towards appropriate goals and actions. This is in accord also with the findings of Erez and Kanfer (1983) and Erez and Zideon (1984) who discovered the most effective goals were those that were self assigned.

Within the context of goal setting, perceived weaknesses such as those in Figure 2.3 might be practically addressed as follows:

- Determine how important the quality is for the athlete. This can be accomplished by inviting the athlete to rate how they would ideally wish to be on each quality. This seems particularly important given that the qualities are not wholly self generated. A rating of ten implies a long-term goal (Jones, 1993). Undertaking such a process corresponds to Garland's theory of goal setting which asserts that a goal is an image of a future level of performance the athlete wishes to achieve (Garland, 1985).

- Ascertain if the athlete anticipates any disadvantage in accomplishing the ideal level. A boxer might, for example, consider a fast start to be fraught with danger because it prevents him from 'sizing up his opponent's weaknesses'. As Tschudi (1977) suggests, where an athlete construes a disadvantage in what might otherwise be considered an ideal state, there is resistance. At this juncture the coach and psychologist have to address the athlete's reasoning for resisting change if any future training programme focused on that area is to be effective. The concern of the boxer in Figure 2.3 about starting a bout on the offensive was overcome by discussing the evidence collected from two major championships which demonstrated the advantages of an early lead. The boxer also examined video evidence of his own performances which suggested that 'sizing up' of the opponent could be expedited.

- Consider what possibilities or options are available for enabling the athlete to achieve the goal. This will invariably be coach or psychologist led, given they are in the Kellyan sense more knowledgeable about the available techniques for enhancing performance. However, the decision over which particular course of action to take necessitates the athlete's involvement because, as Kelly (1955) intimated in his supervisor–student metaphor, the process of change is enhanced where each participant contributes their expertise.

Performance Profiling offers a means by which the coach and psychologist can understand the athlete's unique way of perceiving themself in relation to what they consider important in facilitating a top performance. Undertaking such a task enables the coach and psychologist to work with the athlete in developing training programmes apposite to the athlete's needs. This chapter has described an evolution of the process whereby a profile has been designed to enhance the athlete's awareness in relation to the particular demands of a major change in the way performance is judged. Thus whereas the Performance Profile assesses the athlete's notions of important aspects of performance, the recent development examines the athlete's assessment of performance against a template of agreed qualities. Whilst this development requires extra vigilance in terms of ensuring the athlete understands the qualities, the rest of the process bears a close resemblance to Performance Profiling.

Performance Profiling has the potential to enhance the delivery of sport psychology services (Jones, 1993). It is increasingly being adopted by coaches and psychologists as a framework for analysing the athlete's needs and for monitoring progress towards agreed and self generated goals. The technique is additionally being employed to assist coaches and psychologists to grapple with issues imposed on them by rule alterations, as this chapter has illustrated. Of primary importance, Performance Profiling encourages the move towards more idiographic approaches in applied sports psychology, a stance persuasively suggested by Martens (1987) and Smith (1988).

Acknowledgements

I am grateful to the Sports Council for their support through the Sports Science Support Programme for providing the framework to enable me to apply these psychological approaches. I am further indebted to Ian Irwin and Marcus Smith for their encouragement and ideas in the development of Performance Profiling. This chapter owes a lot to Emma Hiley, who guided the shape of the manuscript. Finally, to the host of amateur boxers who have readily contributed to the process of Performance Profiling I owe a great deal.

References

Banniers, D. (1983) Personal construct psychotherapy. *British J. Hospital Medicine*, 7, 72–74.

Bannister, D. and Fransella, F. (1986) *Inquiring Man: The Psychology of Personal Constructs*. London: Croom Helm.

Boutcher, S.H. and Rotella, R.J. (1987) A psychological skills educational programme for closed skill performance enhancement. *The Sport Psychologist*, 1, 127–137.

Bull, S.J. (1991) Personal and situational influences on adherence to mental skills training. *Journal of Sport and Exercise Psychology*, 13, 121–132.

Button, E. (1985) *Personal Construct Theory and Mental Health*. Beckenham: Croom Helm.

Butler, R.J. (1989) Psychological preparation of Olympic boxers. In *The Psychology of Sport: Theory and Practice* (J. Kremer and W. Crawford, eds) pp. 74–84. Leicester: British Psychological Society.

Butler, R.J. (1993) Some thoughts on Barcelona 92. *World Amateur Boxing Magazine*, 1, 8–9.

Butler, R.J. (1995) *Sports Psychology in Action*. Oxford: Butterworth-Heinemann.

Butler, R.J. and Hardy, L. (1992) The performance profile: theory and application. *The Sport Psychologist*, 6, 253–264.

Butler, R.J., Smith, M. and Irwin, I. (1993) The performance profile in practice. *Journal of Applied Sports Psychology*, 5, 48–63.

Erez, M. and Kanfer, F. H. (1983) The role of goal acceptance in goal setting and task performance. *Academy of Management Review*, 8, 454–463.

Erez, M. and Zideon, I. (1984) Effects of goal acceptance on the relationship of goal difficulty to performance. *Journal of Applied Psychology*, 69, 69–78.

Fransella, F. and Dalton, P. (1990) *Personal Construct Counselling in Action*. London: Sage.

Garland, H. (1985) A cognitive mediation of task goals and human performance. *Motivation and Emotion*, 9, 345–367.

Gordon, S. (1990) A mental skills training programme for the Western Australian State cricket team. *The Sport Psychologist*, 4, 386–399.

Jones, G. (1993) The role of performance profiling in cognitive behavioural interventions in sport. *The Sport Psychologist*, 7, 160–172.

Kelly, G.A. (1955) *The Psychology of Personal Constructs*. Vols I and II. New York: Norton.

Kelly, G.A. (1977) The psychology of the unknown. In *New Perspectives on Personal Construct Theory* (D. Bannister, ed.) pp. 1–19. London: Academic Press.

Martens, R. (1987) Science, knowledge and sport psychology. *Sport Psychology*, 1, 29–55.

Ravenette, A.T. (1977) PCT: an approach to the psychological investigation of children and young people. In *New Perspectives in Personal Construct Theory* (D. Bannister, ed.) pp. 251–280. London: Academic Press.

Ravey, J. and Scully, D. (1989) The cognitive psychology of sport. In *The Psychology of Sport: Theory and Practice* (J. Kremer and W. Crawford, eds) pp. 37–48. Leicester: British Psychological Society.

Ravizza, K. (1986) Increasing awareness for sport performance. In *Applied Sport Psychology: Personal Growth to Peak Performance* (J.M. Williams, ed.) pp. 32–56. Palo Alto, California: Mayfield.

Ravizza, K. (1989) Applying sports psychology. In *The Psychology of Sport: Theory and Practice* (J. Kremer and W. Crawford, eds) pp. 5–15. Leicester: British Psychological Society.

Smith, R. (1988) The logic and design of case study research. *Sport Psychology*, 2, 1–12.

Thomas, L.F. (1979) Construct, reflect and converse: the conversational reconstruction of social realities. In *Constructs of Sociality and Individuality* (P. Stringer and D. Bannister, eds) pp. 49–72. London: Academic Press.

Tschudi, F. (1977) Loaded and honest questions. In *New Perspectives in Personal Construct Theory* (D. Bannister, ed.) pp. 321–350. London: Academic Press.

Weinberg, R.S. (1994) Goal setting and performance in sport and exercise settings: a synthesis and critique. *Medicine and Science in Sports and Exercise*, 26, 469–477.

Weinberg, R.S., Bruya, L. and Jackson, A. (1985) The effects of goal proximity and goal specificity on endurance and performance. *Journal of Sport Psychology*, 7, 296–305.

Winter, D.A. (1992) *Personal Construct Psychology in Clinical Practice*. London: Routledge.

3

The test of attentional and interpersonal style (TAIS) and its practical application

Ian Maynard

Sport: Cycling

Among the many psychological variables that have been studied in the area of human performance, the field of attention is of particular importance. Nideffer (1976a) has claimed, 'it is hard to imagine a variable more central to performance than the ability to direct and control one's attention'. Within the field of sport Maynard and Howe (1989) contend that regardless of whether an individual is learning or performing in a sport setting, attention to the most appropriate cues remains the critical variable. However, in spite of the tremendous importance of the control of attention, or in simplistic terms, concentration, very little has been done to systematically train athletes to concentrate more effectively (Nideffer, 1992).

The concept of attention can be viewed in at least two distinct ways according to Reis and Bird (1982). From the information processing viewpoint, attention is said to be the process that actively selects the inputs to, operation in, and response from, the central operating space, thereby determining the direction of behaviour (Kahneman, 1973; Klein, 1976). Differential psychology, in contrast, proposes that individuals have a characteristic style of attending to stimuli, which is viewed as a personality trait or individual difference variable. Furthermore, it has been proposed that some persons generally attend to stimuli in a very broad, externally-oriented manner, while others tend to be narrow in attentional scope and more introspective. Because of this, it is assumed that people with different attentional styles will process different cues (Bird and Cripe, 1986).

Based upon theoretical constructs proposed by Broadbent (1957), and upon reviews by Silverman (1964) and Wachtel (1967), Nideffer (1973, 1976b, 1981) developed a theory of attention. This theory states that the concept of attention can be dichotomized in two dimensions. The first dimension can be viewed as an internal–external continuum in which the focus of attention is directed either inwards towards the individual, or towards the external environment. The second dimension refers to the width of the focus (narrow to broad), indicating the number of elements to which one can attend in a stimulus field. A narrow focus of attention would facilitate performance in a situation which demands concentration on limited stimuli (for example, a free-throw in basketball). Conversely, during a rugby union game the scrum-half (a primary decision-maker) must frequently attend to a number of incoming stimuli and make his or her decisions accordingly. This situation would require a broad focus of attention.

Nideffer suggested that certain sports require a particular integration of the direction (internal to external) dimension with the focal width dimensions, in order for an individual to perform adequately. He further proposed, that for an individual to function effectively that person's attention must correspond to the environmental demands; should that not be the case, mistakes will occur. An appropriate attentional style, therefore, would seem to be an important determinant of sport performance (Figure 3.1).

Nideffer (1976c) used golf to exemplify such a series of attentional shifts. Selection of a golf club requires a broad external focus to take into consideration certain factors such as distance, the lie of the ball, weather conditions and location of hazards. A broad internal focus then becomes necessary to integrate this new information with what is already known of past performance under similar conditions. Once the situation is analysed, attention must focus narrowly and externally on the execution of the swing itself, rejecting irrelevant thoughts. Following the shot, a narrow internal review may be necessary to evaluate and mentally replay the performance.

Nideffer (1976a) contended that attentional style may be utilized to predict performance across a variety of situations. The concept that performance may be predicted on the basis of attentional processes suggests that the ability to control focus of attention is constant across competitive situations. Nideffer (1980) further suggested that individuals have a dominant style of attention and consequently tend to demonstrate certain related strengths and weaknesses. He hypothesized that when under pressure or in stressful conditions, athletes find it increasingly difficult to control and shift attention, and at such times are more likely to rely on their dominant style. Nideffer (1981) also recognized the implications that an attentional focus would have

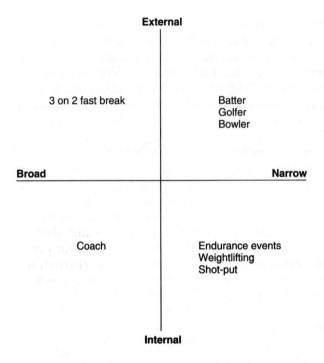

Figure 3.1   *Nideffer's model of attentional focus*

which is either too broad or too narrow. Too broad a focus allows an overload of information to interfere with appropriate decision-making; too narrow a focus causes one to become over analytical in assessing the situation.

In an attempt to assess these hypothesized individual differences, Nideffer (1976b, 1976c) developed a personality inventory, the Test of Attentional and Interpersonal Style (TAIS). The test contains seventeen subscales, six assessing attentional processes, two involved with behavioural and cognitive control, and nine mapping interpersonal style. The six subscales that reflect attentional processes are broad external attentional focus (BET), overloaded by external stimuli (OET), broad internal attentional focus (BIT), overloaded by internal stimuli (OIT), narrow attentional focus (NAR) and reduced attentional focus (RED). High scores on three of the six attentional subscales reflect positive attentional traits (BET, BIT and NAR), while high scores on the remaining scales reflect negative attentional traits (OET, OIT and RED). Subscales BET and BIT are compared to determine the athlete's predisposition to a particular directional preference, external to internal. The comparison between the sets of paired subscales BET/OET, BIT/OIT and NAR/RED, reflect an individual's attentional competencies along the bandwidth dimension (Table 3.1).

Table 3.1   *Attentional Subscales of the Test of Attentional and Interpersonal Style (TAIS)*

BET Broad External	High scores on this scale are obtained by individuals who describe themselves as being able to integrate effectively many external stimuli at one time.
OET Overloaded by External Stimuli	The higher the score, the more individuals make mistakes because they become confused and overloaded with external stimuli.
BIT Broad Internal	High scores indicate individuals who see themselves as able to integrate effectively ideas and information from several different areas. They are analytical and philosophical, good at planning and anticipating consequences.
OIT Overloaded by Internal Stimuli	The higher the score, the more mistakes individuals make because they confuse or distract themselves by thinking about too many things at once.
NAR Narrow Focus	The higher the score, the more effective individuals see themselves with respect to being able to narrow attention when they need to.
RED Reduced Focus	A high score on this scale indicates that the individual makes mistakes because his or her attention is too narrow.

The use of the TAIS for research in sport

The TAIS has demonstrated good internal consistency and high test–retest reliability (Nideffer, 1976b). Predictive validity has also been supported in a number of studies. For instance, Nideffer (1976b) indicated that the TAIS was an effective device for predicting the differences between good and poor college-level competitive swimmers. Likewise, Aronson (1981) and Zaichkowsky (1980) examining the attentional processes of gymnasts and elite track athletes, respectively, found the TAIS to be a strong predictor of successful performance. Using discriminant function and multiple regression techniques, the investigators found independently, that the TAIS was associated with 40–60 per cent of the performance variance.

In contrast to these results, there have been studies which have failed to replicate the discriminatory functions of the TAIS. Vallerand (1983), when assessing attentional style and decision-making in performers of different ability levels found the TAIS subscales unable to differentiate between ability groups. In particular, Vallerand investigated the 'Scan' (higher BET, BIT and INFP scales) and 'focus' (low OET and OIT, but high NAR scales) factors of performers in the basketball situation. No differences were found between three ability groups in terms of these factors.

Other researchers (Etzel, 1979; Landers *et al.*, 1981; Van Schoyck and Grasha, 1981) have questioned aspects of the underlying attentional dimensions of the TAIS as proposed by Nideffer. For example, Van Schoyck and Grasha (1981), categorizing 90 subjects in three different skill levels, sought to examine the way in which attentional processes vary as a function of one's skill. As part of the study, the investigators developed a sport-specific measure for tennis (T-TAIS), adapted directly from the TAIS. The authors proposed that Nideffer's two-dimensional model of attentional style should be supported by the nature of the intercorrelations among the subscales. Intercorrelations for many of the subscales on both instruments were high, thus suggesting the subscales are not independent. Both attentional dimensions, direction and width, were also found within the same scales (BET, BIT, OET and OIT) of the TAIS. Van Schoyck and Grasha (1981) further contended that if the direction and bandwidth of attention were adequately assessed by the TAIS and T-TAIS, the subscales possessing the two dimensions would be negatively correlated. Results revealed high positive correlations for the directional attentional elements, indicating common factors among subscale pairs (BET, BIT and OET, OIT). The conclusions implied direction may not be a significant component of the scales and the concept of width may be multidimensional.

In response to these criticisms of the TAIS, Nideffer (1987, 1990) made a number of astute observations. Initially he suggested that notions of statistical independence are relative. He suggested that although a correlation of 0.7 accounts for approximately 50 per cent of the variability between two scores, it also leaves 50 per cent of variance unaccounted. Hence, although it may be concluded that one failed to find evidence for independence of the variables, one also cannot conclude that this does not exist. Nideffer (1987) indicated that the use of response sets, by subjects, can improve predictive validity, by making the questionnaire more situation-specific and also give subjects an 'anchor' or frame of reference to whom they compare themselves. Such an anchoring system should improve the inventory's ability to discriminate across levels because subjects would then mentally compare themselves and their performance with the entire population, as opposed to subjects of a similar ability to themselves.

Finally, Nideffer also questioned the previously mentioned authors' understanding of the theory underlying the development of the TAIS, because they failed to manipulate the level of arousal within tasks. This is because it is only under conditions of increasing arousal that Nideffer (1990, p. 290) suggests the attentional preferences of subjects begin to affect performance.

> 'Unless researchers manipulate arousal, unless they look for within-subject changes, and unless they control for response set influences, they cannot expect to find the relationships that they have been hypothesizing or to account for much of the variance in those studies designed to examine the predictive validity and/or reliability of the TAIS.'

A series of more recent studies which have subjected the TAIS to factor analyses have also criticized the inventory's attentional dimensions of width and direction (Dewey *et al.*, 1989; Bergandi *et al.*, 1990; Ford and Summers, 1992). In response, Nideffer (1987, 1990) offers some compelling arguments in favour of the TAIS. He suggests that the TAIS is basically a personality inventory, and personality is not a strong predictor of performance. He further indicates that critics have consistently utilized only six or seven of the eighteen subscales of the TAIS and have expected them to be highly predictive of athletic performance. Finally, Nideffer notes that as a consequence of these factor analyses, researchers have tended to reduce the number of attentional variables and produce fewer, but more general, concepts such as scanning and focusing (Van Schoyck and Grasha, 1981) or effective attentional style and ineffective attentional style (Bergandi *et al.*, 1990). He suggests that collapsing scales in this way, may make sense for a researcher who needs to reduce the number of variables under investigation, but it does not make sense for the practitioner who is trying to provide feedback to an individual. He contends that people in sport are well aware of the need to become more specific in their training programmes, not less specific. However, Ford and Summers (1992) in considering Nideffer's contentions did conclude the overall evidence does indicate poor factorial validity for the TAIS attentional-style subscales. The significant item-scale overlap and the large interscale correlations found in theirs and other studies (Van Schoyck and Grasha, 1981; Vallerand, 1983; Dewey *et al.*, 1989) suggest that most of the items may be measuring a smaller set of factors than intended. They further suggest that fewer than six factors are measured by the TAIS attentional subscales and that little evidence indicates that the test adequately discriminates according to the direction dimensions.

The inadequacies of the general TAIS have led to the development of sport-specific versions of the TAIS. For example, as previously mentioned Van Schoyck and Grasha (1981) developed a sport-specific test for tennis (T-TAIS) and compared it with the TAIS for internal consistency, test–retest reliability and predictive validity. For the T-TAIS, Van Schoyck and Grasha (1981) rewrote each item of the Nideffer test for the subscales of BET, OET, BIT, OIT, NAR, and RED. Results of the analysis revealed that the internal consistency and the test–retest reliability of the tennis-specific test were superior to the parent test. The T-TAIS was also a better predictor of tennis playing ability than the TAIS.

Albrecht and Feltz (1987) also assessed the extent to which the attentional subscales of the TAIS and a sport-specific version of those scales could predict baseball/softball batting performance (Batting-TAIS). Like the situation-specific test of T-TAIS, the Batting-TAIS demonstrated higher levels of reliability and internal consistency than the parent test. In terms of predictive validity the Batting-TAIS was again superior to the TAIS. The sport-specific version of the test demonstrated positive correlations between effective attentional subscales and performance, whereas the TAIS did not. As one would expect, and as is the case with most situation-specific personality tests, the predictive validity of the test is enhanced when an interactional model between the person and the situation is used. However, Summers and Ford (1990) contend that sport-specific versions of the TAIS, although improving concurrent and predictive validity in some cases, have not dramatically improved the measurement of attentional styles in sport. They further suggest that where sport-specific versions of the TAIS attentional subscales are constructed as parallel versions of the parent instrument, the same measurement problems encountered in the general TAIS would carry over to sport-specific versions. In conclusion these researchers state that there is mounting evidence that the TAIS attentional-style subscales lack construct validity. This could simply be due to the test scales' poor operationalizations of the model of attentional style, but is more likely that the model of attentional style is inadequate. Although intuitively appealing Ford and Summers (1992) contend that Nideffer's model of attentional style is almost certainly an over simplification of attentional operation and they suggest the test could be broadened to incorporate dimensions such as flexibility, selectivity, maintenance and capacity (Etzel, 1979).

Interpretation and feedback of the TAIS attentional subscales

In this section I shall outline how I have used the TAIS as one method of assessing athletes and coaches. I should stress that along with the TAIS I personally like to talk extensively with the athletes, coaches and/or important others, get the athletes and coaches to keep logs and diaries, as well as get the athletes and coaches to complete one or two psychometric tests. By use of a triangulation of methods within the assessment phase of a consultancy, it is more likely that a good array of strengths or weaknesses may be identified, and also the consultant can take confidence if aspects are highlighted by more than one method of assessment.

I specifically utilize the TAIS to assess concentration via the attentional subscales, but have found the control and interpersonal subscales very useful for gaining insights into athletes or coaches as individuals, and the potential strengths and weaknesses of their working relationship. I should state that I always administer and provide formal feedback on the full questionnaire, but for the purpose of this paper will only illustrate and explain the attentional subscales of the inventory.

When administering the TAIS I attempt to control the subjects' response set by asking them to respond in a sport-specific way, as well as give them a comparison group. Feedback from the TAIS is used, along with other sources of information, in the design of a mental skills training programme and to provide an educational focus for the subject. I should also add that I have never used the TAIS in a group situation, although Nideffer (1992) advocates that the tool does have a role in this scenario.

Scores on the attentional subscales of the TAIS for two different international cyclists are presented in Figures 3.2 and 3.3. (A summary of the formal feedback on the attentional scales including interpretation and recommendations for each cyclist will follow each figure.)

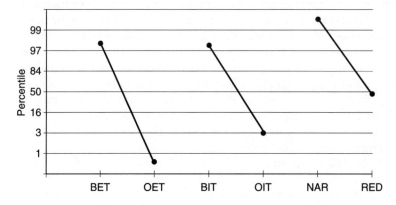

Figure 3.2 *Cyclist A – International amateur sprinter (track specialist)*

Cyclist A – Track Sprint Specialist

Columns 1 (BET), 3 (BIT) and 5 (NAR) identify positive aspects of your attentional style. The column that is the highest on your profile NAR (column 5), is probably your attentional strength or favoured concentration system. This would indicate that you see yourself as having the ability to narrow as you require. It is usual to combine this with the next highest effective score (either BET or BIT) to discover if you tend to narrow externally or internally, but as both are visually about the same, I would suggest that you can focus either towards the environment (a particular 'cue') or internally towards yourself (a particular thought or feeling), as you require.

It is also useful to try and identify your attentional weaknesses at this stage. However, your effective subscale scores being so much higher than 'their' paired ineffective subscale scores, suggests that you do not have any obvious weaknesses. I should point out that you may have a slight tendency to narrow too often, especially under pressure. Quite simply, you are overusing your attentional strength when perhaps it is not the appropriate concentration system to be using.

BET/OET – Broad External Focus of Attention

Broad external focus is like having a wide angle lens on a camera. It allows you to be aware of everything going on around you. An athlete who scores highly on BET is able to 'read and react' appropriately in busy situations. High BET athletes are often said to have a 'good street sense'. BET is essential for team sports where players need to be actively aware almost continuously of the flow of the entire game in order to spot the open player, or know where and when to make a move. For individual sports, high BET scores may be more a distraction than a help. Hence, you should be aware when it is important to revert to your strength and 'narrow-in' onto the relevant cues in your environment. As mentioned previously, this will tend to happen anyway when you find yourself in a pressure situation.

Your OET score indicates how easy it is for you to be distracted by unimportant things around you. The higher your OET score, the more difficult it is for you to switch off your overloaded broad external system and focus on details. Because your BET is so much higher than your OET score, I would suggest you would very seldom become overloaded by your environment in the cycling situation.

BIT/OIT – Broad Internal Focus of Attention

If you were asked to plan your next three years of training and competition you would be using your broad internal attentional system, that is, you would have to analyse, organize and plan; deal with a lot of information at once; recall information, mix it with what is happening at the moment, and draw some logical conclusions. You are using your BIT system if you 'look before you leap', but be aware that an athlete who is focusing internally has forfeited (temporarily) some of his or her ability to react to environmental changes.

Your high BIT score indicates that: you will rarely be involved in anything without first fully analysing what it means and projecting the anticipated results or consequences; you often fail to hear everything said to you because your mind has raced ahead as you think you know what is going to be said; you look away to where the ball is supposed to go rather than staying focused on the ball until the action is completed.

You may be analytical under pressure. You may make mistakes because of a tendency to over analyse. You may spend too much time inside your head, and not enough time paying attention to what is going on around you. However, once again because your OIT score is visually so much lower than your BIT score, I would suggest the overload situation I have described will seldom occur, but it is worth being aware of the problem.

NAR/RED – *Narrow Focus of Attention*

Your NAR score indicates your ability to concentrate in a focused way, to discipline yourself, and to avoid being distracted. High scorers can easily become absorbed, that is, give their undivided attention to one thing (either externally or internally). They are extremely dedicated and have a great ability to follow through on even boring routines. High scorers practise with a sense of purpose few people have.

Your NAR score would indicate: you are likely to become even more narrowly focused under pressure, making mistakes possibly because you fail to consider alternatives; you have difficulty altering plans, hearing new ideas; time deadlines and multiple demands are stressful; your training sessions may be too long or you may not consider including things important to others.

Although your effective subscale (NAR) is much higher than the ineffective (RED) and so the vast majority of the time you will be in control, the RED score is at an average level. This suggests that very occasionally you may make errors of under-inclusion, for example, not taking in sufficient cues from your environment to make valid decisions.

In summary, I should state you have an exceptionally effective attentional profile. I have indicated one or two factors that will only very seldom impinge upon your concentration, but being aware of these factors will be more than half way to ensuring they do not have a detrimental effect on your performance.

60 *Sports Psychology in Performance*

Cyclist B – Road Based Stage-racing Specialist

Columns 1, 3 and 5 identify positive aspects of your attentional style. The column that is clearly the highest NAR (column 5), is your attentional strength or favoured concentration system. Likewise the column which is the lowest BIT (column 3) is probably your attentional weakness. It should also be remembered that for different reasons your attentional strength can also become problematic, especially under pressure. This is because you will tend to overuse the system with which you feel most comfortable, even when it may not be the correct system to use; hence mistakes will be made.

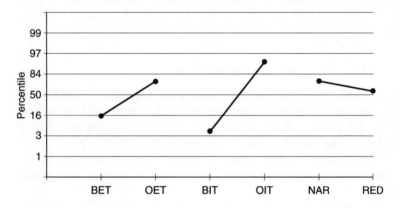

Figure 3.3 *Cyclist B – International professional stage-racer (road-specialist)*

BET/OET – Broad External Focus of Attention

The low score for BET suggests that situations where you have to attend to a great deal of external information at once will be problematic, and hence stressful. Likewise, because your OET score is higher than your BET score you will: have difficulty paying attention; tend to shy away from busy situations because of your relative difficulty in dealing with large amounts of information; probably feel more comfortable in one-on-one situations; be highly distracted by your environment, so having to concentrate when conditions are 'noisy' is certain to increase both frustration and errors.

BIT/OIT – Broad Internal Focus of Attention

Because your BIT score is low any situation requiring extensive use of your analytical ability is likely to be stressful for you; long range planning will make you feel pressured; you will probably let your attention wander to other systems with which you are more comfortable; you would rather just read a book than analyse its style.

Your OIT score being visually so much higher than your BIT score indicates your tendency to be distracted by your own thoughts, which keeps you from noticing what is going on around you; this is often termed 'paralysis by analysis'. This suggests you may get 'stuck inside your head' thinking too many thoughts, rather than acting upon cues from your environment. You will get confused by having a lot of information to process internally; you prefer your own thoughts and feelings to what is going on outside in your surroundings; any pressure to switch from your thoughts to dealing with the environment may be stressful.

NAR/RED – Narrow Focus of Attention

Your high score on NAR indicates you can be easily absorbed and give your undivided attention to one thing (either internally or externally). You are extremely dedicated and have a great ability to follow through on even boring routines. Your score suggests that you will practise with a sense of purpose few people have. NAR being your attentional strength suggests you are likely to become even more narrowly focused under pressure, making mistakes because you fail to consider alternatives; you have difficulty altering plans or hearing new ideas; time deadlines and multiple demands are stressful; your professionalism may result in training or practising so narrowly or repetitively that you are seen as boring to others.

The RED score reflects the tendency for your concentration to go awry, that is, to focus too much on matters which are irrelevant to your best performance. Your RED score being almost on a par with NAR suggests you feel pressure a great deal of the time; you are probably a worrier, and find it difficult to forget your fears and distractions without getting some help from outside.

In summary, I should state that there are aspects of your attentional profile that you and your coach may feel you need to work upon. I will identify these problem areas and suggest some strategies that may help when you find yourself under pressure. I suggest you discuss these strategies with your coach, manager or whoever you see as appropriate and between us we can make the techniques specific to your needs, and of course specific to your sport.

You will tend to suffer from external overload, where there is too much 'noise' (from the crowd, team-mates, coaches/managers, other cyclists), too much movement around, or just too many complex things to watch or listen to. You will also probably suffer from internal overload, where there are too many thoughts rushing through your head, too many coaching or tactical points to think about or too many conflicting negative statements.

Our first strategy will involve you learning some techniques that will allow you to more readily control your level of arousal. As these techniques are mastered and become skills, you will be more able to cope with the pressures of competition. Firstly, you must learn to tell yourself that pressure is not necessarily a negative experience. We must try and understand that the rush of adrenalin that competition brings, which causes the bodily symptoms that we perceive as anxiety (that is, sweaty palms, racing heart-beat, muscle tension or butterflies) are merely the body's way of telling us that it is ready to compete, not something that should upset us. Likewise, in your mental skills training programme, we will include a technique, such as applied relaxation, that will help you cope with these bodily symptoms of somatic anxiety, if and when you feel they are getting out of your control.

The pressure of competition often also forces us to think negatively; for example, we may start to doubt our ability to do ourselves justice in this race. These negative thoughts are the major symptom of cognitive anxiety. Cognitive anxiety may also increase when we start to interpret the bodily symptoms of increased arousal as a negative experience. Hence, whether it is the competition itself that causes us to think negatively, or our interpretation of increased bodily arousal, the net effect will be an increase in cognitive anxiety or negative thoughts. The best way to deal with these negative thoughts is to try to stop them before they damage your performance. Getting rid of negative thoughts helps you regain the proper focus of attention to the task at hand, your cycle race. Learning the skill of thought stopping involves concentrating on the undesired thought briefly, then using a cue or trigger to stop the thought and clear your mind. The trigger can be a simple word like 'STOP' or an action like squeezing the handlebars of the bike (you will need to decide what is the best natural cue that works for you). The next stage will be changing negative thoughts to positive thoughts (countering), which we may use to redirect our attention or provide encouragement and motivation.

A further strategy that helps reduce over-arousal induced by the pressure of competition involves the development of a process orientation to cycling, rather than an outcome orientation. During training, especially in sports such as cycling that require a great deal of commitment and sacrifice on your part, you will probably motivate yourself by thinking about outcomes: 'If I win the race, I'll get a lot of media attention. By making these sacrifices I can get the recognition and financial rewards I want.' Once the competition begins, however, an outcome focus can become very negative. Thinking about the importance of winning the race or the failure that losing the race will bring, typically induces more anxiety. Hence, we must not place so much importance on the outcome (during the competition), but rather focus on the process of performing as opposed to the outcome. For example, you might focus on some technical aspects of your body position when riding, or perhaps focus on generating a rhythm. Over time, you will realize that maintaining this type of focus will help the outcome take care of itself.

Applied relaxation, thought stopping, countering and developing a process orientation will require a great deal of practice; do not expect overnight success. These techniques are best restricted to practice and low pressure races, until you feel they are well-learnt skills. We will discuss the development and use of these strategies in more depth, when next we meet and decide if you wish to include them in your mental skills programme.

A second series of strategies that you may consider, involves the development of some clear and well-learnt performance plans. Attempting to make decisions when under pressure will ultimately only lead to a greater sense of overload. Therefore, being able to refer to pre-made decisions (where possible) will help you to cope with the high pressure situations. Performance planning may involve short-term refocusing techniques or more long-term race tactics. Before races you can identify important task-relevant performance cues to 'look at' or 'attend to' when you have become distracted, or develop an alternative race strategy if your major tactics are not working. These types of pre-made plans will help overcome potentially stressful situations induced by having to make decisions under pressure. A similar concept called objective analysis will involve the identification of where errors have occurred and the role that concentration mis-match has played during a race. A greater awareness of strengths and weaknesses within your concentration will be an important part of your overall performance analysis strategy. In all aspects of your cycling our aim will be to eliminate the poor elements of your performance and recreate the good elements, as a means of improving performance consistency.

Summary

The two examples of TAIS feedback illustrated highlight the potential diversity in attentional styles even within elite performers from the same sport. Although both cyclists had a similar attentional strength, the first example would closely approach Nideffer's (1981) effective profile, whereas the second would equate much more to an ineffective profile. It should also be noted that the actual attentional demands of the two disciplines within the same sport are also vastly different. The sprinter would seldom have more than one or two important cues of which to be aware, whereas the environment of the road-racer would be both more complicated and constantly changing. I should further state that the strategies outlined for the second cyclist were felt to be appropriate to them in their situation; more definitive accounts for improving concentration in sport are available (Weinberg, 1988; Nideffer, 1992; Schmid and Peper, 1992). As a final rather ironic point, it should also be noted that the second profile belongs to probably the most successful British road-racer of the last two decades. Cyclist B has won international multi-stage road races as well as stages of the Tour de France. His record provides further support for the sceptical who suggest personality is not a good indicator of performance; the more credulous amongst us would ask just how much more successful this rider could have been if these problems could have been dealt with early in his career.

Conclusions

It would seem the majority of recent research has aired serious misgivings about the psychometric properties of the TAIS. Various investigators (Dewey *et al.*, 1989; Bergandi *et al*, 1990; Ford and Summers, 1992) have questioned the factorial validity, construct validity or predictive validity of the tool to the extent that future experimenters may see little research potential in the inventory as it stands. However, although the TAIS may not be a valid test of a theoretical construct, many practitioners would agree it can play important diagnostic and/or educational roles, in the applied setting. The simplicity of Nideffer's (1976a) concept of Attentional Style may be a weakness in the theoretical sense, but serves as its strength in practice. The intuitive appeal of the idea, and the ease with which athletes can understand it, suggests the inventory can be readily adapted for extensive use in sport.

In providing an evaluation of concentration the TAIS allows the practitioner to extract information from the client that would otherwise be difficult to elicit. However, probably the greatest strength of the questionnaire along with this assessment potential, is its use as an initial communication device. The feedback provided by the instrument provides an excellent starting point in the development of a rapport between athlete and sport psychologist, as well as suggesting possible aspects of a mental skills programme. Likewise, a comparison of feedback between coach and athlete can also open lines of communication that previously did not exist, or add considerable insight and understanding to their current relationship.

Like any psychometric measure the TAIS is open to abuse or bias, in that the psychologist can always be accused of setting the agenda. However, as long as the practitioner understands the limitations of the test and psychometric measures in general, uses it as a means to an end, rather than an end in itself, then the TAIS can provide a very useful service.

References

Albrecht, R.R. and Feltz, D.L. (1987) Generality and specificity of attention related to competitive anxiety and sport performance. *Journal of Sport Psychology*, **9**, 231–248.

Aronson, R.M. (1981) *Attentional and Interpersonal Factors as Discriminators of Elite and Non-elite Gymnasts*. Doctoral Dissertation (unpublished). Boston University.

Bergandi, T.A., Shryock, M.G. and Titus, T.G. (1990) The basketball concentration survey: preliminary development and validation. *The Sport Psychologist*, **4**, 119–129.

Bird, A.M. and Cripe, B.K. (1986) *Psychology and Sport Behaviour*. St. Louis: Times Mirror/Masby College Publishing.

Broadbent, D.E. (1957) A mechanical model for human attention and immediate memory. *Psychological Review*, **64**, 205–215.

Dewey, D., Brawley, L.R. and Allard, F. (1989). Do the TAIS attentional style scales predict how visual information is processed? *Journal of Sport and Exercise Psychology*, **11**, 171–186.

Etzel, E.F. (1979) Validation of a conceptual model characterising attention among international rifle shooters. *Journal of Sports Psychology,* **1,** 280–291.

Ford, S.K. and Summers, J.J. (1992) The factorial validity of the TAIS attentional style subscales. *Journal of Sport and Exercise Psychology,* **14,** 283–297.

Kahneman, D. (1973) *Attention and Effort.* Englewood Cliffs, NJ: Prentice Hall.

Klein, R.M. (1976) Attention and movement. In *Motor Control; Issues and Trends* (G.E. Stelmach, ed.). New York: Academic Press.

Landers, D.M., Furst, D.M. and Daniels, F.S. (1981) *Anxiety/Attention and Shooting Ability: Testing the Predictive Validity of the Test of Attentional and Interpersonal Style (TAIS).* College Park: North American Society for the Psychology of Sport and Physical Activity.

Maynard, I.W. and Howe, B.L. (1989) Attentional styles in rugby players. *Perceptual and Motor Skills,* **69,** 283–289.

Nideffer, R.M. (1973). *Test of Attentional and Interpersonal Style.* San Diego: Enhanced Performance Associates.

Nideffer, R.M. (1976a) *An Interpreter's Manual for the Test of Attentional and Interpersonal Style.* Rochester, NY: Behavioral Research Applications Group.

Nideffer, R.M. (1976b) Test of attention and interpersonal style. *Journal of Personality and Social Psychology,* **34,** 394–404.

Nideffer, R.M. (1976c) *The Inner Athlete.* New York: Cromwell.

Nideffer, R.M. (1980) Attentional focus – self assessment. In *Psychology in Sports* (R.M. Suinn, ed.). Minneapolis, MN: Burgess.

Nideffer, R.M. (1981) *Predicting Human Behavior: A Theory and Test of Attentional and Interpersonal Style.* San Diego: Enhanced Performance Associates.

Nideffer, R.M. (1987) Issues in the use of psychological tests in applied settings. *The Sport Psychologist,* **1,** 18–28.

Nideffer, R.M. (1990) Use of the Test of Attentional and Interpersonal Style (TAIS) in sport. *The Sport Psychologist,* **4,** 285–300.

Nideffer, R.M. (1992) Concentration and attention control training. In *Applied Sport Psychology – Personal Growth to Peak Performance* (J.M. Williams, ed.). California: Mayfield Publishing Company.

Reis, J.A. and Bird, A.M. (1982). Cue processing as a function of breadth of attention. *Journal of Sport Psychology,* **4,** 64–72.

Schmid, A. and Peper, E. (1992) Training strategies for concentration. In *Applied Sport Psychology – Personal Growth to Peak Performance* (J.M. Williams, ed.). California: Mayfield Publishing Company.

Silverman, J. (1964) The problem of attention in research and theory in schizophrenia. *Psychological Review,* **71,** 352–379.

Summers, J.J. and Ford, S.K. (1990) The test of attentional and interpersonal style: an evaluation. *International Journal of Sport Psychology,* **21,** 102–111.

Vallerand, R.J. (1983) Attention and decision making: a test of the predictive validity of the Test of Attentional and Interpersonal Style (TAIS) in a sport setting. *Journal of Sport Psychology,* **5,** 449–459.

Van Schoyck, S.R. and Grasha, A.F. (1981) Attentional style variations and athletic ability: the advantages of a sport specific test. *Journal of Sport Psychology*, 3, 149–165.

Wachtel, P.L. (1967) Conceptions of broad and narrow attention. *Psychological Bulletin*, 68, 417–429.

Weinberg, R.S. (1988) *The Mental Advantage – Developing your Psychological Skills in Tennis*. Champaign, IL: Leisure Press.

Zaichkowsky, L.D. (1980) *Attentional and Interpersonal Profiles of World Class Track Athletes*. Unpublished Study. Boston University.

4
A theoretical perspective of performance evaluation with a practical application

Tim Holder

Sport: Table Tennis

Introduction

Within the world of sport there are a plethora of individuals, associations and institutions that are constantly evaluating the performance of sportsmen and women in a critical, and in many cases, ruthless manner. It is no surprise then that in the field of sports science there has been considerable research into the way in which the process of evaluation takes place and the most effective methods to evaluate. One crucial question to be addressed is who is best equipped to evaluate sporting performance. Some sport scientists take the view that *post hoc* analysis of performance can be a highly structured, often computerized, objectively based evaluation; an approach adopted by those interested in notational analysis. Proponents of this viewpoint often argue (Hughes, 1993) that, due to attentional selectivity, the performer and coach are often in difficult positions to evaluate a particular performance due to the subjective basis for their evaluations. Others have argued strongly for the benefits of the development of reflective performers and the role to be played by the components of self regulation (self monitor, self evaluate and self consequate) within sporting situations (Kirschenbaum, 1984; Vallerand, 1987; Biddle, 1991; Sinclair and Sinclair, 1994). Also, more radically Rejeski (1981), when discussing the field of exercise psychology stated that, 'knowing what people think they are doing may well be more important than knowing what they are doing'.

In sport there are two main types of evaluations that can occur for the performer involving feedback as a source of information in both internal and external evaluations.

- External evaluation is carried out by another person or system outside of the performer. This can take the form of video feedback or feedback from the coach who has observed the performance.
- Internal evaluation is carried out by the performer through an awareness of the constituents which form actions and the outcome of the action performed.

Both external and internal forms of evaluation gather different forms of knowledge about performance which can be used to ultimately benefit subsequent performance. If knowledge of results (KR – information about the outcome of the action) and knowledge of performance (KP – information about the way the movement was performed or the process of performance) are integrated through the use of either external or internal evaluation or a combination of the two, then correction mechanisms and learning strategies can be put into place to aid future performance through accelerated learning.

With the basic elements of evaluation and feedback in mind, the principal emphasis for work in this area of applied sports psychology was established to be to investigate performances from the perspective of the individual performer. In adopting this approach it was important to develop a method of helping the performer by gaining access to, and subsequently working with, the individual perceptions resulting from competitive achievement situations.

In the following sections the research supporting the method of performance evaluation is described and subsequently the practical development of the Performance Evaluation Sheet is traced, and its modification over time discussed.

Theoretical basis for performance evaluation structure and procedure

Assessment and evaluation occur in many areas of normal life, from achievement of targets for productivity in the workplace to the intellectual evaluative process through examinations and coursework in educational establishments. The large amounts of literature that investigate the role and effectiveness of self evaluation and the process of finding answers to the questions 'What did I do well?', 'What did I not do well?' and 'What caused the performance to be the way it was?' began with research into the attributes of examination performances in education.

In the 1970s Bernard Weiner began investigations into the nature of people's reactions to achievement situations and developed a model which takes as its starting point 'that following an achievement outcome, individuals will engage in causal search to determine why a particular outcome occurred' (McAuley, 1992a). Weiner developed the model (Table 4.1) essentially for use in education and in its original formulation included four major attributions: ability, effort, task difficulty and luck. These elements were formalized into the two-dimensional structure shown below where the attributions were categorized with respect to the dimensions of locus of control and stability.

Table 4.1   *Weiner's (1972) model of causal attribution. Reprinted with permission from Weiner (1974)*

	Locus of control	
Stability	Internal	External
Stable	Ability	Task difficulty
Unstable	Effort	Luck

From work completed in attributional search it is clear that there are specific elements that affect the times at which attributions take place and the manner in which they are completed. For example Weiner (1985) stated that attribution search is more likely to be engaged in as a result of an unexpected event (e.g. an underdog winning) and that 'non attainment rather than attainment of a goal ... promotes attributional search'.

The process of attribution may serve a number of roles for the individual, team or organization involved. For example, such a process may help to stimulate change in the form of adaptation in order to survive, or may in many cases serve as a mechanism for someone to gain a better understanding of themselves and the situation in which they were striving to achieve.

It seemed clear that when attempts were made to apply the original model (Table 4.1) to other spheres of achievement such as sport the number of possible elements and the type of attribution profile encountered may be significantly different (e.g. Roberts and Pascuzzi, 1979; Rejeski and Brawley, 1983). The model shown in Table 4.2 extends Weiner's original model to the competitive sporting environ-

Table 4.2 *Model of attributions in sport. Reprinted with permission from Roberts and Pascuzzi (1979)*

	Locus of control	
Stability	Internal	External
Stable	Ability	Coaching
Unstable	Effort	Luck
	Unstable ability	Task difficulty
	Psychological factors	Teamwork
	Practice	Officials

ment which provides a rich source of attributions. It is clear that many of the attributions in sport may form ideal opportunities for performers to use as excuses; for example, officials are often blamed for bad performances.

By working with attribution profiles of winners and losers many researchers have found evidence for what has become known as a self serving bias in attributions (e.g. Brawley and Roberts, 1984; McAuley, 1985). In its simplest form this bias shows winners to attribute to more stable and internal factors and losers to unstable and external factors (using Weiner's two dimensions). Many researchers have argued that the biasing does not form a consistent relationship (Bradley, 1978; McAuley and Gross, 1983; Riordan *et al.*, 1985) and that the concept needs to be altered to fit different achievement situations (Mark *et al.*, 1984).

Subsequent to this Mullin and Riordan (1988) discovered that 'self-presentational bias is weakest at the level of questions focusing on individual performance which is contrary to what one would expect' (McAuley, 1992b). This raises the question as to whether another format for investigating performance in achievement situations may not be more appropriate.

Weiner's (1986) most recent formulation of the attribution process (Figure 4.1) indicates important advances made in this research area and highlights specifically the importance of not simply describing the attribution profiles but formulating mechanisms of how such attributes affect attitudes towards future achievement scenarios. This circularity of the attribution process indicates the importance of the fields of affect, expectations and motivation for sports performance and offers ways in which these fields may be integrated through attributes.

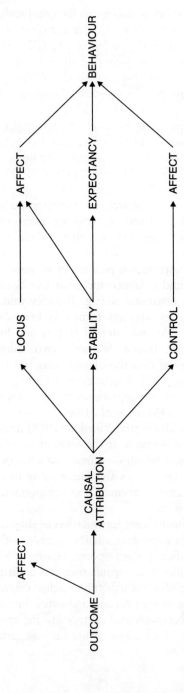

Figure 4.1   *The causal attribution process. Reprinted with permission from Weiner (1986)*

Expectancy has been shown to be an integral part of the attribution process in that it sets forth to aid anticipation of the prospective performance to be evaluated. The factor which Weiner's (1986) model establishes as crucial to the power of the overall process is that of affect or emotion and how this is influenced not only by the outcome but by the attribution profile itself and hence in a circular fashion influences future performance situations.

Only within the last decade has research into the affective consequences of performance and of subsequent attributions made, been closely investigated. For example McAuley *et al.* (1983) investigated the links between affect and the causal dimensions of locus of causality, stability and controllability (as assessed by the Causal Dimensions Scale (Russell, 1982)) and found strong links for winners, with the controllability dimension influencing affect greatest. Further studies conducted by McAuley and Duncan (1990) and Vallerand (1987) have focused on the intuitive (or subjective) evaluation and the reflective (deliberate) evaluation of performances and found both types to have strong links to affect. Vallerand (1987) also pointed strongly to the importance of perception of success and failure as opposed to objective success or failure measures as the most potent influence on affect.

The research into attribution is deeply embedded in the evaluation of performance through cognitive processes within the individual. Weiner's (1986) model extends this initial position by indicating relationships between factors which influence future behaviours. Cognitive Evaluation Theory (Deci, 1975) indicates further areas which can be influenced greatly through the evaluation processes (of which attribution is a prime example). Ryan *et al.* (1984) state that, 'any event which affects people's feelings and perceptions of self determination or of competence can affect their intrinsic motivation'. Therefore the influence of perceived competence and self determination can be seen as crucial factors which sports coaches should attempt to nurture through an evaluation procedure.

Harter's (1978) Competence Motivation Theory similarly suggested that 'positive feelings of competence and perceptions of personal control over outcomes, in turn would be associated with higher levels of actual achievement' (Weiss *et al.*, 1986a).

Another factor of great importance, which can both feed into and feed off the evaluation process in a cyclical manner, is that of situation-specific self confidence or self efficacy (Bandura, 1977). Any evaluative process of a competitive situation should work in some manner to influence positively the individual's self efficacy. Being able to evaluate a performance and establish areas of success regardless of the outcome appears to be one method through which this could be achieved.

The role of goal setting and the reliance on performance and process goals as opposed to outcome goals has been shown to enhance the perceived success of performers (e.g. Burton, 1989) and should, within Harter's and Deci's theories enhance intrinsic motivation (McAuley and Tammen, 1989). The use of goal setting has, as an integral feature, the use of an evaluative procedure in the form of goal assessment.

To gain greatest benefit from an assessment the performer's knowledge of what happened is paramount. As Weiss *et al.* (1986) state when talking about young performers, 'by improving the child's understanding of why he or she succeeds or fails, his or her level of intrinsic motivation and physical achievement will improve'. Therefore, it can be seen that it is paramount to utilize a method of evaluation which enables some level of control over factors which relate to cognitions in achievement situations, such as competitive sport, to benefit performers and coaches.

The choice of what sort of evaluation procedure is adopted and how it is operationalized with performers will often depend upon which of the influential factors are felt to be most important to highlight. The evaluation procedure outlined below attempts to utilize important principles from the theoretical background and relevant research outlined above, and to work within this to the benefit of performers. The major emphasis in the following sport-specific example is that of encouraging the performers to internalize their evaluation in concert with self monitoring benefits highlighted by Vallerand (1987) and Rejeski (1981). In this way the performer is aided in the search for improvements in subsequent performance incorporating factors which are within their control. The areas which the Daily Performance Evaluation Sheet (Figure 4.2) attempts to influence are

- Goal setting – The ability to set appropriate goals based on previous performances.
- Perceived competence – Appropriate goal setting should enhance the perception of competence of the individual performer.
- Process orientation – Establish and maintain performers' efforts through goal setting on the process of performance rather than on outcomes alone.

DAILY PERFORMANCE EVALUATION

NAME: DATE: COMPETITION/PRACTICE

YOU **MUST** HAVE AS MANY POINTS IN THE POSITIVE COLUMN
AS YOU DO IN THE NEGATIVE

POSITIVE ASPECTS	NEGATIVE ASPECTS
TECHNICAL	
TACTICAL	
PSYCHOLOGICAL	

OVERALL HOW DO YOU FEEL YOU PERFORMED

GENERAL COMMENTS:

Figure 4.2   *The Daily Performance Evaluation Sheet*

- Affect – Attempt to heighten awareness and subsequently exert some level of control over emotional state both before and during performance.
- Intrinsic motivation – Control over competence will encourage the development of intrinsically motivated behaviour.
- Self efficacy – Increased awareness of the positive aspects of the individual's performance to aid situation-specific self confidence.
- Rationality – Through evaluating in a balanced manner each performance can be established as a platform from which to learn.

Development of the Daily Performance Evaluation Sheet

When developing the performance evaluation tool it was essential that some underlying principles that could be targeted were identified, and the three principles of simplicity, effectiveness and feedback mechanisms guided the development of the table tennis performance evaluation sheet from the beginning to the current status of the process.

Simplicity

Within sports science it is my experience that many coaches and performers develop a mystique about sports science and what it can do. This is often based upon experiences of complex concepts, models and jargon which can confuse and form communication barriers, rather than aid in opening pathways through which performance can be enhanced. Therefore the primary principle for the performance evaluation sheet was that of simplicity – not only in the concepts that were included (which as they are of a sport-specific nature are more readily accepted by performers) but in the structure and layout of the sheet itself.

A simple tool not only aids performers in all age groups and levels of experience to utilize it, but also increases the possibility that the performer will become self sufficient in its use in the shortest, and most effective, time period.

Effectiveness

A tool such as the Performance Analysis Sheet, however simple or complex it may seem, needs to be effective in succeeding to influence the psychological status of the performer either in the short or the long term. The effectiveness of the evaluation sheet needs to be monitored closely when first using it with an athlete. Subsequent meetings to recap or assess progress may prove useful in the long term.

In the early phases when beginning to use such a method with a performer it is crucial (especially with youth performers) that they have access to and use support structures to learn how to use the tool effectively. This is important as many performers have little experience at verbalizing their internal thoughts and feelings and probably have even less experience of writing down these evaluations.

Coach and sport psychologist

The first line of support and facilitation should be the coach and the sport psychologist either working independently at different times, as access to performers determines, or preferably in conjunction with each other. This aids in the coordination of advice and feedback given to performers. The types of activity which the coach and sport psychologist would enter into in their supportive roles would be the following:

- Highlight from the outset that the tool is an aid to learning from each performance and that having acted upon the factors identified an acceleration in improvement should subsequently occur.
- Work through specific performance evaluations with the performer and compare coach perceptions to player perceptions.
- Indicate through the use of examples of completed Performance Analysis Sheets areas of their performance that should be prioritized.
- Work closely with the performer in operationalizing short-term goals in areas which were highlighted by the particular evaluation.
- When conducting the long-term occasional monitoring sessions use this time to establish consistent trends in the evaluation forms. Both positive and negative evaluations can serve to highlight areas for long-term or out of season goal setting, particularly in the adaptation of technique.
- Verbally reinforce the written words highlighting the strengths as well as the weaknesses.

At all times the coach and sport psychologist acting in this supporting role should be trying to equip the performer with the skills to evaluate their performance more effectively themselves and encouraging them to become more self determining. In this way the performer will be more able to play a major role in planning and carrying out the steps to their technical, tactical and psychological progression.

Video

With the progression of technology and the increased availability and enhanced simplicity of operating video equipment this tool to aid in performance evaluation should not be undervalued. A note of caution when using video with performers who have not seen themselves perform on screen before is that they understand that it is a method to help them learn more about the types of things they do in a performance. What can occur, and which can have quite severe short-term effects on self confidence and motivation to continue, is that the performer sees themself on video for the first time and the image they see does not in any way correspond to the image they have in their mind of how they perform. (It is my experience that this discrepancy in image is rarely that they are better than they thought they were.) If this support mechanism is used an awareness of this potential problem should be highlighted to the athlete and the fundamental role of the video as a learning tool forcefully communicated. The use of video as a source of feedback can make the process of completing the Performance Evaluation Sheet a more comprehensive and effective technique.

Another aspect of the effectiveness of the tool which should be acknowledged, and was an integral feature in its design, is the open endedness of the categories. As can be seen from the form (Figure 4.2) it is not a structured questionnaire-based performance analysis itemizing distinct aspects of performance (e.g. Orlick, 1986a). It was felt that this approach formed an over restrictive feedback mechanism for the performer and that performers would access a higher quantity and quality of information from a more freeform evaluation procedure. In such a format the requirement of initial guidance and advice as outlined above helps the performer to establish their own way of using the form specifically tailored to their needs within a loosely structured base.

Feedback mechanisms and log development

The third and final principle underlying the performance evaluation sheet was to provide a written feedback mechanism for performers which, over the course of months or a season, could develop into a useful, and possibly essential log of performances. The essential features of such a log would provide the opportunity for

- long-term planning
- a move away from evaluation based on outcomes to those based on factors that are more in the performers control, i.e. the processes
- a valuable resource of information about improvements made and recurring problem areas
- more structured debate on the status of the performances with coaches, other players, parents and important others, thereby improving the performance related communication channels.

Using the concept of a log leads both the athletes and coach away from the idea that performance analysis is totally a short-term process and that all benefits are from the immediate feedback delivery which it can produce.

With these underlying principles and goals in mind the sheet itself was developed. Many factors emerged in the early stages of using it which were then considered and utilized in the metamorphosis from the initial format to the Performance Evaluation Form shown in Figure 4.2.

Sport-Specific Nature

It was clear that the tool needed to be specific in the parameters it evaluated to service the needs of performers within the sport in which it was to be used. Within the principle of keeping the open-ended nature of the sheet, the categories were chosen in consultation with some of the top performers in order to establish those which were seen to be essential. It is not surprising that the categories which were felt to encompass the vast majority of table tennis performance were those of technical, tactical and psychological factors. Physical fitness was not perceived as such an important area to evaluate as the performance is rarely influenced by this factor in such a fundamental way as the technical, tactical and psychological factors in a highly skilful sport like table tennis.

Age group specific

The sheet developed for the senior squads, although essentially the same as that later adapted for the younger performers (Figure 4.2), did not contain the user friendly affective response drawings (the smiling, neutral or sad faces). These were added to the Junior (under 17) and Cadet (under 14) performers' versions as this supplied information about feelings associated with importance of events in relation to pre- and post-competition and could also give information about the person's outcome or process orientation. Many of the young performers had a good deal of problems with learning from each performance situation, and as Orlick (1986b) stated, Performance Evaluation Forms 'allow *you* (the performer) to examine your own performance to learn as much as possible from that performance'. Unfortunately most of the younger performers were found to evaluate their performances solely in an outcome oriented fashion. Many assessments were full of emotionally linked evaluations which were rarely, if ever, converted to a learning based analysis (Figure 4.3).

WIN PLAY WELL   WIN PLAY BADLY   LOSE PLAY WELL   LOSE PLAY BADLY
SOME LEARNING NEGLIGIBLE LEARNING NEGLIGIBLE LEARNING SOME LEARNING

Figure 4.3   *Emotional responses to outcomes that can inhibit maximizing learning*

Using tools such as the Performance Analysis Sheet with young performers is wholly appropriate when it is considered that experienced child performers are more able to integrate information related to performance from a variety of sources and that 'children develop an internal set of performance criteria or standards they can then use in subsequent performance situations to make independent judgements of their skill competencies' (Horn and Hasbrook, 1987).

Rule

As the initial users of the sheet fed back to coaches and the sport psychologist it became apparent that the perception by the performers of the use of the sheet was to identify the countless negative parts of a performance. This negative bias was certainly something which the performance evaluation concept was attempting to avoid rather than to encourage and so the formation of a simplistic, but ultimately very successful, rule was an important addition to the overall effectiveness of the process. The rule was simply

● You must have as many items in the positive column as you do in the negative column.

This helped enormously in evaluating performances regardless of the outcome in a way which drew on the good aspects and highlighted the bad aspects in a balanced and realistic fashion. Many performers found it difficult to think of any positive aspects to their performances as they saw all the good things that they had done as simply being what they should do and accepted them as prerequisites to good performance. Performers accepting what they are good at in written form in the positive aspects column is just as important in the performance evaluation process as the identification of the areas for improvement in the negative aspects column.

When to use it and how often

Essentially this is left up to the performer themselves to decide but the following recommendations are made to all performers:

● Use at competitions sparingly (players can play up to fifteen games of table tennis in a one day tournament and so logistically it is impossible for each competitive match to be analysed) but **always** use it to evaluate the whole day's play and pick out certain key performances to evaluate in a more detailed fashion (video can help enormously).
● Use within practice sessions comprising work on particular technical aspects evaluating fine details with the coach.
● Within practice sessions when simulating matchplay use it as you would in the competitive situation.
● If problems occur in evaluating performances outside the competitive environment then it is helpful to set a goal for that particular training session and evaluate performance to that target.

Having used the Performance Evaluation Sheet and seen the effect that it has on attitudes to training and competition it is interesting to note the uses that performers found with the evaluation, and some of the short- and long-term benefits observed by performers, coaches and the sport psychologist.

Benefits of using the Daily Performance Evaluation Sheet as the method of achievement evaluation

There are many benefits which can be split into those which occur more readily in the short term (one to three months) and those which require a longer period to come to fruition.

Short-term benefits

Self awareness

Performers become more aware of the positive and negative aspects of their performance in technical, tactical and psychological terms which enables them to begin a period of change if this is necessary through the following methods.

- Setting of short-term goals. The Daily Performance Evaluation Sheet is designed so that the negative aspects column can be used by performers and coaches alike as a 'things to work on' list for the period following the analysis.
- Enhance self efficacy. Due to the insistence upon the rule for equality between number of items in the positive and negative columns the performer always has some elements of performance which they can use to enhance, or to maintain, their current feelings of self efficacy. Reinforcement of such factors may increase the strength of, and establish resistance to changes in, the individual's self efficacy.
- Development of positive self statements. The positive aspects of performance can be used to help to formulate positive self statements which can be used prior to subsequent performances to aid in the controlling of efficacy.
- Develop rational and logical critique. The process of filling in the Daily Performance Evaluation Sheet helps the performer to establish a rational and logical search through the performance and to complete an holistic evaluation.

Performers and coaches find such a tool easy to relate to and use which enhances the work of the sport psychologist and helps performer, coach and sport psychologist to work as a team to mutual benefit.

Long-term benefits

Log of progression

The development of a log can help to indicate long-term progression and act as an acute reminder of the great strides made over a period of time.

Identification of frequently occurring problems

Some performance difficulties which occur once or twice over a significant period of time can often be ignored. A long-term benefit can occur when a similar problem occurs infrequently, but regularly, especially in certain scenarios where opportunities to access information are sparse (e.g. coping with a major championship final).

Transformation in attitude towards success and failure

Through a regular emphasis upon evaluating performance by analysing the processes of performance in preference to the outcomes the performers adapt and change in the focus of their competitive experiences. They become more able to learn from both defeats and successes whilst still maintaining a drive to achieve.

Conclusion

In conclusion it can be seen that, through the setting up and appropriate implementation of a sport-specific performance evaluation system, there are numerous benefits which can be accrued for the coach, sport psychologist and, most importantly, the performers themselves.

For the coach the benefits in the use of an evaluation tool are to be found primarily in encouraging the mutual agreement with the performer of individual planning schedules and in so doing enabling the coach to become a more effective, facilitating influence in the development of the performer.

For the sport psychologist, performance evaluation establishes a simple and effective method of introducing and implementing a range of psychological skills and increases the likelihood of influencing a large range of psychological factors that can affect performance. Also, possibly the greatest benefit of using Performance Evaluation Sheets for the sport psychologist is that they complement the overall programme with any individual, team or group in that they create an environment where performer, coach and sport psychologist work together.

For the performer, benefits can occur through performance evaluation in areas such as increased awareness, intrinsic motivation and self efficacy and can provide a potent means of establishing logical and rational evaluation procedures which can lead to accelerated learning. Furthermore, alterations to perceptions of competition can be achieved, which when coupled with a greater sense of control and influence over preparation and performance, can lead ultimately to greater opportunity for each individual to access their potential in the sporting arena.

References

Bandura, A. (1977) Self efficacy: Toward a unifying theory of behavioural change. *Psychological Review*, **84**, 191–215.

Biddle, S. (1991) Interpreting success and failure. In *Sport Psychology: A Self Help Guide* (S.J. Bull, ed.). Marlborough: Crowood Press.

Bradley, G.W. (1978) Self-serving biases in the attribution process: a re-examination of the fact or fiction question. *Journal of Personality and Social Psychology*, **36**(1), 56–71.

Brawley, L.R. and Roberts, G.C. (1984) Attributions in sport: Research foundations, characteristics and limitations. In *Psychological Foundations of Sport* (J.M. Silva and R.S. Weinberg, eds) Champaign, IL: Human Kinetics.

Burton, D. (1989). Winning isn't everything: examining the impact of performance goals on collegiate swimmers' cognitions and performance. *The Sport Psychologist*, **3**, 105–132.

Deci, E.L. (1975) *Intrinsic Motivation*. New York: Plenum.

Harter, S. (1978) Effective motivation considered: Toward a developmental model. *Human Development*, **21**, 34–64.

Horn, T.S. and Hasbrook, C.A. (1987) Psychological characteristics and the criteria children use for self evaluation. *Journal of Sport Psychology*, **9**, 209.

Hughes, M. (1993) *A Manual of Notational Analysis for Squash*. Unpublished manuscript.

Kirschenbaum, D.S. (1984). Self-regulation and sport psychology: nurturing an emerging symbiosis. *Journal of Sport Psychology*, **6**, 159–183.

Mark, M.M., Mutrie, N., Brooks, D.R. and Harris, D.V. (1984) Causal attributions of winners and losers in individual competitive sports: toward a reformulation of the self-serving bias. *Journal of Sport Psychology*, **6**, 184–196.

McAuley, E. (1985) Success and causality in sport: the influence of perception. *Journal of Sport Psychology*, 7, 13–22.

McAuley, E. (1992a). Self-referent thought in sport and physical activity. In *Advances in Sport Psychology* (T.S. Horn, ed.) p. 102. Champaign, IL: Human Kinetics.

McAuley, E. (1992b) Self-referent thought in sport and physical activity. In *Advances in Sport Psychology* (T.S. Horn, ed.) p. 105. Champaign, IL: Human Kinetics.

McAuley, E. and Gross, J.B. (1983) Perceptions of causality in sport: an application of the Causal Dimension Scale. *Journal of Sport Psychology*, 5, 72–76.

McAuley, E. and Tammen, V.V. (1989) The effects of subjective and objective competitive outcomes on intrinsic motivation. *Journal of Sport and Exercise Psychology*, 11, 84–93.

McAuley, E. and Duncan, T.E. (1990) Cognitive appraisal and affective reactions following physical achievement outcomes. *Journal of Sport and Exercise Psychology*, 12, 415–426.

McAuley, E., Russell, D. and Gross, J.B. (1983) Affective consequences of winning and losing: an attributional analysis. *Journal of Sport Psychology*, 5, 278–287.

Mullin, B. and Riordan, C.A. (1988) Self-serving attributions in naturalistic settings: a meta-analytic review. *Journal of Applied Social Psychology*, 18, 3–22.

Orlick, T. (1986a) *Psyching for Sport: Mental Training for Athletes*. Illinois: Leisure Press.

Orlick, T. (1986b) Psyching for Sport: Mental Training for Athletes. p. 80. Illinois: Leisure Press.

Rejeski, W.J. (1981) The perception of exertion: a social psychophysiological integration. *Journal of Sport Psychology*, 4, 305–320.

Rejeski, W.J. and Brawley, L.R. (1983) Attribution theory in sport: current status and new perspectives. *Journal of Sport Psychology*, 5, 77–99.

Riordan, C.A., Thomas, J.S. and James, M.K. (1985) Attributions in a one-on-one sports competition: evidence for self-serving biases and gender differences. *Journal of Sport Behavior*, 8, 42–53.

Roberts, G.C. and Pascuzzi, D. (1979) Causal attributions in sport: some theoretical implications. *Journal of Sport Psychology*, 1, 209.

Russell, D. (1982) The Causal Dimension Scale: a measure of how individuals perceive causes. *Journal of Personality and Social Psychology*, 42, 1137–1145.

Ryan, R.M., Vallerand, R.J. and Deci, E.L. (1984) Intrinsic motivation in sport: a cognitive evaluation theory interpretation. In *Cognitive Sport Psychology* (W.F. Straub and J.M. Williams, eds) p. 232. New York: Sport Science Associates.

Sinclair, G.D. and Sinclair, D.A. (1994) Developing reflective performers by integrating mental management skills with the learning process. *The Sport Psychologist*, 8, 13–27.

Vallerand, R.J. (1987) Antecedents of self-related affects in sport: preliminary evidence on the intuitive–reflective appraisal model. *Journal of Sport Psychology*, 9, 161–182.

Weiner, B. (1974) *Achievement Motivation and Attribution Theory.* p. 6. Morristown, NJ: General Learning Corporation.

Weiner, B. (1985) "Spontaneous" causal thinking. *Psychological Bulletin,* 97(1), 74–84.

Weiner, B. (1986) *An Attributional Theory of Motivation and Emotion.* Berlin: Springer-Verlag.

Weiss, M.R., Bredemeier, B.J. and Shewchuk, R.M. (1986a) The dynamics of perceived competence, perceived control, and motivational orientation in youth sport. In *Sport for Children and Youths: Proceedings of the 1984 Olympic Scientific Congress* (M.R. Weiss and D. Gould, eds). p. 90. Champaign, IL: Human Kinetics.

Part Two

5

Developing confidence

Sheelagh Rodgers

Sport: Ice Skating

'If you think you can win, you can win.
Faith is necessary to victory.'
William Hazlitt

Confidence may be defined as a firm trust or belief; a faith or assuredness especially in the outcome of something (Chambers Dictionary). Confidence in oneself can be defined as the belief or degree of certainty that individuals possess about their ability to be successful in a particular situation or task. Confidence can be seen to be synonymous with self belief.

Butler (1996) discusses a model of self belief that describes four different components of confidence; two descriptive and two evaluative facets. The descriptive elements are those of self image and self vulnerability and the evaluative elements are self esteem and self belief (Figure 5.1).

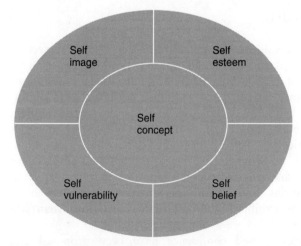

Figure 5.1 *A conceptualization of self. Reproduced with permission from Butler (1996)*

- Self image is the system of characteristics that are available to an individual in defining him or herself.
- Self vulnerability is the perception of changes in the self that are construed under stressful circumstances.
- Self esteem is the evaluation of the self along the characteristics that are used to describe the self.
- Self belief is the estimate of one's ability to execute a task successfully.

The way one sees oneself (the self construct) is subdivided using the descriptive elements of self image and vulnerability and the evaluative elements of self esteem and belief. To promote confidence or belief an athlete needs to become aware of their own characteristics and how they may alter over time, or in stressful situations.

The value that is placed by an individual on their own characteristics, and the athlete's ability to execute a task successfully, enable an evaluation to be made by the athlete, of what they personally are capable of successfully performing.

Through understanding themselves and having expectations about their ability to perform, an athlete will begin to develop a model of their abilities and how they might be used to carry out given tasks, whether these are small, such as landing a double axel correctly, or large, such as performing a complete ice skating programme.

Theoretical models

The area of self confidence or self efficacy has been a subject of interest for sport psychologists and researchers alike. Experiments have demonstrated relationships between an individual's expectations of their performance and the outcome of their performance in laboratory settings (Feltz, 1982; Feltz and Mugno, 1983) and in field settings (Gould *et al.*, 1981). The identification of effective strategies for enhancing efficacy has also been studied (Gould and Weiss, 1981; Feltz, 1982; Feltz and Mugno, 1983). Results from these studies have generally shown that positive relationships exist between an individual's expectations and motor performance and that more successful athletes exhibit higher efficacy expectations than less successful athletes.

Various theories of self confidence have been proposed and researched. Early research owes much to the theories of achievement motivation developed by McClelland and Atkinson (1953). According to this model, motivation to achieve and fear of failure are the primary factors determining whether a person will approach or avoid an achievement situation. The model of achievement motivation is a complex behavioural mathematical approach to explaining the need to achieve (n Ach). A simplified version of the model proposes that two factors determine an athlete's n Ach. These factors are the motive to achieve success (Ms) and the motive to avoid failure (Maf).

Increased interest in self confidence research parallels a declining interest in the achievement motivation theory of McClelland and Atkinson. However, McClelland and Atkinson's model has not been dismissed or rejected. The construct of self confidence is very similar to n Ach. The confident athlete has high motivation to succeed and a high expectation of success.

Bandura's (1977) theory of self efficacy has recently proved influential. The notion of self efficacy is synonymous with an individual's belief that he or she is competent and can succeed at a particular task. An individual who enjoys a high level of self efficacy enters into a competitive situation with enthusiasm and self confidence.

The degree of self efficicacy possessed by an individual will determine whether that person will approach or avoid an achievement situation. While the concepts of self confidence and self efficiency may not be absolutely identical, it is clear that they are similar. Bandura's theory of efficacy (1977 and 1982) proposes that self efficacy is fundamental to competent performance. In competitive situations, the higher the level of self efficacy the higher the performance accomplishments and the lower the emotional arousal.

The model further states that self efficacy is enhanced by

- successful performance
- vicarious experience
- verbal persuasion
- emotional arousal.

The most important of these four factors appears to be successful performance.

According to Bandura, successful performance raises expectations for future success; failure will lower these expectations. Once strong feelings of self efficacy develop through repeated success, occasional failures will be of small consequence. Feelings of self efficacy lead to improved performance, while a lack of these feelings will result in a slackening of performance. In a successful performance the athlete's sense of mastery is influenced (e.g. 'If I have done it in the past, I can do it again.'). Weinberg *et al.* (1979) demonstrated the strength of such information by showing that if the athlete focused on performance accomplishments it enhanced both efficiency and subsequent performances.

Vicarious experience is the most vulnerable source of information because it is inferred from social comparison (e.g. 'If they can do it, so can I.') and not from personal experience. However Feltz (1982) and Feltz and Mugno (1983) found modelling did improve efficacy and performance. The most critical aspect of Bandura's theory is repeated success through participatory modelling. In participatory modelling the subject first observes a model perform a task, then the model assists the subject in successfully performing the task. The subject is prevented from failing. As a result of repeated success, strong feelings of self efficacy develop.

Verbal persuasion is suggested by Bandura to be a weak source of information because there is no experiential basis for the athlete. Mahoney (1979) has carried out research within sports settings which confirms this finding.

Emotional arousal and its control or otherwise undoubtably affects performance. The theoretical basis is that self efficacy is increased following performance where an athlete can control the physiological signs of arousal. However, research findings do not confirm this, showing that whilst management of anxiety symptoms can result in an increased sense of mastery over the arousal control, this does not necessarily demonstrate an increase in feelings of self efficacy (Bandura, 1977). Because arousal is only one of several sources of efficacy information, and not necessarily the most dependable one, extinguishing anxiety arousal is rarely a sufficient condition for eliminating defensive behaviour.

An extension of Bandura's model relates to the use of cognitive techniques for dealing with anxiety (Beck and Emery, 1985). As Bandura (1982) has shown, increasing a person's sense of confidence can decrease their levels of anxiety. Psychologist and athlete can work together to develop ways for the athlete to increase his or her confidence in the feared area. This may involve dealing with negative thoughts by challenging the assumptions behind them, and by using such methods as risk taking in certain areas, e.g. testing out skills in performing a difficult jump on the ice. Knowledge of what is required in a specific jump can reduce anxiety and increase self confidence, and the ability to handle any performance task can increase a person's sense of confidence. Restructuring one's cognitive beliefs can result in a change of behaviour and can lead to changes in emotions. For example, a skater who believes they cannot successfully land a double axel jump, although the evidence is present, can try and access the thoughts that were present whilst attempting the jump, and any negative thoughts such as, 'I can't do this jump' can be explored and challenged. The thought may be further interpreted as 'I did not get enough height for the jump and I knew the landing would be wrong'. This may lead to the skater trying the jump and aiming for more height, which results in a successful accomplishment of the task, which in turn leads to a feeling of more confidence when performing that task in the future.

Another idea that has influenced opinion on the subject of confidence is the 'goodness of fit' model postulated by McCoy (1977) who argued that self belief is an awareness of how well a person will match up to the task before them. Where there is a 'goodness or fit' between how they actually perform, then the individual will experience confidence. Where there is a discrepancy between expectation and performance, the person experiences guilt (they have behaved in a way they would not have anticipated of themselves). Note that this model equally describes a person's lack of confidence in 'goodness of fit' terms as it does a person's sense of confidence.

Butler (1996) has used a combination of McCoy's 'goodness of fit' and Bandura's self efficacy model to give an integrated model of confidence. When performing a given task, a person estimates how effective they might be in successfully completing the task. Belief that they will be successful suggests high self efficacy, and belief in an unsuccessful outcome results in low self efficacy. Should the estimate of efficacy be validated either with success meeting the expectation of high self efficacy (e.g. in the case of a skater who expects to succeed in landing a specific jump and does so) or when low self efficacy is met by failure (e.g. when a skater has not completely learnt a new jump, i.e. they understand that they must land on the blade in a certain way but fail to grasp the necessity of speed and height before entering the jump, they expect to fall when executing the jump on the ice and then, because of inadequate knowledge, do fall over), this match between the outcome of the event and the person's expectations gives a 'goodness of fit' which confirms their ability or inability. Achievement or incompetence strengthens the person's self belief.

Should the estimate of efficacy be invalidated this may lead to feelings of hostility or guilt. Hostility is the individual's effort to maintain a view they have of themselves despite evidence to the contrary. The person attempts to rationalize, or excuse themselves for the performance. For example, the skater who does not expect to pull off a certain jump may do so and be surprised, but put it down to beginner's luck, whilst the experienced skater who falls over an easy jump may complain that this is due to poor ice surface.

Invalidated estimates of self efficacy may more commonly lead to feelings of guilt. Guilt occurs when an individual must change the way they view themselves. A skater who has never managed to land a difficult spin and then demonstrates a perfect spin may feel guilt because they will have to re-appraise their belief in their ability to carry out that specific spin.

The athlete will estimate how their feelings of self efficacy will affect their performance in a given task, and this is driven through their own self belief. This estimate can be helped through working with coaches or sport psychologists.

Developing confidence

An important task for anyone working with athletes, such as coaches or psychologists, is to help athletes improve their self confidence or belief in their own abilities. Research suggests that focusing on performance achievements may be one way that can enhance an athlete's confidence. Feltz and Doyle (1981), Feltz and Weiss (1982), Weinberg *et al.* (1985) and Gould *et al.* (1977) have proposed techniques which may assist an athlete increase his or her confidence. Gould *et al.* (1977) found that thirteen strategies were used, at least to some degree, to enhance self efficacy by coaches, who felt that all techniques were at least moderately effective. These were

- Encouraging positive statements – These are statements that emphasize the qualities and attributes of the athlete, as they are seen by the coach or other support staff.
- Acting confidently – The athlete can act in a confident manner, by modelling a confident performance.
- Reward statements (praise) – This is best delivered with emphasis, and is genuinely directed and follows immediately after a successful attempt or accomplishment.

- Feedback – This is the immediate relaying of information about a performance, either of an objective nature (e.g. time) or subjective (e.g. commenting on improved technique).
- Setting goals – This may involve working on strengths and fine tuning certain techniques that an athlete is good at performing, or setting new tasks to learn and perform.
- Emphasizing readiness and physical preparation – This will involve statements that stress how well the athlete has prepared, and emphasizes that any arousal is a signal of the athlete's preparedness to compete.
- Framing positively – This involves the delivery of instructions in a way which does not mention what is *not* expected (e.g. don't lift your arm too high on that move) which carries information and an expectation about how the person should *not* perform. Information about behaviour should be framed in a positive manner (e.g. keep your arms tucked in during a spin).
- Visualization – This gets the athlete to picture herself re-living a successful performance or to picture himself accomplishing a forth-coming event.
- Reflecting on own abilities – This encourages the athlete to assess his or her performance, particularly following success.
- Verbal persuasion – This involves persuading, coaxing or enticing the athlete in some way to demonstrate that they are capable and able to perform successfully.
- Analysing performance – This allows the evaluation of training and competitive performance to be made in a way that will highlight successes and encourages athletes to believe they are the result of ability rather than effort, which suggests a stable attribute rather than one which alters at each performance.
- Emphasizing advantages – This focuses on the athlete's superiority or perceived edge over other competitors.
- Focusing on performance – Focuses on the behaviour(s) demon-strated by the athlete which account for success and not on the success itself (performance not outcome).
- Expecting success – This provides an expectation of success because of previous successful performances and because every-thing that was possible has been done in the preparation for the event.

Effective confidence building techniques will work for some athletes but not for others. What is helpful to one person may be disastrous when used with another person. There are many individual differences and feedback techniques that motivate and are useful to one athlete, yet may destroy another's self belief and set up an uneasy relationship between coach and athlete. Techniques are no substitute for 'knowing the athlete'.

Coaches, too, need confidence in the techniques that they employ, and self evaluation or evaluation and assessment by another person can help a coach learn and successfully apply techniques that help an athlete develop confidence.

The athlete also will know what inspires and instils confidence in him or herself. Too frequently the athlete is not consulted about what works for them, or re-evaluation does not occur. When being coached, what worked as a junior may not be effective as a senior. Techniques may need to change and be re-emphasized as the athlete changes or is more successful.

Working with ice figure skaters

There are numerous situations within ice skating where a skater will need self confidence. For example, a skater needs to be confident about his or her ability to jump, to project himself or herself so that judges and audiences feel there is something special about that skater, or simply just to compete. Self confidence can affect a skater's results, particularly where there are two parts to a skater's programme, a first section of about two minutes termed the 'short programme', and the second section of four minutes called the 'free programme'. Points are awarded for jumps and spins of differing abilities (technical merit) and for artistic interpretation (fitting the programme to the music). A bad performance in the first section can frequently affect how the skater prepares for the second part, and poor self confidence will not aid a good successful performance. In learning new routines or jumps, individual or pairs skaters need to develop confidence. Confidence is important in landing a jump; failure can mean falling and hurting oneself on ice, a surface that is far from user friendly! Pairs skaters require confidence; a lift must be made and held, one partner having belief in her partner that she will not be dropped and the male partner remaining confident that he can hold the lift.

This section considers how techniques for developing self confidence have been used with ice skaters. To date most of these techniques have been taught by sport psychologists. Coaches will often make a request for helping a skater 'develop confidence so they will attempt a jump'. Skaters, too, have referred themselves when coaching techniques have been negative rather than facilitating the development of self confidence.

Skater A

Skater A was a young man who generally performed at a consistent level and whose levels of confidence had remained high. The referral was made following an international competition which had been a disaster for the skater and left him concerned about his future performance.

An analysis of the situation showed that on this occasion the skater had fallen at an early stage in the long competition. The rest of the programme was a tale of disasters, the skater falling on two more occasions and failing to make jumps he knew himself to be capable of doing.

Sessions with the skater consisted of an assessment of the performance and discovering that there had been several successful elements. He had not been expected to obtain a placing in the competition (i.e. within the first four) and our work emphasized that the performance was important, not the outcome. The performance was to reflect certain jumps of graded difficulty and good height in these jumps. His own expectations of success differed from those of his coaches. Feedback had been realistic from the coach and performance, not results, had been emphasized.

Our work consisted of the cognitive restructuring of several statements: 'I blew this competition – I'll fail again', 'I didn't get enough double/triple axels in the programme – I'll get kicked off the squad'. The beliefs that the skater held were that he would be successful at the task. However, the outcome was unsuccessful and he felt guilt, because he had not achieved his aim and there was low efficacy in achieving the task, and no 'goodness of fit' between expectations and outcome.

Belief in the statements was low. The skater knew that performance in competitions was usually good and he could draw on this to expect success in the future. On this occasion the skater was not well prepared; he described feelings of tiredness and lacking the competitive mood; his arousal levels had been low. He analysed his performance and was able to attribute tiredness to a cold that he had just started. Restructuring statements in a positive manner about his strengths and abilities were useful and feedback from the coach and verbal persuasion that 'he could do it' resulted in an increase in belief in his abilities.

At the next competition, the skater used positive self statements and visualized a successful performance. He was well prepared and focused on performing certain elements in his programme to a level with which he would be satisfied. He also had the competitive edge, and the final result was that he won the competition.

Skater B

Skater B was referred by a judge. She had been ill for some period in the year due to a broken ankle. She had not performed at any competitions since a disastrous performance during a major championships the previous year. Her self confidence, normally not a problem, was extremely low and the skater was very anxious. After some discussion it became clear that her training programme was going well, but her involvement with her coach was proving to be a disaster. No feedback was forthcoming, nor was any praise. In fact the coach was very negative about the skater. Feedback was sought from another source who was aware of the skater's abilities. The feedback established that the problem was more than just poor and negative feedback, it was a failed relationship between coach and performer. At this stage work began with the skater to re-build confidence in her abilities through the use of positive statements by acknowledging what strengths and abilities she possessed. She began to focus on her performances and analyse them; visualization became an important tool in working towards success. Visualization involved the skater 'seeing' herself completing a technically accurate performance, with spins and jumps being executed well. The skater imagined a giant television screen and saw a skater (herself) performing at the ice rink. Her movements on the ice were in time to her chosen music, and she saw herself completing the short (two minute) programme. However, praise and feedback remained absent from the coaching sessions and finally the skater made the decision to move to another coach. The techniques she had learnt were useful, but finally confidence was being eroded, not developed, by the coach. Skater B has now begun work with a coach who has done a lot of work in analysing her performance and has used praise and feedback to give knowledge to the skater of her performance. The skater too is more confident and feels that she is now prepared physically and psychologically to enter competitions.

Skater C

Skater C was referred by her coach because she doubted her ability to perform well. She had a history of success, but had recently abandoned a competition in tears. Her arousal levels were very high and at times she had been hyper-ventilating. The work began with techniques to control the panic breathing and this was learnt and used effectively, which gave Skater C a feeling of control in the situations which caused the over breathing.

Belief in her abilities to perform the tasks was good but she was unable to 'feel' confident. We looked at beliefs in her ability which remained high. She knew she could perform a good variety of jumps at a high level, practices were excellent but competitions were disastrous.

Skater C usually demonstrated 'goodness of fit' in that she believed she could perform the task effectively and the outcome was a success. The outcome was not necessarily winning the competition but getting placed within the top ten. The event in question had shown her to be unsuccessful at the task and she felt guilt because she had failed.

We examined her thoughts around the issues of competitions and found that at the last competition her parents had decided to watch, an unusual occurrence as they had realized that their presence did worry Skater C. However, they had not seen her perform for some time, and believed that they could sit in the audience without their daughter's knowledge. Unfortunately, Skater C had seen her parents and this had triggered a series of thoughts, 'I always fail when they watch'. She then expected to fail and did so, validating her belief that she would fail in her parents' presence. This belief was unusual as Skater C usually expected to be successful and the outcome was generally good. The family had forgotten the incident, but on discussion the event had been remembered and could be explored.

Work consisted of discussing what was practical, i.e. did the skater need to be desensitized to her parents' presence? This was decided to be impractical and they agreed not to sit in the audience.

Presentation of confidence involves ensuring that her make up is good, her clothes fit well. When physically ready she feels able to tackle her thoughts and uses positive self statements. Modelling a confident skater has helped her regain some confidence. She continually has to work on the ways in which she might present herself and look confident, but the assistance of a choreographer has proved invaluable in learning how to project herself confidently, through smiling and facial expressions.

Skater D

Skater D was referred by her coach because of a fear of falling on the ice. She did not appear able to learn and execute a new jump, though previously when learning new skills had shown no problems. Unfortunately recent falls had shaken her confidence and produced some painful bruises. The coach had also resorted to giving no feedback. The first move was to organize padding and protection which was to be used when performing the new jump. Secondly, the coach was encouraged to look at his own behaviour and to once again provide praise and feedback, as most of the training was going well, and the skater needs some knowledge about what was good as well as what the problem areas might be. Skater D began to visualize successful performances and made positive statements about the strengths she possessed. Gradually the protection worn during the jumps was reduced and the coach began to make positive statements of what was expected rather than saying what was not working. Verbal persuasion was employed once the protective padding was removed and the skater began to attribute success to her own ability. For example, at first when trying the jump the ice skater believed she would fall and hurt herself. This fear was relieved by the use of padding, so that the skater believed that if she fell she would not be hurt. Gradually, the padding was removed and the skater did not fall, and her belief in her own effectiveness increased – 'I can do it'. The level of efficacy was raised, and as the outcome of the task resulted in success, her belief in her own effectiveness was increased.

Those techniques that appear to have been particularly effective with ice skaters have involved the use of the 'goodness of fit' model where skaters have looked at their estimation of outcome in a given task and how the outcome of that task has validated their belief system.

Uses of positive self statement that build on the beliefs held have helped the skaters build more confidence about their performance. Belief in ability to do it has resulted in good achievements for the skaters.

Coaches and judges too have been able to help build the skaters' beliefs in their own ability through the use of praise and feedback, which has frequently been missing from their previous repertoire of responses.

Analysing performance and making attributions has been useful for some skaters. It assists them in highlighting success and what has worked for them. Visualization skills can assist the skaters in 'seeing' and mentally rehearsing a performance.

Techniques such as those described in the section of 'Developing confidence' have been used successfully with several ice skaters with whom feedback has proved to be very important and the use of performance profiling techniques as used by Butler and Hardy (1992) have proved to be of benefit. Performance profiling is introduced to the athlete as a means of shedding light on how they are currently feeling about their preparation for competition. The constructs that the athlete perceives as constituting the fundamental qualities of elite performance are elicited. By rating themselves as they perceive themselves to be now and how they want to be (their ideal) the skaters are able to chart their progress, and work on those areas they perceive to be important. Profiling with the coach has also been of benefit in that any discrepancies between what skaters perceive to be important attributes and what coaches believe to be important can be discussed (Figure 5.2).

Anxiety management and reduced levels of self confidence have been two main areas where work with the ice figure skaters has recently been concentrated. The results of the work need to be evaluated and analysed to report confidently on the usefulness and success

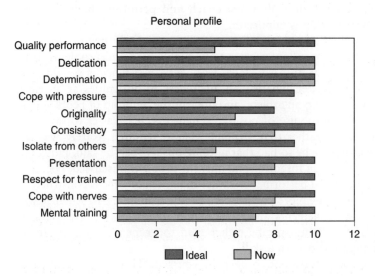

Figure 5.2 *General performance profile for an ice figure skater*

of these techniques, but reports from the skaters themselves are encouraging and should promote further developments in this field.

Summary

In conclusion, the following points have been useful in working with ice figure skaters:

- Knowledge of the skater. This has involved getting to know the skater. It has involved close collaboration with skaters and coaches to learn how the athlete sees their sport and performance, and what qualities and beliefs are important to them. With specific individual knowledge a coach can learn to give constructive feedback to individual athletes which accounts for personal preferences. Knowledge of athletes enables coaches and psychologists to find techniques that will enable individuals to learn tasks and improve on their skills.
- Performance profiling has allowed the skater to generate their own list of abilities and characteristics that they perceive to be useful to them as skaters to enhance their own performances.
- Profiling has allowed discussion of how a skater's view of themselves has varied from a coach's viewpoint. Setting aims and objectives can be difficult when coach and performer have different views on what is important.
- Analysing and evaluating performance, both in training and competitions, allow success to be highlighted and problems to be monitored at an early stage. Frequently assistance is sought only after a disaster, whereas an awareness of difficulties at an early stage can help an athlete, and prevent the build-up of problems.
- Encourage the use of positive statements. It is easier to say what *not* to do rather than explain what is required. Rarely will the performance be so bad that nothing positive can be said. However, praise is often forgotten and only the problems discussed. Focusing on the actual performance rather than the outcome is constructive. The outcome represents the end product, and the performance will consist of elements and parts that worked/looked good/could be removed. Being specific rather than too general helps an athlete change and relearn a skill.
- Act confidently and believe in yourself. This can facilitate the projecting of a confident and successful image. Use all the tech-

niques that help you feel good, and if you believe you can do it, this belief means you can.

References

Bandura, A. (1977) Self efficacy: towards a unifying theory of behavioural change. *Psychological Review*, 84(2), 191–215.

Bandura, A. (1982) Self efficacy: mechanism in human agency. *American Psychologist*, 37, 122–147.

Beck, A.T. and Emery, G. (1985) *Anxiety Disorders and Phobias – A Cognitive Perspective*. New York: Basic Books.

Butler, R.J. (1996) *Sports Psychology in Action*. Oxford: Butterworth-Heinemann.

Butler, R.J. and Hardy, L. (1992) The performance profile: theory and application. *The Sport Psychologist*, 6, 253–264.

Feltz, D.L. (1982) A path analysis of the causal elements in Bandura's theory of self efficacy and anxiety based model of avoidance behaviour. *Journal of Personality and Social Psychology*, 42, 764–781.

Feltz, D.L. and Mugno, D.A. (1983) A replication of the path analysis of the causal elements in Bandura's theory of self efficacy and the influence of autonomic perception. *Journal of Sport Psychology*, 5, 161–277.

Feltz, D.L. and Doyle, L.A. (1981) Improving self-confidence in athletic performance. *Motor Skills: Theory into Practice*, 5(2), 89–96.

Feltz, D.L. and Weiss, M.R. (1982) Developing self efficacy through sport. *Journal of Physical Education, Recreation and Dance*, 53(2), 24–26 and 36.

Gould, D.A. and Hodge, K. (1989) An exploratory examination of strategies used by elite coaches to enhance self efficacy in athletes. *Journal of Sport Psychology*, 31, 128–140.

Gould, D. and Weiss, M. (1981) The effects of model and task on self-efficacy and muscular endurance. *Journal of Sports Psychology*, 3, 17–29.

Gould, D., Weiss, M. and Weinberg, R. (1981) Psychological characteristics of successful and nonsuccessful Big Ten wrestlers. *Journal of Sport Psychology*, 3, 69–81.

Gould, D., Hodge, K., Peterson, K. and Petlichkoff, L. (1977) Psychological foundations of Coaching: Similarities and differences amongst intercollegiate wrestling coaches. *The Sport Psychologist*, 1, 293–308.

Mahoney, M.J. (1979) Cognitive skills and athletic performance in *Cognitive–Behavioral Interventions: Theory Research and Procedures* (P.C. Kendan and S.D. Hollon, eds) pp. 423–443. New York: Academic Press.

McClelland, D.C., Atkinson, J.W., Clark, R.W. and Lowell E.I. (1953) In *The Achievement Motive*. New York: Appleton – Century Crofts.

McCoy, M.M. (1977) The reconstruction of emotion. In *New Perspectives in Personal Construct Theory* (D. Bannister, ed.). London: Academic Press.

Weinberg, R.S., Bruya, L.D. and Jacks, N.A. (1985) The effects of goal proximity and goal specificity on endurance performance. *Journal of Sport Psychology*, 7, 296–305.

Weinberg, R.S., Gould, D. and Jackson, A. (1979) Expectations and performance: An empirical test of Bandura's self-efficacy theory. *Journal of Sport Psychology*, **1**, 320–331.

6

Developing team cohesion and empowering individuals

Brian P. Miller

Sport: Hockey

Many elements of psychological preparation are important in the build-up to a major sporting event, but when dealing with team sports I tend to concentrate on two major components: developing team cohesion, and empowering individual players. This chapter will be based around an explanation of how these two aspects were dealt with during the Olympic build-up period.

Team cohesion

Membership of and involvement in groups is a fundamental feature of modern society. Birth brings membership to one of society's strongest and most significant groups, the family. As human beings mature, so they are exposed to many other influential groups in different social settings. In short, from cradle to grave we are all part of formal and informal groups. Groups have a powerful and significant impact on our lives.

Since the turn of the century behavioural scientists have been interested in evaluating, observing and otherwise recording the behaviours within groups. Social psychologists in particular have analysed the interactions between the individual members of a range of groups. In the last twenty years a great deal of attention has been focused on sporting groups as a source of research data, and psychologists all over the world have examined successful teams, squads and clubs in an effort to determine the 'special factors' that influence sporting performance.

Most sporting activities involve groups or teams. Even those sports which are typically described as being 'individual', including tennis, athletics and swimming, occasionally have team events (the Davis Cup in tennis, for example) which require athletes to work as a group.

Group performance has always been a relevant practical issue as many coaches and administrators around the world devote considerable time, effort and money to maximizing team performance.

Surprisingly though, much of the research conducted in the area of applied sports psychology has focused on individual performers in sport, and there is a relative dearth of information concerning team athletes. Obviously, all teams and groups are made up of individuals so any variables that influence individual athletes will also operate on individuals within groups. However, the team situation introduces a whole range of new variables as athletes interact with one another.

Group performance will always add the element of interaction among members. According to Shaw (1976), 'A group is defined as two or more persons who are interacting with one another in such a manner that each person influences and is influenced by each other person.' The degree of interaction might well differ among different sports teams, but it is nevertheless present. In fact it is this interaction factor that sets apart a group from a mere collection of individuals.

There is a difference between a group and a crowd. Some of the properties that make up this difference are a sense of shared purpose, structured patterns of interaction, interpersonal attraction, personal interdependence, and a collective identity. Sports groups should be thought of as a collection of interdependent individuals, coordinated and orchestrated into various task-efficient roles for the purpose of achieving some goal or objective that is deemed important for that particular team (Yukelson, 1984).

Models of group performance

What makes a group effective? How can team athletes improve the overall performance of their team? Psychologists working in industrial or educational settings have studied productivity or performance for several decades. While their findings may not always be directly relevant to the sporting arena, some of their theoretical models are invaluable. Throughout this chapter, I shall refer to the Australian Olympic Women's Hockey Team of 1988 and the British Olympic Women's Hockey Team of 1992 as examples of sporting groups who underwent an extensive psychological programme in the build-up to their successful Olmpic campaigns. It is hoped that the principles used with these teams will help to illustrate some of the theoretical issues discussed in this chapter.

Figure 6.1 *Steiner's (1972) model of group effectiveness*

One such conceptual framework was developed by Steiner (1972) (Figure 6.1) and it has been applied and extended by a number of sport psychologists in the last fifteen years. The essence of Steiner's theory is that a group's actual productivity is equal to potential productivity minus losses due to faulty process. Actual productivity or performance is what the group actually does. It is the performance that is attained. Potential productivity is the group's best possible performance given its resources and the task demands. The group's resources comprise all relevant knowledge, abilities and skills of the individual members, including overall level and distribution of these talents. Process, everything the group does while transforming its resources into performance, is a critical but vague part of Steiner's model. Group processes are the actual steps or actions taken individually or collectively by group members to carry out the group task.

When individuals work in groups communication, coordination and interaction are necessary. Process is subdivided by Steiner into two general categories, coordination losses and motivation losses. Steiner's model is classically described using a hypothetical tug-of-war team. In the case of a two-man team, each individual might be capable of pulling 100 kg. Thus, the potential productivity is 200 kg. However, in a controlled trial the actual performance is only 180 kg. The group has experienced a decrement of 20 kg or 10 per cent, and this is probably due to the inability of the two athletes to coordinate their efforts and/or because each athlete was inclined to let the other athlete do most of the work. The result is a process loss of 10 per cent.

This idea of process loss was fundamental to the psychological skills programme developed specifically for the women's hockey teams. If Steiner's model is extended into the competitive arena it becomes obvious that process loss must be reduced. If Team A is to be more effective than Team B there are three contrasting scenarios that will make this possible (Figure 6.2).

---

(1) Team A possesses greater relevant resources than Team B, and experiences fewer process losses than the opposition.
(2) Team A possesses greater relevant resources than Team B, but experiences approximately equal process losses.
(3) Team A possesses approximately equal relevant resources, but experiences fewer process losses.

Figure 6.2   *Steiner's model extended to sporting matches*

Clearly the role of the sport psychologist is to work on reducing the amount of process loss that occurs. In any Olympic context, most of the teams will be fast, strong, powerful, skillful, and experienced. A team could not rely on winning the gold medal because of the first and second scenarios. During the course of a tournament a team must be capable of winning within the third scenario. In other words, the teams have comparable relevant resources, but the amount of process loss is different. This is one key element to a successful psychological programme with a team or squad. It might be surprising to learn, therefore, that there is relatively little applied research material available in this area.

Research findings

It does not seem unreasonable to assume that the most successful sports groups are those with the better individual athletes. Individual ability has been described by Gill (1986) as '... probably the most important resource for sports groups. Perhaps the most accepted maxim by both researchers and practitioners is that the best individuals make the best team.'

However, the relationship between individual ability and group performance is not perfect. Researchers from social psychology have shown that there is a positive relationship between individual ability and group performance, but the relationship is moderate at best and is mediated by task and situational factors.

The human resources available to any group must be relevant to the task. Task demands and the requirements imposed by the task will determine the relevant resources. In other words, an Olympic rowing eight will meet the requirements for a rowing regatta, but they are less likely to meet those of a gymnastics championships. In the one instance their somatotype is an advantage, but in the latter it is a distinct disadvantage.

Research on individual and group motor performance is limited, but what there is can be divided into two categories. One category focuses on the relationship between individual abilities or resources and subsequent group performance without considering any intervening processes. The other category concentrates on various group process losses, especially the 'social loafing' phenomenon.

In one of the very few studies involving sports teams, Jones (1974) investigated the relationship of team performance (as measured by win/loss records) with individual match statistics for such sports as American football, basketball and baseball. Correlations ranging from 0.60 to 0.90 led Jones (1974) to conclude that group effectiveness was positively related to individual effectiveness in all cases. The relationship was weakest for basketball, with individual statistics accounting for about 35 per cent of team performance variability.

The research conducted by Jones (1974) did not take into account any intervening group processes. By comparison there have been a number of investigations which have examined the so-called Ringelmann effect which is entirely based upon intervening processes. Over 50 years ago a German psychologist named Ringelmann observed individuals pulling on a rope in groups of two, three and eight. As might have been expected the groups pulled harder than individuals, but not with as much force as would have been predicted by simply adding the individual forces together. Eight-person groups did not pull eight times as hard as individuals, but rather only four times as hard. The average individual force for the eight-person group was 49 per cent. The decrease in average individual performance with increases in group size is now known as the Ringelmann effect.

More recently Ingham *et al.* (1974) resurrected the original Ringelmann paradigm with updated controls and modifications. Their results generally supported the Ringelmann effect, although the percentage decrements were not as large. Ingham *et al.* (1974) concluded that the decreases in average performance were due to motivational losses within groups.

Developing out of the work of Ingham *et al.* (1974) came that of Latane *et al.* (1979). They coined the term, 'social loafing' which was also a key element in the preparation of the Australian and British Women's Hockey Teams.

In a series of publications in the period 1979–1981 Latane *et al.* established that social loafing was in part due to a diffusion of responsibility. In other words, when individuals were performing in a group where their precise contribution was hard to identify or measure, the degree of social loafing was greater than when they performed in a task where individual performances or contributions were easily identified. They concluded that identifiability of individual performance is critical and that when individual efforts are lost in the crowd, performance decreases.

Social loafing and individual performance identifiability were seen as important factors in reducing the amount of process loss surrounding the hockey teams. Using a variety of competitive small-sided games and individual goal setting for training and match-play situations, the coaches worked on providing individual feedback to all team members. The players also took an active part in immediate post-game discussions in which they outlined their thoughts on the individual and team performances following every match. Across the two year programmes the players became more and more aware of their own performance levels and those of their colleagues. The players took more responsibility for their own actions both on and off the field, and the coaches used an empowering coaching style which helped the athletes to retain their sense of initiative and self-determination.

In general, sports coaches would agree that there is a need to reduce coordination and motivation losses within a team. The difficulty lies in knowing what to do to achieve this. In a situation where the coach has a choice of athletes available, identifying athletes who possess individual interactive skills as well as physical talent could greatly reduce the coordination losses to which Steiner referred. However, if there is no choice available, coaches need to direct their efforts towards developing these interactive skills. There is little or no research in this area of sports psychology, but experience has shown that it is an area which can reap great reward. By utilizing a range of off-field discussion sessions, the hockey sides were able to evolve into units whose interactive skills were finely tuned. By developing a series of specific responses to on- and off-field events the teams were able to work towards the one goal of pride-in-team performance.

An example of this approach concerned a strategy for dealing with on-field injuries which necessitated a break in play while the doctor or physiotherapist came onto the pitch. There was a well-defined policy which meant that individual players came together as a group during any such short break. One player was asked to look towards the coaches on the bench to receive any pre-planned, strategic hand signals, while another positioned herself to see the progress being made with the injured player. The team would need to quickly resume their playing positions as the treatment concluded and it was important that the players knew what was going on. The rest of the team were drilled to be listening to the captain's comments or discussing things in small groups, but there was also this 'look-out' who told the other players to break up and return to the play.

At first sight this tactic may seem trivial and unimportant, but it was important that the players felt that they were controlling all of the controllable factors within their sport. If there were things that could be controlled, such as the on-field injury programme, the warm-up, the half-time team talk and the post-game discussion, then the agreed approach was that the team members would control these items to the best of their ability. Other uncontrollables, such as an umpire's decision or an unlucky stick deflection, were uncontrollable and as such were to be ignored.

The Australian victory against the Koreans in the 1988 Olympic final provided that team with a good test of the on-field injury strategy. An Australian player accidentally hit the hockey ball into the face of a Korean player and the game was immediately halted. The injury looked worse than it actually was, but nevertheless the player needed treatment. The Australian team went through their usual injury scenario. They came together as a group, received a signal from the bench and discussed the state of play. All of this went on against a backdrop of 27 000 screaming Korean fans who were very unimpressed by the event. By comparison all the Korean players rushed in to help their fallen colleague. Two coaches and two medical personnel also joined in the throng which meant that the Korean players were involved in an undisciplined, unmanaged break in the middle of the biggest game of their lives. Presumably their thoughts were not on the immediate hockey-related issues, but rather on the injury to their colleague. In the minutes that followed this interruption, the Australian players were able to settle into a style and mode of play which allowed them to dominate the game. In contrast the Koreans were unable to gain control and the incidence of unforced errors increased dramatically.

While there are many factors that could have contributed to this situation, there is no doubt that the Australian players were able to focus on the mechanisms of success while the Koreans allowed themselves to be distracted and influenced at a crucial time in the game. In other words, there were coordination losses occurring and the actual productivity decreased. It is suggested that by careful planning and forward thinking it is possible to reduce this by establishing mutually agreed strategies which form part of a contingency management programme. Coordination losses can be reduced to a minimum if the principle of controlling the controllables is adopted.

It is possible to focus on performance outcomes alone in sport. If the team wins on a Saturday afternoon, then things must be going well. However, the reality of the situation is that key interactive behaviours may be overlooked if this over simplistic approach is followed to its extreme. The coach's goal must be to identify individual behaviours that contribute to group performance and work to increase the identifiability and recogition of those behaviours.

Once the appropriate individual behaviours have been specified, strategies to encourage and reinforce those behaviours are needed. Most coaches are aware that feedback is a key element in this situation. Research has suggested that individuals work harder and more successfully when provided with individual feedback within a group situation.

Gross (1982) examined social loafing and the influence of group and individual feedback on a group motor task. Although four-person groups did not exhibit social loafing, possibly due to identifiability and evaluation potential in the group task, feedback effects were observed. Groups who received feedback of both individual and group times improved performance more than did groups who received only group feedback or no feedback.

Encouragement and reinforcement can also be used to supplement pure information feedback. However, it is recommended that extrinsic rewards are not emphasized at the expense of intrinsic motivation. According to Gill (1986), 'Thus, verbal encouragement and specific, informative evaluations of positive behaviours will be likely to be more effective and have fewer negative consequences than adding extensive extrinsic reward systems.'

In summary, it is important that coaches identify the individual behaviours that contribute to desired group performance. It is equally important that in order to make actual performance closely reflect potential performance there is a need to make sure these individual behaviours are recognized and rewarded in order to reduce the process losses within the team situation. While the available research is minimal and often poorly defined, the tactics employed by successful coaches across a variety of team sports suggest that this is the most efficient route to performance enhancement.

Team and group cohesion

The term 'cohesion' comes from the Latin word *cohaesus* which means to cleave or stick together. Not surprisingly, the term cohesion has been used by social psychologists to describe the tendency of groups to stick together and remain united.

Cohesion reflects the strength of the bond among individual members within a group. Cohesiveness is so fundamental to groups that it has been suggested that there is no such thing as a non-cohesive group – it would be a contradiction in terms.

Cartwright and Zander (1968) developed a useful model of cohesion which has been variously modified to suit the sporting context (see Carron (1982) as an example). Figure 6.3 represents a summary of the forces which have been identified as determining the levels of group cohesion.

Team cohesion can be described as a function of determinants and consequences. Determinants of team cohesion reflect those factors that lead to the development of cohesion among team members. Consequences of team cohesion reflect those factors that are believed to occur as a result of cohesion among members.

Carron (1982) stressed the need to view cohesion as a dynamic process which is reflected in the tendency for a group to stick together and remain united in the pursuit of its goals and objectives. Importantly, Carron's definition suggests that there are at least two important dimensions to team cohesion, task cohesion and social cohesion. Social cohesion reflects the degree to which the members of a team like each other and enjoy each other's company. Task cohesion reflects the degree to which members of a group work together to achieve a specific and identifiable task. This task is usually associated with the purpose for which the team or group was formed. For example, the 1988 and 1992 hockey teams had the general task of winning an Olympic gold medal, and specifically to do this they would try to score more goals than the other team in every match they played.

The two types of team cohesion could work independently of each other. It is possible that a team with high levels of social cohesion have low levels of task cohesion. For instance, a team of recreational

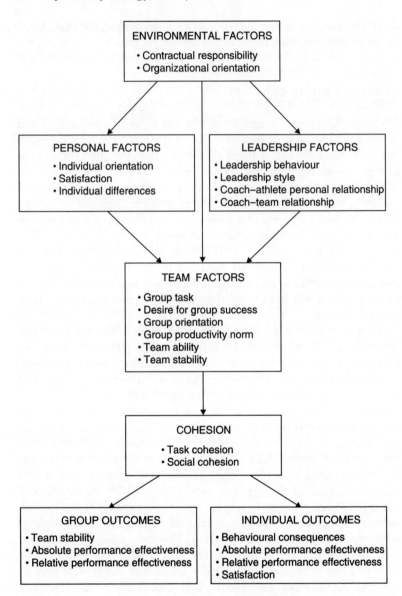

Figure 6.3   *Carron's (1982) model of cohesiveness in sport*

basketballers or a veterans' rugby side are likely to be driven by social goals rather than task goals *per se*. They will, of course, try to win matches, but perhaps they are more concerned with the interactions that occur after the game than during it.

In a similar vein, it is possible that a team will be very focused on a task goal, but have little interest in social objectives. Indeed, anecdotal sporting literature is littered with examples of very successful professional clubs who are torn apart by social problems, but because of their 'professional' approach to their sport they are prepared to 'bury the hatchet' on a Saturday afternoon in an effort to achieve victory.

There are a number of properties associated with cohesiveness. A major property is communication. The level of communication relating to task and social issues increases as the group becomes more cohesive. Group members are more likely to talk openly with one another and, perhaps more importantly, they are more prepared to listen to each other's views. As cohesiveness increases so does the exchange of useful, relevant task information.

Another important property that develops with increasing cohesiveness is conformity. There is a greater conformity to group standards for behaviour and performance in cohesive groups. As a group increases its cohesiveness, its members place increasing value on social approval and the opportunities to interact with other group members. They show an increasing tendency to adhere to the group norms and to give way to the group influence.

Perception is another interesting property that changes with increasing cohesiveness. The perception that a group has about itself and about other groups also gets slightly distorted with increased cohesiveness. This can make the introduction of new faces (when players or coaches have retired from the sport, for example) more difficult within a successful, cohesive team. Specific, deliberate strategies have to be adopted in such circumstances in order to reduce the possibility of players or officials being shunned by the group.

The nature of cohesion-performance relationships in different sports

Studies which have examined the effect of cohesion upon levels of performance have failed to produce consistent results. While some research has suggested that successful teams are also more cohesive units, this has not been replicated in all sports or situations. For instance, basketball teams have tended to provide data suggesting a positive link between cohesiveness and performance (Klein and Christiansen, 1969; Martens and Peterson, 1971; Arnold and Straub, 1972). However, other authors have reported a negative relationship. Lenk's (1969) work with rowing is one example, and McGrath's (1962) work with rifle teams is another. Landers and Luschen (1974) were the first to put forward a theory which could reconcile these differences. They felt that the task structure and demands could account for the results.

The task dimension originally proposed by Landers and Luschen (1974) was *coacting* versus *interacting*. In interacting teams the total group effort is a product of teamwork. This situation has been described by Thomas (1957) as high means-interdependence. By comparison, in a coacting situation the group product is achieved via the summation of individual group members' efforts. This is described as low means-interdependence. An athletics or rifle team would be an example of a coacting team, while the major field games of soccer, rugby, hockey, etc. would typify interacting sports.

According to Carron and Chelladurai (1979) it is only within those sports or activities which require interactive dependence that cohesiveness will contribute to improved performance because of improved coordination. In coactive situations cohesiveness is unrelated to performance success. Carron and Chelladurai (1979) summarize by saying, 'Sports differ in the degree to which task interdependence is required of participants; the degree of task interdependence present affects the type of coordination necessary, and the type of coordination necessary affects the degree to which group cohesiveness is a mandatory factor in performance outcome.'

More recently, Slater and Sewell (1994) focused on the relationship between cohesion and performance in university hockey teams. The results of their study showed that a positive relationship exists between team cohesion and performance outcome. That is, high cohesiveness is associated with more successful performance.

On a practical level, there are a number of exercises that can be carried out with any given group of athletes that can help to promote both task and social cohesion. Traditionally they take the form of educational sessions and are useful for bridging any real or perceived gaps between the older and younger members of any team or squad.

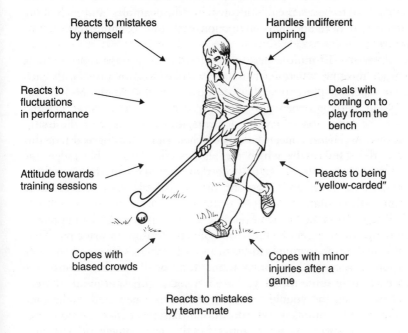

Figure 6.4 *An example of a team building exercise from hockey*

During 1987–1988 and 1991–1992, the women's hockey teams completed a number of such exercises in the build-ups to Seoul and Barcelona, respectively. One such session was known as 'the perfect player'. Figure 6.4 is taken from the Australian players' training diaries used on their European tour of 1988, and it formed the basis of the session. Basically, the players were asked to develop a profile of how they thought the perfect or model player would react in certain situations that might affect an international hockey player taking part in the Olympic Games.

The squad divided into four groups of four players. Within each group the athletes nominated a spokesperson and a 'minute taker' who would keep notes of their group's discussions. Each group included a mixture of experienced and less experienced players. These small groups were allowed 30 minutes in which to come up with their ideas on how the perfect player would react to the various hypothetical situations. It was important to present the players with hypothetical situations that were common or at least feasible within their sport. There had to be a sense of realism about the examples, and each of the items was developed in conjunction with the coaching staff of this team.

After the 30 minute period, the four small groups returned to a larger meeting where each issue was discussed in turn, with each spokesperson presenting their group's opinions. At the end of this session there had been a great deal of discussion as to what was and was not acceptable behaviour or strategies for dealing with these situations. A general concensus was reached and it was agreed that this was the standard by which the players could justifiably judge one another. It is interesting to note that the views of the Australian players in 1988 and those of the British players in 1992 were extremely similar.

The importance of such exercises was that players had an opportunity to contribute to the formation of team strategy or principle. They also had an opportunity to listen to each other's views and to agree upon an accepted task orientation. Additionally, such sessions were used to help unite the players from a social cohesion point of view. They helped the younger players settle into a new and challenging situation. In summary, the educational nature of these sessions was useful in providing opportunities for the development of both task and social cohesion.

These hockey teams were also introduced to another approach which was designed to promote improvements in both elements of cohesion. If a team is involved in a tournament they will have to play several matches spread over several days. Most World Cup and Olympic competitions are based around such a format. It is important that when one game is completed, players and coaches learn from that game, discuss the implications of it, and then put that game out of their minds as they prepare for the next encounter. Because that game is over, there is no point in worrying about it as the result is already in the record books. It is vital that players are assisted to analyse a performance honestly and accurately. They learn from it, but win, lose or draw, they must not dwell on it.

Although this strategy would be regarded as commonsense in the cold light of day, it is easier said than done when the athletes are involved in a vital competition. It is very likely that in the face of a disappointment, players may be tempted to over-analyse and be over critical of themselves, their team-mates or the coach. Typically, this does not make a positive contribution to subsequent pre-match preparation. It can lead to the development of cliques or disaffected factions within the group.

The Australian hockey team started to use the idea of post-match de-briefing sessions in 1987. During these sessions players were asked a variety of questions. They might be asked to name the thing with which they were most happy from their own performance, and the thing with which they were least happy. Conversely, they might be asked to give one key point about their individual game and one about the team performance, or perhaps only the forwards or the defenders or the substitutes might be asked for their opinions.

Importantly, there was always an opportunity for any player to give her view on any aspect of the game. Finally, and always at the end of the player input, the coaches would give their thoughts on the match. As part of the empowering coaching style adopted by the two coaches, they thought it important not to stifle any player contributions by dictating the theme of the meeting with their own observations. These sessions, known as post-game analysis or PGAs, were utilized after every practice game, every test match or every Olympic encounter, irrespective of the match result. They allowed the players to 'put the game to bed' and concentrate on the next game. This approach helped to improve task cohesion and reduced the opportunities for any destructive social factors to develop.

Developing team cohesion

While most researchers stress the need to be able to measure cohesion accurately, most coaches do not focus on this element. They tend to rely upon an intuitive feeling for how well the team sticks together. However, they are very interested in ways that might allow the team to become more cohesive and, they hope, more successful.

The following methods have been used successfully in the past by the current author. They can be employed with athletes from a range of sports and with a variety of age groups. Some of these are cited in Yukelson's (1984) excellent work on group motivation. They are principles around which the psychological preparation of any sports team can be based. While the research concerning cohesion and performance is somewhat equivocal, there is no doubt that coaches prefer to work with a team that is cohesive and united in purpose. While it is acknowledged that there have been some notable exceptions to the rule, it is generally accepted that sports teams should be cohesive units. This is particularly true with regard to task cohesion.

The replacement process

Within every team, squad or club there will be a turnover of athletes. People will move away from the area, or they will simply retire from the sport due to injury, age or changing priorities. Thus a major problem can exist with the assimilation of new players.

While experienced teams are not always winning teams, losing teams are generally more inexperienced. It is important to retain that element of experience and stability while preparing for major championships. Coaches and senior athletes need to be sensitized to the possible effects of the team dividing into the 'mature' players and 'young' players. Such education exercises as 'the model player', and 'what if ...' (Miller, 1988) can be helpful in this context, but the attitude of key personnel is probably more important than any one-off psychological team-building session. The replacement process is inevitable within every group, so it is important that any disruption is kept to a minimum. It requires an intellectual commitment from the existing personnel to achieve this.

Open communication channels

It is important that effective communication occurs between coaches and athletes. The foundation for this communication is trust and mutual respect. Ideally coaches should strive to establish an atmosphere where individual players feel that their contributions are welcomed and appreciated. Sarcasm and ridicule play no role in this process, and it is important to note that communication is a two-way process. Both the coach and the athlete have a responsibility towards each other for making it work.

Pride in the group

Pride comes from the self-satisfaction that goals set by individuals and the group have been achieved. Goal setting can go a long way towards achieving pride in the team's efforts. Individual goals should be established for both professionalism issues as well as performance goals. Table 6.1 includes some of the professionalism goals that have been used by athletes in the past. Basically, they can be focused on any of the off-field issues that might affect on-field performance.

As well as these individual goals, team goals should be discussed and targeted. Typically, these goals should focus on the process of

Table 6.1 *Professionalism goals*

'To eat only nutritious food while on road trips.'

'I will try hard to get on with all the other athletes on tour.'

'Use my walkman for recreation and relaxation on long trips during the tour.'

'Ensure I do not react to suspect refereeing in a negative way.'

'Make sure I get a daytime sleep every day.'

'Make sure I do mental rehearsals at least once a day.'

'I will try to be a supportive member of the team, especially when on the bench and when others are feeling a little down.'

'Keep reasonable hours during the trip and be aware of my room-mates' wishes.'

'Accept the desires of the majority of the squad and support their decisions.'

'Ensure I am mentally prepared to train intensely, thereby using each training session as an opportunity to develop.'

'Take the opportunity to learn from the older players.'

'I won't overeat at breakfast, even if they lay on "the works".'

'Set goals for each training session/game and constantly evaluate my progress.'

'Focus on controllables, and stay single-minded.'

---

success rather than the outcome. The 1988 hockey team wanted to win the Olympic gold medal, but that was not their stated goal. Rather they were concerned with ensuring that they controlled all of the controllable variables, and took each game as a separate entity. They were to retain their focus on the 'here and now', rather than concentrating on the consequences of any one result. For example, 'If we win this match today, we will be in the semi-final tomorrow', or 'We only need a draw today to make next week's play-offs'.

During the build-up period to Seoul and Barcelona the players were encouraged to set themselves goals for each training session. Goal setting for matches and tournaments is now a commonly accepted practice, but using goals for training sessions was slightly more unusual. Most importantly, the goals that were established had to be evaluated. There is little point in conducting goal setting exercises if the loop is not closed by the final step of evaluation. This is where the coach is so important in teaching players to be able to self-evaluate. Obviously the coach provides feedback concerning goals and objectives, but it is preferable if the athletes can also initiate the process and evaluate their own performance.

The uniqueness of group goals has been highlighted by Mills (1984) who noted that a group's goals are not the sum of the personal goals of group members. Results from Brawley *et al.* (1993) have suggested that the group variable of cohesion is greater among those individuals who perceive that their team engages in group goal setting for competition. Following on from their earlier research Brawley *et al.* (1992) are happy to conclude that, 'when groups are less involved in participative group actions such as setting team goals, the degree to which group unity and other group goal-related variables are perceived is correspondingly less'. An important element of the mental preparation of both the Australian and British Women's Hockey Teams of 1988 and 1992, respectively, was to promote this sense of involvement in such activities as team goal setting.

Common expectations of behaviour

Behaviour norms need to be conducive to the goals the group is striving to achieve. It is suggested that philosophy on behaviour standards is stated explicitly. Athletes should be able to discuss the topic and then formulate a plan to which all players should agree. Ambiguity and lack of clarity can be disastrous at this stage and it is important that all personnel are striving towards the same clearly-stated goal.

Living in an Olympic village for nearly a month may be regarded by some as a glamorous past-time. However, the village lifestyle comes complete with distractions and temptations, and it is important that athletes control their free time quite tightly. The temptation is to become absorbed into the 'circus-like' atmosphere. Athletes have a lot of time on their hands because they are doing very little training at this stage of their preparation. They can find themselves walking around the shopping complexes or going off to watch some of the athletes from other sports train or compete. By themselves, any one of these events is not going to disrupt performance, but if the athlete slips into this 'tourist' mode over a number of days it can seriously impair performance.

Recognize excellence

Individuals who excel within their designated role should be recognized and verbally rewarded with praise. Some coaches are loathe to do this within a team context for fear of causing resentment and jealousy. However, the coach's goal should be to have all members of the team fulfilling their individual goals, and thus it is important to let players know that their efforts are appreciated. Such recognition can serve to get athletes ego-involved rather than just task-involved.

At one time it seemed unfashionable to praise team athletes. The coaches seemed to spend most of their time being critical of their charges and trying to correct faults. Of course, correction is an important part of the coach's role, but it is only one. In an effort to establish increased self esteem for both individuals and the team, it is vital that athletes are striving towards a performance that brings with it praise and recognition. The coaching style has a direct bearing on this process.

Conclusion

Team athletes play their sport within a group. These groups are dynamic and are influenced by many external factors. In order for these team athletes to achieve their full potential they need to share common goals with their team-mates. The group needs to have an effective communication system that promotes goal achievement.

Any team that seeks to make actual productivity relate closely to potential productivity (Steiner, 1972) must work to promote cohesiveness within its ranks. Coordination losses and motivation losses need to be minimized if a team is to fulfil its potential. By eliminating social loafing and by increasing individual performance identifiability, the coach can help to create an efficient working unit. If negative influences are not reduced or removed the coach will have difficulty in concentrating on the technical and tactical elements of team preparation. In the worst cases the coach may be left working with a crowd rather than a group.

However, there are a number of principles and a number of techniques that can be employed with sports teams that can help to promote a co-operative environment. While the research in this field is scant, there are many practical examples of the empowering coaching style being successful in this area, and it is to be encouraged and promoted.

References

Arnold, G.E. and Straub, W.F. (1972) Personality and group cohesiveness as determinants of success among inter-scholastic basketball teams. *Proceedings Fourth Canadian Symposium on Psycho-Motor Learning and Sport Psychology*. Ottawa: Health and Welfare Canada.

Brawley, L.R., Carron, A.V. and Widmeyer, W.N. (1992) The nature of group goals in sport teams: a phenomenological analysis. *The Sport Psychologist*, **6**, 323–333.

Brawley, L.R., Carron, A.V. and Widmeyer, W.N. (1993) The influence of the group and its cohesiveness on perceptions of group goal-related variables. *Journal of Sport and Exercise Psychology*, **15**, 245–260.

Carron, A.V. (1980) *Social Psychology of Sport*, p. 249. Ithaca, NY: Mouvement Publications.

Carron, A.V. (1982) Cohesiveness in sports groups. Interpretations and considerations. *Journal of Sport Psychology*, **4**, 123–138.

Cartwright, D. and Zander, A. (1968) *Group Dynamics: Research and Theory*, 3rd edn. New York: Harper and Row.

Gill, D.L. (1986) *Psychological Dynamics of Sport*. Champaign, IL: Human Kinetics Publishers.

Gross, J. (1982) Effects of knowledge of results upon individual performance on a motor task under alone and group situations. PhD thesis, dissertation. University of Iowa (unpublished).

Ingham, A., Levinger, G., Graves, B. and Peckham, V. (1974) The Ringelmann effect: studies of group size and group performance. *Journal of Experimental Social Psychology*, **10**, 371–384.

Jones, M.B. (1974) Regressing group on individual effectiveness. *Organisational Behaviour and Human Performance*, **11**, 426–451.

Klein, M. and Christianson, G. (1969) Group composition, group structure and group effectiveness. In *Sport, Culture and Society* (J.W. Loy and G.S. Kenyon, eds) pp. 397–408. Toronto: Macmillan.

Landers, D.M. and Luschen, G. (1974) Team performance outcome and the cohesiveness of competitive coacting teams. *International Journal of Sport Sociology*, **9**, 57–71.

Latane, B., Williams, K. and Harkins, S. (1979) Many hands make light work: the causes and consequences of social loafing. *Journal of Personality and Social Psychology*, **37**, 823–832.

Lenk, H. (1969) Top performance despite internal conflict: An antithesis to a functionalistic proposition. In *Sport, Culture and Society* (J.W. Loy and G.S. Kenyon, eds) pp. 393–397. Toronto: Macmillan.

McGrath, J.E. (1962) The influence of positive interpersonal relations on adjustment and effectiveness in rifle teams. *Journal of Abnormal and Social Psychology*, **64**, 365–375.

Martens, R. and Peterson, J. (1971) Group cohesiveness as a determinant of member satisfaction in team performance. *International Review of Sport Sociology*, **6**, 49–61.

Miller, B.P. (1988) Touring skills: Learning to cope. *Excel*, **4**, 3–5.

Mills, T.M. (1984) *The Sociology of Small Groups*, 2nd edn. Englewood Cliffs, NJ: Prentice Hall.

Shaw, M. (1976) *Group Dynamics: The Psychology of Small Group Behaviour*, 2nd edn. New York: McGraw-Hill.

Slater, M.R. and Sewell, D.F. (1994) An examination of the cohesion–performance relationship in university hockey teams. *Journal of Sports Sciences*, **12**, 423–431.

Steiner, I. (1972) *Group Process and Productivity*. New York: Academics Press.

Thomas, E.J. (1957) Effects of facilitative role interdependence on group functioning. *Human Relations*, **10**, 347–356.

Yukelson, D. (1984) Group motivation in sport teams. In *Psychological Foundations of Sport* (J.M. Silva and R.S. Weinberg, eds) pp. 229–241. Champaign, IL: Human Kinetics Publications.

Part Three

7

The individual consultation: the fall and rise of a professional golfer

Richard Cox

Sport: Golf

In October 1992 Billy Crooks (not his real name), a 26 year old professional golfer, made an appointment to see me. He told me he had been playing golf since he was nine years of age and as a professional for the past six years. He had won his own club championship at 15 and, in 1986, had been the leading amateur in Scotland. At that time the media had held out great hopes for him, though one newspaper had described him as 'self-centred', a criticism that had affected him adversely ever since.

He had continued to improve by his own standards until 1990 but then levelled off. As he spoke to me during that first meeting he described himself as physically fit, for he ran regularly and trained in a local gymnasium three times a week. He was also a non-smoker and someone who drank only occasionally. Thus, at 6' 3" tall, lean and hungry looking, whatever problems he had were unlikely to revolve around a lack of physical fitness.

By his own judgement he was technically competent and, at various times, had been taught by all the top professional coaches, including Bob Torrance, John Jacobs and David Leadbetter. Earlier that same year, 1990, he had played in the Scottish Open for the first time and played badly. In his own words, he felt 'tight and under pressure'. During the week that followed he had finished third in the qualifying round for the British Open. However, because of the pressure he felt under, he nearly pulled out before the tournament had even begun. To quote his own words,

> 'Things came to a head when I qualified for my first British Open. But, instead of looking forward to it, all I could feel was pressure. It got to the stage where I almost didn't want to play. As a result, when I did play, I played so far below my potential it wasn't true.'

He recalled he had decided to play mainly because of his father but that, as he stood on the first tee, his mind was flooded with negative thoughts mostly based around what he thought he was expected to do. It never became clear during this or subsequent meetings precisely who was doing 'the expecting', as he maintained throughout that no pressure ever came from people around him. Needless to say, given that he had asked me to help him, he played badly in that British Open and remembered thinking that he 'would rather be fishing than playing golf'.

In terms of diagnosing what his problems were I did not, as many psychologists might have done at this point, ask him to fill in a questionnaire of any kind. I know of no questionnaire that can tell me which course of action to take with any client and experience has shown them to have a poor track record in this respect. Of course, advocates of questionnaires will argue otherwise but overuse and misuse of, for instance, personality inventories in the early days of British sports psychology made me, and many others in this field (see, for instance, Rushall 1979), sceptical about their worth in any type of work outside academic life.

For almost twenty-five years now I have espoused the philosophy of the science of human behaviour known as Behaviourism (Skinner, 1974). To a behavioural psychologist everything a person thinks, feels, says and does are forms of 'behaviour' and constitute legitimate subject matter for study. More importantly, perhaps, a behavioural psychologist sees Man as a complete entity rather than as a mind within a body that somehow operates independently from that body. Thus, a person's cognitive behaviour (thinking) can be studied through what he says (verbal behaviour) and does, and his emotional behaviour (feelings) through how and when he says and does things.

Behavioural psychologists believe that all forms of human behaviour are products of the interactive effects of one's environmental experiences and influenced to some degree by one's genetic endowment. They also believe that almost all types of problems experienced by normal people in everyday life can be solved by a number of techniques which, collectively, are referred to as Behaviour Modification (Martin and Pears, 1992).

The most important characteristic of Behaviour Modification is its strong emphasis on defining problems in terms of behaviour that can be measured in some way and how it uses changes in the behavioural measure of the problem as the best indicator of the extent to which that problem is being solved. Its treatment procedures and techniques are ways of rearranging an individual's environment to help that individual to function more effectively in the society in which he lives. Behaviour Modification techniques emerged from the laboratory and, therefore, they can be described in precise detail. Consequently, Behaviour Modification emphasizes that a particular intervention was responsible for a particular change in behaviour and therefore places high value on accountability on everyone concerned.

Obviously, this is a very simplified introduction to the concerns of the behavioural psychologist and to develop it is not relevant to present purposes. My task here is to document how I was to help Billy, if at all possible, and I began by exploring his answers to a series of questions emanating from the three basic questions any behavioural psychologist would ask himself in this situation:

- What was Billy's history of reinforcement and punishment?
- What stimuli were operating on him at that moment in time?
- What was his level of deprivation of those stimuli at that moment in time?

For a full discussion of these three questions and how comprehensive answers to them all could lead to an explanation of the behaviour of an individual, at any one moment in time, in sporting contexts, see Dickenson (1976).

These three questions are easy to pose but extremely difficult to answer, even when the individual in question is well known. I had never met Billy before which meant they would always be impossible to answer comprehensively. Nevertheless, they provided the frame-work for our discussion during that first meeting and for all others thereafter. It was not difficult to conclude from that discussion that Billy had created a negatively reinforcing environment for himself in terms of playing tournament golf. All his recent 'history of reinforce-ment' from matchplay at that level was negative both in terms of results and how he perceived himself as a player. Consequently, he was experiencing what the layman (and psychologists adopting alter-native, theoretical stances) might call 'a lack of confidence and low self esteem'. These feelings were part of the 'stimuli operating on Billy at that moment in time' and he was therefore 'currently deprived' of sufficient, successful performances to reinforce himself positively as a professional golfer worthy of the name.

More specifically perhaps, it became clear from that discussion that Billy was almost certainly a classical 'self-instructor', who was focusing predominantly on external stimuli and particularly so each time he struck the ball.

I based this conclusion primarily on his answers to two questions in particular. Firstly, I asked him what he thought about as he swung his club to play a shot. His first response was to say, 'Nothing'. However, further questioning revealed that he was typically thinking self-instructions and technical thoughts. For instance he would say such things to himself as, 'Keep your left wrist cocked' and 'Clear your left hip'. If he failed to carry out these self-instructions, as all too often he did, he would follow them up with a negative value judgement (verbal behaviour) about either his lack of ability or intelligence, or both. Secondly, I asked him if he was aware of what he did with his breathing during his swing and particularly during the downswing. Again, he couldn't tell me to begin with but, after simulating a few swings, decided that he probably drew breath on his backswing and held it during his downswing which is what most golfers do, from novice to professional. Moreover, much of the way in which he evaluated his performances was determined by what he thought other people would think of him. Thus, he wasn't playing primarily for himself as all elite sportsmen and sportswomen should do. Even worse, many of his self-instructional thoughts, at the point of striking the ball, were phrased either negatively or in avoidance terms. This had evolved through being very successful in his early days and thereby being positively reinforced to a high degree but less so in recent years and the fact that certain individuals were criticizing his lack of recent success. As a consequence, he was beginning to doubt his own ability to ever succeed at the levels he thought he was capable of playing.

In the same way as patients visiting their GP's surgery expect some tangible form of remedy for their ailments, so clients consulting a sport psychologist expect to leave with some form of action they can take which, through discussion and explanation, they have been led to believe will help them. This is true, irrespective of the theoretical stance adopted by the sport psychologist. If not, then the sport psychologist should refer them to someone who *can* help them. Before seeing Billy again I asked him to attempt to do two things on the driving range where he practised. First, to hear himself breathe out audibly at the moment he struck each shot and, secondly, to hold a picture in his mind at those critical moments of precisely where he wanted the ball to land. Being an intelligent young man Billy immediately asked for an explanation because, to use his own words, he had 'tried enough gimmicks already to last him a lifetime'. He had also heard of others being recommended such behaviours but had never understood why.

My reason for asking him to breathe out at the moment of striking the ball was that we can only be doing one of three things with our breathing at any one moment in time – breathing in, holding it or breathing out. Only breathing out is compatible with either maintaining or reducing muscular tension. Thinking in negative avoidance terms typically has the effect of increasing muscular tension (Rushall and Potgeiter, 1987) so if he was tensing unnecessarily during his swing then breathing out would go someway towards reducing the tension, particularly in his jaw, chest and shoulders. It was also the easiest behaviour he could change as his first step towards creating a feeling of being in control of himself rather than external factors controlling him. The reason for asking him to picture in his mind exactly where he wanted the ball to go was to replace his negative self-instructions with more positive thought content. It would also facilitate what Gallwey (1981) described as a state of 'relaxed concentration' and thereby allow him to strike the ball with less inhibiting stimuli operating at the precise moment he made contact. What I did *not* tell him was that these behaviours would change his focus of attention from external stimuli, which were largely the cause of so much negative reinforcement for him, to internal stimuli which, I believed, would go a long way towards redressing the imbalance he was experiencing in his golfing life; such an explanation was simply not necessary at that time.

He agreed to try these recommendations and we arranged to meet at the driving range in one month's time. I chose the driving range for our next meeting for two reasons. Firstly, to empower him by meeting on territory more positively reinforcing to him than to me and, secondly, to watch him actually hit a few balls and to discover, closer to first hand, precisely what he was attending to as he struck the ball. The reason for the one month's interval between meetings was to allow him sufficient time to practise the two behaviours recommended, particularly as he had two 'pro-am' tournaments during that month.

Our initial discussion during that second meeting revealed that he had been able to achieve both behaviours recommended but with only minor rewards. He reported that he 'had felt slightly more relaxed' during the two 'pro-am' tournaments and 'less self-critical' but not any happier with the quality of his stroke play. My immediate response was to remind him of how many years it had taken to develop to the point where he had sought help from me and not to expect miracles in the first few weeks which is a typical expectation of many elite athletes when they consult a sport psychologist for the first time.

Much of the first half of that session revolved around target practice. I chose target practice as I believed he was skilful enough to do this successfully and thereby gave him an opportunity to be positively reinforced in my presence. He showed he could hit a target, or get very close to it, at 200 yards, both with deliberate fade and hook if asked to. Therefore, I concluded that he was sound technically just as he had said he was during our first meeting.

For some inexplicable reason (given that I was and never will be a golf coach) he then introduced a problem into the proceedings which he believed he had (because he had been told often enough by fellow professionals) at the top of his backswing. He was closing off the club face by allowing his left wrist to become uncocked. This, he said, was causing him to hit with too much of a hook particularly on his tee shots. However, when he was actually playing golf he wasn't aware of himself doing it. Now, awareness exercises in golf were explored and documented thoroughly by Gallwey (1981) and so I asked him, in typical Gallwey fashion, to pose with his club face in the wide open position at the top of his backswing and then to do exactly the opposite, i.e. with the club head in the fully closed position. We decided that a score of one was to be given for the club face fully closed and five for fully open. I asked him to hit a few balls and focus on where he felt his club head to be, regardless of what happened to the ball, and to score each stroke between one and five. I then asked him to reproduce different scores at will and I started with the two extremes – he was to produce a five followed by a one and I alternated these demands for the next thirty shots. We then moved to twos and fours for the next thirty shots, slipping in the occasional one and five. He found it easier to reproduce one and two than he did four and five and predictably his fours, and very often his fives also, produced perfect results. In other words, what felt slightly open to him was in fact the exact position of the club face he was seeking at the top of his backswing.

We discussed this at some length and he practised developing his awareness of the position of the club head for the remainder of the session. Thereafter, we discussed the fact that he had the qualifying tournament in three week's time for the European Tour the following year. The qualifying tournament was to take place in Spain and it would involve more than seven hundred professional golfers competing for less than one hundred places. How should he approach it given that he had never qualified for this tournament in six years of trying? As someone who had never been more than an infrequent spectator at golf tournaments this was another very difficult question for me to answer. However, I reminded him of the three things we had worked on so far – breathing out during his downswing, visualizing where he wanted the ball to land and developing awareness of the club head at the top of his backswing. Given that Locke *et al.* (1981) had found that goal setting improves performance and that Burton (1989) maintained that setting goals around performance was more effective than around the outcome, I recommended that he set his goals around these three behaviours and that his evaluation of his performance should be in terms of how well he managed to do them for each shot he played in the tournament.

He was reluctant to accept this advice at first and quite obviously wanted me to talk to him in terms of scores and finishing positions which are the most powerful reinforcers available to a golfer but, as I pointed out, he had tried focusing on such outcome goals six times before and had sought my help as a result. Therefore, what was the point in carrying on in the same way as before? I quoted an aphorism to him which I had personally composed and used many times previously with various athletes in a wide range of activities:

'Get the performance right
and
you will get the result you deserve.'

He needed to focus on the performance and let the outcome take care of itself. But what was the performance in his terms and when and how should he focus on it? We finished that second session with Billy agreeing to try focusing his attention on, first, the club head position at the top of his backswing and, secondly, on breathing out throughout the downswing and follow through whilst holding a picture in his mind of where he wanted the ball to land. He would attempt to adopt this strategy for all tee and fairway shots throughout the qualifying tournament.

Recommendations and advice from sport psychologists can often have a dramatic effect. This may, or may not, be due to the quality of such recommendations and advice, and it is not my intention here to question the efficacy of sport psychologists. However, many athletes are in a state of desperation when they consult with a sport psychologist and will try anything that is suggested to them. As with the world of medicine, we can never be certain that it is the *substance* of the advice given that helps the athlete rather than the fact that *something* has been given – the placebo effect. What it is intended to guard against is sport psychologists believing they have a cornucopia of panaceas ready to select from and administer during the first and possibly the only consultation they have with an athlete. Life is seldom that simple and it came as no great surprise to me that Billy returned from the qualifying tournament, some four weeks later, for our third meeting having failed to qualify for the 1993 European Tour. However, he was pleased with what he had discovered about his ability to focus his attention on kinaesthetic feedback as he was striking the ball but he had learned that changing his normal focus of attention at these crucial moments would take more than one tournament to accomplish. He resolved to practise what had been set in motion over the coming winter months with the hope of improving his competitive results at the start of Spring 1993. Thus, evidence was to hand that already he was being more positively reinforced by attending to internal stimuli concerning his actual performance than he was by external stimuli concerning the outcome of his performance.

This brought us to the subject of practice and what he usually did in his practice sessions. When I asked him about this, his reply was that he 'would normally hit a thousand balls a day'. When I asked him what for, he replied, 'to groove in his swing'. I asked him how he knew if he was grooving in his swing insofar as he usually practised on his own. He didn't know but he believed he must be because 'that was what all professionals did in practice'. I pointed out to him that without somebody there to provide feedback, or a video camera and monitor to provide instant replay pictures, he might well be grooving in an actual error. I then explained the relationship between the demands of the game, the most important of which is to hit as few shots as possible, and the nature of practice, and I asked him next time he practised to reduce his session to one hundred and twenty balls or less, depending on how he felt, but to make every shot count. Furthermore, insofar as professional golfers rarely get to hit two balls in succession from the same spot I wondered why he practised doing just that. So, for instance, for putting practice, I asked him to position twenty balls in a circle of some six foot radius around a hole and to play them at random and record the outcome. He would then graduate to a similar practice from twelve feet and ultimately from eighteen feet recording the outcome of every shot on a copy of the recording sheet illustrated in Figure 7.1. We also devised a system of recording whether a shot was either left or right, short or long in relation to the target, and how well he had maintained his visual focus throughout his shot, which would enable him to see how consistent he was. This is illustrated in Figure 7.2. For practical purposes this was reduced to A6 in size and reproduced as a small notepad consisting of eighteen sheets of paper. Thus, it could be used in competitive golf without drawing attention to oneself. (It can be slipped into a side pocket of a golf bag and used whenever one's opponent is playing a shot.) The result is a detailed account of each hole in a round of golf which provides more objective and detailed feedback than memory alone and, as Drowatzky (1975) observed, 'Without feedback, any change in performance and subsequent improvement would be impossible'.

If he was on a driving range he was to use at least three different clubs alternately, choose three different targets, one for each club, and aim his shot at the appropriate target, again recording details of each shot in terms of long or short, left or right of the target. This, of course, was in conjunction with the skills he had already started to practise whereby he would breathe out at the point of striking the ball and hold a picture in his mind of exactly where he wanted the ball to go to.

When Billy departed at the end of the sessions it was with enthusiasm and looking forward to the practice he was going to put in over the winter months, which was a change from his usual attitude to practice. I didn't see Billy for almost six months after that meeting as I had left it to him to contact me when he felt ready to. This he did in May 1993 and it was a much changed person that I ushered into my office for our fourth meeting. He told me he had been practising hard throughout the winter, in the ways we had discussed, and had played only a few minor club tournaments just to keep his hand in. He had also been reading widely in the field of sports psychology, such was his enthusiasm to learn more about the subject, and had been much impressed by Jim Loehr's (1986) book *Mental Toughness Training for Sports*. Much more importantly though he had been experimenting with his breathing pattern and instead of breathing out only on his downswing he had discovered that if he breathed out throughout the whole of his swing then he felt much more in control of the situation. To do this he would take up his stance and breathe in at that point. He would then start breathing out for a count of five before he even

Distance	6′			12′			18′			6′			12′			18′		
Accuracy Shot	√	1 2 • 4 3	X	√	1 2 • 4 3	X	√	1 2 • 4 3	X	√	1 2 • 4 3	X	√	1 2 • 4 3	X	√	1 2 • 4 3	X
1																		
2																		
3																		
4																		
5																		
6																		
7																		
8																		
9																		
10																		
11																		
12																		
13																		
14																		
15																		
16																		
17																		
18																		
19																		
20																		

Figure 7.1   *A recording sheet for putting in golf*

Hole number_____ (_____ Yards/metres) Par____

Shot number	Club chosen	Target chosen	Quality of visualization before each shot			Outcome 1 2 T 4 3 (Record distance from target)	Fade or draw (slice) (hook)		Correct choice of clubs	
			Good	50/50	Poor		F(S)	D(H)	Yes	No
1										
2										
3										
4										
5										
6										
7										
8										

Figure 7.2 *A recording sheet for each hole played in golf*

moved his club backwards and it was on the count of six that he would begin his backswing and, thereafter, his downswing. So, by the time he had struck the ball and finished his follow-through he had probably been breathing out continuously for a period of between ten and twelve seconds. Moreover, he breathed out sufficiently loudly for him to be able to hear himself and tried to maintain the same level of volume throughout the whole swing. He was much happier with this breathing pattern than the one we had worked on earlier, which only required him to breathe out on the downswing and he reported that, from that moment on, this was the breathing pattern he intended to practise and refine.

I was pleased for him because this represented one of the changes he could control which I had referred to much earlier in our meetings. There is no point in trying to change anything, if you do not feel in control of it, because every athlete has to take responsibility for whatever changes they make to their sporting performance. Furthermore, I told him that it was a good example of a *specific* change. Too many elite athletes attempt to bring about gross changes in their performances, which are often not possible anyway, and they fail to concentrate on the specifics of performance anywhere enough. So, for instance, we had discussed that instead of putting to get within two feet of the hole from putts twenty feet out, he should actually aim at the back of the cup. In other words, every putt he took, no matter how far away, should be aimed to hit the back of the cup which is the only part of it that is visible. He reported that a lot of golfers he knew aimed to get their first putt from twenty feet or more to within a two foot radius of the cup so that they could be more or less certain of holing out on their next shot. My understanding was that if you could get the first putt down you saved a shot so why not aim to hole out first time, rather than to just get it into the vicinity? Moreover, since the cardinal sin in putting in golf is to leave the ball short, aiming at the back of the cup means that the shot should always be long enough, which would go a long way towards avoiding the negatively reinforcing consequences of the golfers' expression 'Never up, never in'.

Billy had mixed fortunes during the summer and autumn of 1993. His two high points came, first, in July, when he broke the course record at one of Scotland's major championship courses and, secondly, and perhaps even more importantly, in the autumn, when he qualified for his first ever European Tour. Both were magnificent achievements for which he received considerable public acclaim. Nevertheless, in between those two high points, he had several frustrating performances in which he lacked the level of consistency he was seeking.

I did not see him again until after the qualifying tournament for the 1994 European Tour so it was late in November when we met for the fifth time. At that point he was obviously delighted with his success and very much looking forward to 1994 and the European Tour and we spent much of the time together on that occasion discussing how he should cope with the number of tournaments that he would be entering for the first time and the fact that life would be almost continuous tournament golf. He also had another important occasion to look forward to in 1994 as he was due to be married at Easter time.

We discussed his goals for the Tour and again they were very similar to what we had discussed previously. In other words, the goals revolved around controlling the nature of his thought content during performance rather than how many cuts he should be aiming to make or how much money he was hoping to win. Perhaps, most important of all on that occasion, I introduced him to a series of relaxation and mental rehearsal programmes which I had devised earlier. These were all contained on cassette tape which he was to take away with him, but first I worked through them with him so that he was able to experience them and had the opportunity to ask me questions about each programme. I explained that they would enhance his awareness of and control over, firstly, the degree of tension in his voluntary muscles, secondly, his breathing pattern and, thirdly, his ability to think visually rather than verbally.

The tape contained four programmes – two physical relaxation programmes, the first being a comprehensive version and the second a shortened version of Jacobsen's (1938) progressive muscle relaxation technique. The third programme was a mental relaxation programme based around specific details in a visualized, quiet room and the fourth a controlled breathing programme. The last, I explained, he could use at a moment's notice out on the golf course, if he felt the need for it, as it involves controlling the amount of breath one takes in over a certain period of time (initially for five seconds) and also releasing it in a similar, controlled way. We practised these four programmes together and discussed them at some length before he left with the cassette tape.

The next time I saw him, our sixth meeting, was just after his wedding at Easter time of 1994. He told me that he had missed the four cuts in tournaments immediately prior to the wedding and had felt shattered, emotionally and physically, for the first four days after it. He had taken a week off from golf and had returned to the Tour to make the next two cuts, at which he was delighted. So, at that point, he had made six out of eleven cuts and had won approximately the amount of money he was expected to, although obviously he had hoped for much more. Perhaps more importantly, however, he reported that he felt he lacked organization in his life. Having recently been married and having to consider another person for the first time, he felt disorganized when he was away on the Tour.

In an attempt to help him overcome this feeling I introduced him to the concept of a pre-competition strategy (Rushall, 1979). I gave him a copy of the plan illustrated in Figure 7.3 and asked him, before the first day of his next tournament, to enter, firstly, his tee-off time, secondly, his practice start time and then any other deadlines he had to meet for that day. Thereafter, he was to enter the time he wanted to get up that morning, when and what he wanted to eat, when he expected to be making telephone calls, when and where he planned to do his full warm-up routine and anything else he felt he needed to do in order to be ready for the first tee. All of these events added up collectively to what was to be his 'primary strategy'. I then asked him to consider if any of these events could be delayed or interrupted for any reason. If so, then he was to enter a secondary, or 'coping', behaviour alongside the primary behaviour such that he had a plan of action that would always give him the feeling of being in control of the contingencies of reinforcement that influenced his life, rather than the other way round. With his day now planned with behaviours he had chosen to pursue, his pre-competition strategy was designed to preclude the development of anxiety due to having time on his hands and not knowing how to cope with it.

His pre-competition strategy was also to include events after he had finished his round of golf because that point in time marked the beginning of his preparation period for the second round of the tournament. Thus, he was to set aside time for evaluating his pre-competition strategy for the first round and to decide what, if anything, he should do differently to prepare for the next round. It was also to include time for relaxing and socializing before retiring that evening as he would most likely spend much of the time available talking 'shop' with other golfers on the Tour and this might not be the most profitable way to prepare for the following day – he had to guard against any eventualities in this respect.

One of the positive developments in his game he reported at that meeting was that he had become totally aware of what his last 'swing thought' was before he struck the ball but that he lacked control over it. For instance, on one occasion he remembered thinking technically and, as a result, he 'hit the ball straight right'. He also reported that the breathing pattern he had decided upon had now become an integral part of his swing and he could never envisage himself going back to doing anything else. Moreover, he had never felt overawed in any

Event: Date: Time of day:

Approx time	Primary strategy	Coping strategy (if primary strategy is not possible)	Post-event evaluation (√ or X)
6.00 am			
6.30			
7.00			
7.30			
8.00			
8.30			
9.00			
9.30			
10.00			
10.30			
11.00			
11.30			
12.00 noon			
12.30 pm			
1.00			
1.30			
2.00			
2.30			
3.00			
3.30			
4.00			
4.30			
5.00			
5.30			
6.00			
6.30			
7.00			
7.30			
8.00			
8.30			
9.00			
9.30			
10.00			
10.30			
11.00			

Figure 7.3   *Pro-forma for a pre-competition strategy*

competition as he had done in the 1992 British Open. As a consequence, he had decided that one of his goals should be 'relaxed
concentration' or, as he put it, 'trying not to perform'.

He had finished in the top 20 per cent in the Italian Open, scoring
a total of level par over the four rounds and he was pleased with his
performance. However, he had tried a 'swing thought' of 'brushing
the tops of daisies' for three inches before his club connected with the
ball. This had worked successfully at the driving range previously but
he was not happy with this in competition. He felt that he had no feel
for either deliberately hooking or fading his tee shots to reach a
particular target. So, he decided to concentrate his 'swing thoughts'
on visualizing what the ball was going to do after he had hit it. This
gave him much more feel for the shape of the ball flight. It also helped
him to concentrate more fully on what he was doing. He had also
worked on his putting and particularly on trying to hit the back of the
cup on every occasion with notable success.

This brings this account up to the time of writing, at which point
Billy is half way through the 1994 European Tour. He has learned to
appreciate that he is, in one sense, just beginning his professional
career, despite having been fully engaged in it for six years. He has
also come to change his perception of his own age. Hitherto, he had
felt that he was 'getting a bit past it'. Now he appreciates that, at 28,
he is a comparatively young man and that time is on his side as a
professional. At the time of documenting this account Carl Mason has
recently won the Scottish Open at 44 and Nick Price the British Open
at 38.

Billy has yet to get his driving, chipping and putting all working
well at the same time. For most of the European Tour so far this year
he has been able to report, from his detailed diary, that one of these
three and, on occasions, two of these three have been going well but
always one of them has been letting him down. He is beginning to
appreciate that the conditioned inhibition he developed, over six years
of relative failure by his own standards, has run deep. To some extent,
it has become ingrained and it will take at least another year on the
European Tour and, perhaps, even another after that before he is able
to play to his full potential. He definitely needs to decide on one
specific, overall strategy for his drives, one for his chip shots to the
green and one for his putting and to work at these over a prolonged
period of time now.

I think it is important that I now see him play in a proper tournament as, this far, I have only seen him hit a golf ball at the driving

range. Perhaps, there is a need for me to actually caddy for him because not only would I like to see him play but also to discuss with him, immediately after each shot, precisely whether he felt he was able to carry out the strategy decided for that shot. To this end, I know he has yet to develop the discipline of recording his observations about each shot he plays in a tournament and I would like to help him achieve this. Hopefully, the evaluation session in the clubhouse after each round would provide sufficient feedback for him to appreciate the benefits of being as specific as possible in his approach to playing golf. At the top level of any sport the participants are all more-or-less as skilful as one another. What is likely to separate them is their ability to focus their attention, at precisely the right moment, on the most relevant stimuli concerning performance. Of course, other factors are important and influence performance in various ways such as temperament, character, fitness and nutrition. However, insofar as the contingencies of reinforcement that each of these factors brings to bear upon the individual's performance are important considerations, so they can be manipulated and changed to be more effective through Behaviour Modification techniques. Essentially, this represents the long-term goal that Billy and I have set for the work we shall do together over the next two or three years.

References

Burton, D. (1989) Winning isn't everything: examining the impact of performance goals on collegiate swimmers' cognitions and performance. *The
Sport Psychologist*, 3, 105–132.

Dickenson, J. (1976) *A Behavioural Analysis of Sport*. London: Lepus.

Drowatzky, J.N. (1975) *Motor Learning Principles and Practices*, p. 99.
Minneapolis, MN: Burgess Publishing Company.

Gallwey, T.W. (1981) *The Inner Game of Golf*, p. 79. London: Jonathan
Cape.

Jacobsen, E. (1938) *Progressive Relaxation: A Physiological and Clinical
Investigation of Muscular States and their Significance in Psychological and
Medical Practice*, 2nd edn. Chicago: University of Chicago Press.

Locke, E.A., Shaw, K.N., Saari, L.M. and Latham, G.P. (1981) Goal setting
and task performance, 1969–1980. *Psychological Bulletin*, 90, 125–152.

Loehr, J. (1986) *Mental Toughness Training for Sports*. Massachusetts, USA:
Donnelly and Sons.

Martin, G.L. and Pears, J.J. (1992) *Behaviour Modification: What it is and
how to do it*, Hemel Hempstead: Times/Mirror Mosby College Publishing.

Rushall, B.S. (1979) *Psyching in Sport*. London: Pelham.

Rushall, B.S. and Potgeiter, J.R. (1987) *The Psychology of Successful Competing in Endurance Events*. Pretoria: South African Association for Sport Science Physical Education and Recreation.
Skinner, B.F. (1974) *About Behavourism*. New York: Alfred K. Knopf.

8

An educational approach: the design, implementation and evaluation of a psychological skills training programme

Deirdre Scully and John Kremer

Sport: Golf

Increasingly, sport psychologists are being considered as part of a very important back-up team of sport scientists including dieticians, physiotherapists, physiologists, biomechanists and others whose sole responsibility is to devise packages and programmes which athletes and coaches can implement with a view to enhancing sporting performance. The increased demand for sports psychology services has led to a concomitant rise in the number of mental skills training programmes both of a general nature (Albinson and Bull, 1988; Terry, 1989; Orlick, 1990) and sport specific (Rotella and Bunker, 1981; Kubistant, 1988; Weinberg, 1988). However, one difficulty with the many mental skills training programmes available is that they have been advanced without any evaluation of the programmes, which makes it difficult for coaches or, indeed, sport psychologists to know the relative merits of the numerous programmes currently available. This significant failing has been highlighted in a number of recent review articles assessing the future of applied sports psychology research (Weinberg, 1989; Hardy and Jones, 1994; Vealey, 1994). Fortunately, a change in this regard would appear to be taking place with a variety of evaluative studies assessing the impact of comprehensive intervention programmes (as distinct from studies assessing the effectiveness of isolated psycho-behavioural techniques) currently appearing in the literature (Gould *et al.*, 1990; Brewer and Shillinglaw, 1993; Savoy, 1993; Daw and Burton, 1994).

The purpose of this paper is to outline the development and implementation of a specific psychological skills training programme for a

group of elite female golfers and to evaluate qualitatively and quanti-
tatively the effects of the programme over a six-month period.
Participant based evaluation was employed which depended on the
creation and perpetuation by the tutors of 'ideal speech situations'
(Habermas, 1970; Giddens, 1985) in which the verbal responses of
the participants were encouraged and valued. These responses were
gathered by the tutors and used in conjunction with the quantitative
evidence to guide proposed changes in policy, planning and action.
This type of evaluation illuminates the participants' experience more
lucidly than quantification alone could and, therefore, facilitates a
more constructively critical approach to programme building in
which the participants' views and opinions are a valued and vital
element. Sports psychology is an applied science and as such provides
a service to sport which, in turn, is made up of aspiring participants
who wish to selectively avail of its prevailing epistemology for the
purpose for sporting advancement. Only a combined approach to
programme building and evaluation will see both sports psychology
and the sport participant prosper.

Participants

The programme participants were members of the Ulster Senior
Ladies Panel from which four individuals would be selected later in
the season to form the Ulster Interprovincial Team. The players
ranged in age from 19 to 38 years ($M = 28$ years) with an average
competitive golf experience of 14 years (ranging from 7 to 24 years).
Player handicaps ranged from scratch through 1 to 5; two players had
played for the Irish National Team for the previous two years, and
one of these players (the scratch player) was working towards
becoming a Golfing Professional during the season in which intervention took place. A pilot sports psychology programme had been run
early in the previous season with seven of these players in attendence.

The Psychological Skills Training Programme for Golf

Due to the overwhelming interest in and support for the previous
season's pilot programme, it was decided that this programme should
have similar content but a slightly different structure. At the request
of the players it was decided to run the whole programme over a

single intensive weekend at Knock Golf Club, Belfast. The programme was team-taught by two sport psychologists with over 16 years of lecturing/consultancy experience between them. Six main sessions were planned, each approximately 1½ hours in length and starting with a short explanatory lecture introduction, followed by a workshop in which individuals practised specific mental skills. A programme folder was also given to each individual and a very thorough handbook of explanations and technique practices was distributed at the end of each session to insert into the ring folder. Open discussion of each session was encouraged in an effort to address any individual problems as they arose. The main topics covered were self-awareness, goal setting, stress management, imagery/visualization, attention control and concentration, and a practical on-course session in which competitive conditions were simulated while playing a nine-hole game. A programme evaluation form was given to each individual immediately after the programme and a follow-up evaluation was distributed at three-month and six-month intervals.

Box 1 shows the overall programme structure. The rationale for the chosen topics was a combination of what individual golfers had requested as being important to them and topics that have been outlined in many applied sports psychology texts as forming the basis for a mental skills training programme. In all cases, a variety of textbooks were consulted in an effort to combine the best elements of a number of established programmes. In addition, efforts were made to include material which has a recognized psychological base, such as cognitive behavioural techniques, rather than using some of less well established popular sources. The elements of the programme will now be outlined along with comments on each component from both the consultants and the participants.

Programme components

1. Self-awareness

It has been suggested by Martens (1987) that the motto of sports psychology should be 'know thyself'. Many programmes start with this topic and a number of practising sport psychologists (Ravizza, 1986; Martens, 1987; Orlick, 1990) emphasize that the 'self-knowledge' gleaned from keeping a sports journal or diary is invaluable in structuring other elements of a mental skills programme. With this in mind the initial session was designed to enable the golfers to become

Box 1: Mental skills training programme for golfers

TOPIC and PURPOSE	TECHNIQUES
Awareness	
To assess the sport's demands on golfer. To explore individual's goals/aspirations. Learn how mental skills programme can assist in performance preparation.	Person profile Questionnaires Discussion
Motivation	
How to get most out of training and competition.	Goal setting
Stress management	
To understand stress and anxiety. To explore the symptoms of anxiety and to learn cognitive and somatic coping techniques.	Discussion Self-directed, Centering, Imagery, Thought control
Imagery/Mental rehearsal	
To understand the different types and the different uses of imagery.	Awareness Vividness Controllability
Attention control	
To control direction and width of attention To cope with distractions and improve concentration.	Attentional switch Distraction control Inner game
Theory to practice	
To use mental skills on the golf course.	Simulation
Evaluation	
To assess programme and to modify for future.	Informal chat Questionnaire(s)

more aware of their psychological strengths and weaknesses. A pre-programme pack containing a number of standard sports psychology questionnaires was sent to programme participants two weeks prior to the scheduled weekend. Golfers were asked to complete the questionnaires and return them in order that scoring could be completed by consultants, in advance of the workshop, and specific profiles established for each participant.

Questionnaires selected included three which have established psychometric properties (Ostrow, 1990) and are reported by Gould *et al.* (1989) as being the most popular and most useful to sport psychologists: Sports Competition Anxiety Test (SCAT); Competitive State Anxiety Inventory-2 (CSAI-2); Test of Attentional and Interpersonal Style (TAIS)) and two which were specifically designed to assess attitudes to golf (Golf Attitude and Behavior Inventory and the Golf Goals Questionnaire, Rotella and Bunker, 1981). The SCAT (Martens, 1977) gives a measure of a player's trait anxiety or underlying personality tendency to be anxious in sporting situations. The CSAI-2 (Martens *et al.*, 1990) measures specific pre-competitive cognitive anxiety, somatic anxiety and self confidence. The TAIS (Short Version) (Nideffer, 1976a) is a self-report measure of attentional style which indicates a player's attentional style in terms of their profile being effective, ineffective or choking.

During the initial introductory session players were returned their scored profiles with an explanation of what the scores meant and were told that these would be used as a basis for discussing psychological skills training. These profiles were merely used to facilitate the self-awareness process and to indicate to individuals possible areas where mental skills training would enhance preparation for golf. Consultants only discussed these results in general terms, such as 'if you scored high (or low) on the SCAT (CSAI-2 or TAIS) then ...', rather than referring to any individual scores. To facilitate group discussion the consultants had prepared a person profile proforma which was intended to guide discussion, in a non-threatening way, around such topics as career goals, sporting goals, lifestyle demands and current need for and use of such psychological skills as time management, goal setting and stress management.

Comments

The golfers seemed to have an amazingly haphazard approach to preparing for golf (both mental and physical) considering their relative success in the sport. Most of the girls admitted that the previous season's pilot programme did instil a more organized approach to training and they agreed that they understood the need for mental skills, but few found that they followed through with their intentions for any length of time. Several remarked on how this session forced them to face up to the fact that they were ignoring an area of their game which needed practice and they made resolutions to make changes where possible. For example, two remarked that they used to practise at lunchtime but had got out of the habit and stated that in future they would try to spend some of that time on either physical or mental practice. Most of the panel agreed that unless they took a more organized approach to their training that they would not be so fortunate in gaining team positions against the upcoming competition from other golfers.

From the organizational point of view two important features were brought to light. Firstly, both consultants and participants agreed that there were too many questionnaires which did not contribute a great deal more than information that came to light through discussion of the issues. This view has been supported recently by Orlick (1989) who favours individual interviews with performers rather than using standard questionnaires. Secondly, both consultants were aware of the need to be sensitive to individuals within the group. Although we were dealing with one coherent group, the players themselves were aware of each other as potential competitors rather than team-mates. A totally open atmosphere would have been difficult to expect given these limitations yet, despite this, most members of the group were willing to be fairly open in discussing their approach to training.

2. Motivation

The pre-programme Golf Attitudes and Behaviour Questionnaire (Rotella and Bunker, 1981) showed that all ten panelists were 'high maximizers', indicating that they were willing to work hard to achieve their goals. Motivation, *per se*, was not seen to be a major problem. However, through the Golf Goals Questionnaire (Rotella and Bunker, 1981) and the group discussion on self-awareness it quickly emerged that none of the players was actually approaching their training in a planned fashion. The majority of the players admitted that they knew they should be more organized about their training but they felt that they lacked the skills to do this. In a sense the players were selling themselves short because on the one hand they had the physical skills and the motivation to do well at golf but by adopting a haphazard approach to their game they were undoubtedly all underachieving. The topic of motivation was therefore approached from the perspective of using goal setting as a motivational tool to improve practice behaviour.

Theoretically, the research evidence to support goal setting is quite strong in the industrial psychology literature (Locke and Latham, 1990) and although the sports literature is rather more equivocal (Locke, 1991) there is ample evidence of both an academic and anecdotal nature (Beggs, 1991; Burton, 1992) to support its use in sport. In particular, a study of top class golfers by Orlick and Partington (1988) showed that good golfers are very goal orientated individuals; they regularly set themselves practice goals, tournament weekly goals, tournament daily goals, etc. The technique of goal setting was introduced by a short explanatory lecture outlining the reasons for goal setting, as presented by Locke and Latham (1990), to increase effort, persistence and to develop strategies to achieve desirable goals. A workshop session then detailed the steps necessary to establish long-term and short-term specific, measurable and attainable goals. It was essential that goals were established on an individual rather than a group basis and therefore golfers used much of the information from the self-awareness session in establishing their own baselines. Goal setting procedures outlined by Martens (1987) and Bump (1989) were used in conjunction with specific golf goal questions posed by Rotella and Bunker (1981). Players were then asked to focus on the most important aspect of their game that they needed to work on and decide on one specific goal in order to complete a 'goal setting exercise'. This exercise would then become their template to work through other areas of their game. A worked example and the goal setting exercise is presented in Box 2.

Comments
The main problem in working through the goal setting exercise was in identifying specific goals rather than vague goals. For example, typically players were stating goals such as 'spend half hour on irons' as opposed to making goals very specific, such as '20 practice shots each for 5, 7, and 9 irons to a specified target, working on a specific aspect of technique'. It was not unusual to find that this aspect of goal setting was difficult as it is one frequently referred to in the applied sports psychology literature (e.g. Gould, 1986). Interestingly, all players agreed that goal setting was very important but they were not convinced that they would take the time to sit down and work out the

Box 2: Goal setting in golf

Example

A player decides that she needs to get her handicap down from five to four. The biggest obstacle to her achieving this is the inaccuracy of her driver although distance is acceptable. Firstly, she needs to assess her current accuracy, e.g. she can hit a large targeted area 30' × 30' which is 130 yards away on average 6 out of 20 attempts. She then sets herself the long-term goal of hitting the target area an average of 15 out of 20 attempts by the start of season (three months away). How will she achieve this? She could work out a *realistic* practice schedule which involves going to the practice ground and taking a minimum of 25 driver shots per day, hitting each shot as though on course aiming for a real or imaginary target. She should also set shorter term goals such as improving from 6 out of 20 to 9 out of 20 in 14 days' time (there will usually be more rapid improvement at the lower skill level and improvement will slow down as she improves). She should record the number of practice balls hit each day and every two weeks she could retest for accuracy by testing over three consecutive days. If her average score over three test days is ahead of time then she could raise her goal to a more challenging one. If progress is too slow she should check to see what the problem is, e.g. correct practice? established target? need more time on one wood?

Goal Setting Exercise

Think of one aspect of your game performance which you would like to improve and start to see how you can put in place a programme to realize your goal.

1. Identify one aspect of performance which you wish to see improved.
2. What skills/qualities need to be developed to bring about this improvement?
3. What routine/practice will help improve this skill/quality?
4. How can you measure or quantify this skill/quality?
5. What is the present level of attainment in terms of this skill/quality?

6. What level of performance would you like to achieve by a certain date?
7. Work out what targets you would like to meet by certain dates, what training routines you must put in place to reach these targets and how you will measure performance. Always remember that timetables can be adjusted to take into account changing circumstances, e.g. illness, injury, other circumstances.

details regularly. This was a problem which tutors attempted to address by reiterating the importance of good goal setting to successful performance and by insisting that although the initial learning phase of goal setting takes time, eventually it would become a quicker process. The golfers were encouraged to get in the habit of at least jotting down two or three specific practice goals each time they ventured to the practice ground, in an effort to ensure they were not simply 'putting in time'. As long as the daily goals set can be measured in some way either subjectively or objectively then there is an obvious route to seeing improvement.

3. Stress management

This session gave a brief explanation of the arousal, anxiety, stress, performance interrelationships, mainly focusing on the detrimental role of competitive anxiety. The self-awareness session had revealed that all ten golfers had relatively high SCAT scores ($M=27$) and each of them in discussion revealed that, in the past, they felt that their high anxiety had affected their game. The notion of self-awareness of their ideal level of arousal was emphasized because although the objective measures of anxiety taken revealed high scores, one or two individuals admitted that they sometimes felt that they needed a relatively high amount of stress to get them 'fired-up' enough for a game. This notion is entirely in keeping with recent advances in the research literature on performance anxiety (Jones *et al.*, 1993). Nevertheless, given the time limitations of the session it was felt that it was most appropriate to focus on arousal reduction rather than methods to increase arousal.

The workshop opened by using biofeedback (heart rate monitors and Galvanic Skin Response apparatus) to show very quickly the effects of even thinking about an important match. Individuals were linked to the various apparatuses and then asked to recall a recent stressful game; they could instantly see the effect of their cognitions on their physiological responses. A variety of cognitive and somatic stress management techniques were then introduced with an opportunity to practise each one in order to emphasize the point that it is important to find the technique which is most appropriate to the individual and the situation. Cognitive techniques included a 'thought stopping exercise' by Bunker and Williams (1986) and a 'rational thinking exercise' by Suinn (1986). These 'pencil and paper' exercises encouraged the players to really listen to their thoughts and record the negative statements they typically make when in trouble on the golf course. They then tried to help each other find ways of turning the negative thinking into positive statements with an appropriate action attached. An example of the thought stopping exercise appears in Box 3.

Box 3: Thought stopping technique

Instructions

Select a situation in which you frequently find yourself thinking negatively. Complete the following worksheet based on that situation.

1. Describe the situation as completely as possible.
2. Identify the particular negative self statements you make in this situation.
3. Specify a term or cue or image that you will use as a signal to stop your negative thoughts.
4. List three realistic, positive and constructive self statements you can use to replace the negative thoughts.
5. Now, imagine the situation, recall the negative thoughts, use your signal to stop those thoughts, and replace them with your positive self statements.

Did you feel less stressed after you replaced the negative thoughts?

Practise using the stop signal and positive thoughts every time you are aware of yourself thinking negatively.

The relaxation techniques presented in the workshop session included a form of self-directed relaxation and an imagery relaxation exercise similar to Suinn (1986) and also the 'quick-fix' centering technique advocated by Nideffer (1985), see Box 4. Other relaxation techniques such as progressive muscle relaxation, deep breathing, autogenics, and meditation were included in the written materials provided, with the advice to players to try each one and decide which

---

Box 4: Centering

1. Stand with feet slightly apart and knees slightly bent with your weight evenly balanced between your two feet. The bend in knees is important and should result in your being able to feel the tension in the muscles in the calves and thighs. Bending counteracts the natural tendency to brace and lock your knees when you become over aroused.
2. Now, consciously relax your neck and shoulder muscles. Check this by making slight movements with your head and arms (see that they are loose and relaxed).
3. Your mouth should be open slightly to reduce tension in the jaw muscles.
4. Breathe in from your diaphragm, down to your abdomen. Inhale slowly and, as you do, attend to two cues. Firstly, notice that you extend your stomach as you breathe. Next, consciously maintain relaxation in chest and shoulders. This helps you avoid allowing your chest to expand and shoulders to rise. It counters the tendency to brace neck and shoulder muscles.
5. As you exhale slowly, attend to feelings in your abdomen and notice your stomach muscles relaxing. Consciously let your knees bend slightly, attending to increased feelings of heaviness as your body presses down towards the ground. The exhalation counteracts the natural lifting of breathing in and the body does begin to feel more steady. As you attend to the relaxing physical cues you stop attending to the things that are causing you to lose control. Now, you have recovered enough to remind yourself of a constructive way in which to deal with the situation you face.

Centering needs to be practised on a regular basis. Many performers build it in as a routine procedure they engage in just before performing, e.g. tee-off, putting, etc.

The goal is to reach the point at which, in the space of a single breath, you can bring your level of arousal to any point you choose.

method suited them best. Instructions regarding the appropriate timing in the use of various techniques was also emphasized in the workshop and stated clearly in the handbooks, e.g. longer and deeper methods of relaxation should never be used within a few hours of playing.

Comments
The process of examining individual thought contents was quite revealing as the golfers became aware of just how negative their thinking sometimes is and the effects of this on their performance. It took most individuals a little time to come up with realistically positive statements to replace the negative ones, but they were encouraged to make sure these statements were ones which they truly believed rather than simply appealing to 'the power of positive thinking'. Consultants encouraged individuals to work together in order to see that their negative thinking was not unique and also to facilitate brainstorming for positive thoughts and actions. This small group atmosphere worked very well with all participants being very open and helpful to each other. The positive self statements made could generally be classified into the three categories identified by Rushall *et al.* (1988) which are task-relevant statements ('slow, smooth swing'), mood statements ('feeling good and strong'), self-affirmation statements ('I putt well from this distance'). Unfortunately, time constraints on the physical relaxation session meant that only some of the shorter techniques could be practised. However, all participants enjoyed the session (possibly because they were tired of listening to us by then!) with most preference for imagery relaxation over the other forms. The majority of players also agreed that they had been trying to incorporate the centering technique introduced in the previous season's pilot programme into their pre-performance routines. This was welcomed by the tutors who had planned to make such a suggestion later in the attention/concentration session.

4. Imagery, mental rehearsal and visualization

Jack Nicklaus once said, 'I never hit a shot, even in practice, without having a very sharp, in-focus picture of it in my head'. In essence, what Nicklaus was referring to is the mental skill of imagery or visualization. Considerable research evidence, both empirical and anecdotal, exists to support the usefulness of imagery as a performance enhancement technique. Empirical investigations of imagery have tended to focus on the role of mental practice in skill acquisition, the role of imagery as a pre-competition cognitive 'psyching-up' strategy and comparisons in the use of imagery by successful and unsuccessful athletes. A number of these studies also explore the various variables thought to mediate imagery effects (for a comprehensive review of these studies see Murphy and Jowdy, 1992). In general, the research evidence attests to the effectiveness of imagery in enhancing skill acquisition and in acting as an effective psyching-up strategy. Where comparisons have been made between successful and less successful competitors it has been suggested that the former claim to use imagery more than unsuccessful athletes. Although criticism has been levelled at much of the research work (see Kremer and Scully, 1994) considerable efforts have been invested in the development of interventions and practical guidelines for the use of imagery in sport.

This workshop session was based on a combination of existing imagery programmes (Suinn, 1986; Martens, 1987; Weinberg, 1988; Orlick, 1990) which advocate the use of imagery for a wide variety of purposes including skill acquisition, skill maintenance, competition preparation and arousal control. Explanations of different types and uses of imagery were presented, followed by examples of how to implement imagery training and a workshop taking golfers through the development of sensory awareness, vivid images and controlling images (see examples in Box 5). At all times it was stressed that imagery involved all of the senses and every effort was made to include suggestions in imagery scripts. Players were also asked to devise their own scripts for particular problems or situations which held meaning for them. Suggestions for the use of imagery were provided along with examples of images used by successful golfers (see Box 6).

Comments
This session appeared to be the easiest for participants to understand and relate to as most golfers already practise imagery in some form. However, the difficulty posed by players being so familiar with a technique is that it is not very easy to convince them of the need to develop that technique and refine it in the same way as they would practise a physical skill. Numerous sport psychologists have outlined strategies to develop the skill of imagery (Harris and Harris, 1984; Vealey, 1986; Martens, 1987; Weinberg, 1988) and a composite of these suggestions was presented in the handbooks with verbal encouragement from tutors to properly develop imagery skills in order to

---

Box 5: Examples of imagery exercises

Image Vividness: Golf Scene

Imagine yourself walking out of the locker room and up to the first tee on a warm summer day. Be aware of the heat of the sun on your face as you leave the shade of the building. Take a deep breath and smell the freshly mown grass. As you walk towards the tee, notice the feel of the ground. Is it hard or soft? Rough or smooth? Now look around the tee area. Look at the other people present, their bags and trolleys. In your mind's eye create an image of the first tee. Become aware of the white competition markers. Notice the box and read the par, distance and stroke index. Now see yourself stepping up to tee off. Feel the heat of the sun on your back as you bend down to tee up the ball. Hear the other people around you gradually becoming quiet. Finally, focus on the feelings you have just prior to teeing off.

Image Control: Stress Inoculation

Most golfers have problems with tensing up, becoming angry, losing concentration or losing confidence. Picture yourself in a situation that usually brings out one of these emotions. It might be missing an easy putt, going out of bounds and dropping a shot, etc. Recreate the situation and especially the feelings that accompany that situation. For example, feel the anxiety experienced when putting under pressure at an important stage of the game, but use one of the stress management techniques learned, e.g. centring, positive talk, imagery, etc. Feel the tension drain out of your body and focus on what you need to do to sink the putt. Again the focus should be on controlling what you see, hear and feel in your imagery.

---

maximize the use of imagery in practice. From the tutorial perspective two specific problems arose which would probably be common to many educational situations. Firstly, there is a slight inconsistency in attempting to present the learning phases of imagery skills in the same session as providing realistic examples of uses of imagery in practice. For example, Vealey (1986) highlights how important it is to develop

Box 6: Images used by championship golfers

The following are a few suggestions from top class golfers of images they use while actually performing the shot – thinking in images stops instructive self-talk.

The Swing

General

One way of making sure you transfer your weight properly is to imagine your legs forming a double K. During the backswing your left knee should move to the right; in the downswing, the opposite movement should take place.

Backswing

To remind you of the proper way to swivel your body to the right, imagine you are playing inside a barrel without touching the sides.

Downswing

To make the club work for you during the downswing and increase its speed, imagine that the club is very heavy and that the ball is a beach ball; hit it so that it rotates inwards.

Bunker Shots

If you are obsessed with hitting the ball and afraid of hitting the sand, you may like to imagine that you are trying to scoop up a fried egg or a cake from the bunker and drop it gently on the green.

Chipping

To avoid breaking your wrists during the backswing or bringing your right hand across your left in the downswing you should imagine your shoulders and forearms as three sides of a triangle which stays the same shape all through the swing.

In a pitched shot, where it is essential that the ball stops quickly on the green, try imagining the ball attached to a parachute which lands it neatly on the green.

Putting

- Imagine you are pulling a toy lorry along on a piece of string.
- Imagine the ball being sucked straight into the hole by a vacuum cleaner from underneath.
- Imagine that the line the ball is to follow is a magnetic track.
- Imagine the hole is much larger than it is, perhaps getting bigger.

awareness before vividness before control, yet, as tutors, we also felt it was important to allow participants to experience how imagery might be used for stress inoculation, for example, which is a fairly advanced use of controlled imagery. We tried to resolve this inconsistency by continually stressing the importance of taking the time to develop the skills presented in the logical sequence outlined in the handbooks before attempting to use imagery in competition. A second problem which arose was that this session was conducted as a group session, yet there were undoubtedly differences in imagery ability. Where possible the tutors tried to elicit major problems and propose alternative suggestions; this worked well for this group as all participants had already had some experience of imagery.

5. Attentional control and concentration

This session started with an explanation of attentional styles and emphasized the importance of being able to shift style according to the demands being faced. According to Nideffer (1976b) attentional demands fall along two dimensions, breadth (either broad or narrow) and direction (internal or external). Breadth refers to the number or range of possible stimuli to be attended. Direction refers to whether the focus is directed internally to the performer's thoughts, feelings and body sensations, or externally to stimuli in the environment. Nideffer (1976b) argues that individuals exhibit a natural tendency to function within a restricted range along each of these two dimensions and this then gives us one of four distinct attentional styles (Broad–External, Broad–Internal, Narrow–Internal, Narrow–External). Problems may then arise if an individual has a predisposition to function within a style that is incompatible with the demands of a particular sporting circumstance. For example, a player with a tendency to favour a Broad–External style may have difficulty coping with the Narrow–External demands of a golf swing. Further difficulties arise when a player is under stress because although we can learn to shift attentional styles according to the demands of the situation, when under stress we tend to revert to our favoured style (Nideffer, 1986).

Golf is one of the few sports where a player is required to use all four attentional styles (Nideffer, 1985). This workshop session focused on the importance of being able to shift attention when required by the task conditions. The TAIS (Short Version) questionnaire completed in the self-awareness session indicated that several players had quite ineffective attentional style profiles. Therefore, the starting point for the workshop was to take players through the different dimensions of attention by exploring the sequence of attention for a golf shot (Rotella and Bunker, 1981), see Box 7. This sequence was then incorporated into individual pre-performance routines (see Rotella and Bunker, 1981; Nideffer, 1986; Cohn, 1990). Individuals were asked to outline their current pre-performance routines and see if any improvement was needed. Attentional requirements at each stage of this routine were emphasized.

Concentration and distraction control elements of this session were dealt with through a variety of practices and exercises adapted from those devised by Albinson and Bull (1988), Weinberg (1988), Bump (1989) and the Inner Game exercises of Gallwey (1978). Concentration exercises included the standard numbers grid technique to emphasize scanning and focusing abilities. Other practices involved either concentrating on a specific object or image for specified periods of time (see Box 8) or else attempting to avoid internal thought distractors when instructed not to concentrate on anything specific (Passive Thinking exercise). Players were also asked to devise ways of including simulation and desensitization techniques into their practices (although this would be dealt with in greater detail in the final session). Finally, the inner game techniques of Gallwey (1978) were proposed as an alternative way of considering all of the psychological skills covered.

Box 7: Sequence of attention in golf

A. Preliminary Phase

1. Broad–External: Gather the information needed to assess the requirements of the shot.
2. Broad–Internal: Examine your personal abilities and preferences.
3. Narrow–External: Select club.

B. Set-Up Phase

4. Narrow–External: Concentrate on the target.
5. Narrow–Internal: Feel the perfect shot.
6. Narrow–External: Think through the intermediate target (1–2 feet ahead) to aid in alignment to final goal.

C. Swing Phase (Shot runs off automatically – think target)

7. Narrow–External: Observe results.
8. Narrow–Internal: Capture the feeling of that shot.
9. Broad–External: Analyse the shot relative to previous correct or incorrect decisions.
10. Narrow–Internal: Visualize and feel the correct swing.

Comments

Most participants agreed that this was one of the most important sessions. All players felt that they could improve their attentional control and were relieved to find that they did not have to concentrate for the entire four hours of a game but could switch on and off between the various styles. Rotella and Bunker (1981) confirm that this is a fairly common misperception in golf that one has to 'concentrate' for the entire period of the game. Tutors stressed that importance of self-awareness again to encourage players to find the style that suits them best while also developing the ability to be flexible and shift as situations demand. It was also interesting to note that many golfers naturally use simulation techniques but not in a formal way and the participants were encouraged to include this exercise in their formal training programme.

Box 8: Concentrating on a specific object

The purpose of this exercise is to help you develop the skill of concentrating on a specific object for an extended period of time.

Instructions

Hold a picture of one of your favourite golf holes in front of you. Study the picture. Study the hole. If any distracting thoughts cross your mind, block them out. Repeat the word 'target' and get your mind back on the golf hole shown in your picture. See how long you can focus your attention on the picture. Time it the first few times you try it.

Practise recognizing distracting thoughts as soon as they enter your mind and eliminate them by repeating the word 'target'. Remember, it is seldom that anyone will play a round of golf without being distracted. You must not stay distracted for an extended period of time.

Initially, practise this exercise in a place that is quiet and which has few or no distractions. In the beginning use a 30 second concentration period followed by a 30 second rest period. As the ability to concentrate increases, extend the concentration period and then shorten the rest period until the concentration period can be held for five minutes.

The difficulty of the exercise can be increased by doing it in more and more distracting situations (e.g. with music, in a room with other people, etc.).

Adaptation

This exercise can be varied in many ways so that you can practise the same skill in as many different situations as possible. The greater the variety of situations in which you practise the better will be the transfer to the golf setting. The principle remains the same — you should gradually attempt to increase the length of time for which you can maintain your concentration on a simple object or task.

Some Suggestions

- Clock watching – say 'now' to yourself every alternate five and ten seconds.
- Counting breaths – add one for each inhalation and continue for one minute.
- Focus on a golf object – shoe, club, ball.

6. Theory to practice

This session was essentially a means of putting into practice on the golf course the techniques covered over the weekend. Two groups of four players (one girl was injured and one did not participate) went out on the course with one tutor with each group. Obviously, these conditions were less than perfect for attempting to put theory into practice, as normally time should be devoted to learning and practising the psychological skills first before attempting to use them in reality (Williams, 1986; Martens, 1987). Nevertheless, given the financial and time constraints in which the psychological skills training programme was taking place it was decided that some form of 'hands on' experience, in the presence of tutors, was better than none. Individuals were required to establish written goals in advance and then the groups were advised of appropriate situations in which to use the various psychological skills used. Each tutor then attempted to maximize the use of 'teachable moments' (Salmela, 1989) or times during the course of playing when circumstances or individuals dictated that an important point of information could be reviewed or introduced. For example, a player who forgot to use her pre-performance routine with disastrous consequences could immediately review the error of her ways, or during the course of walking towards a potentially difficult bunker shot the tutor could remind a player of appropriate imagery, centering and concentration techniques.

Comments
This was a useful exercise even if a little contrived. It was fortuitous that there was one tutor to each four-ball and this enabled quite a lot of discussion and suggestion. As Salmela (1989) suggests, so much of what sport psychologists do is unquantifiable in the sense that one frequently has to step back, observe and wait for that 'teachable

moment'. This was a new departure for the tutors involved and one which we found very usful and encouraging, not least because the participants also agreed that they appreciated this kind of exercise and suggested that it would be useful to have similar sessions several times throughout the season.

Programme evaluation

The majority of studies investigating the effectiveness of mental skills rely solely on changes in performance measures and rarely do investigators explore the more subtle changes in attitudes and opinions associated with psychological skills training. The evaluation of this programme has purposefully combined qualitative and quantitative methods precisely because of the apparent imbalance in favour of quantitative measures and consequent neglect of qualitative indicators. Studies of this nature which explore the participants' reaction to the programme have the potential to help us guide practice in, arguably, more valuable ways than some of the more positivistic approaches currently so popular in sports psychology. Much of this work has tended to overemphasize the quantifiable indicators, particularly those which provide a measure of outcome. In sport, such quantifiable data are difficult to attach to a single factor or intervention strategy. However, strategies of evaluation of both a formative and summative nature offer the evidence of participant experience which is essential to the reflective sport psychologist. Both the participants' and tutors' formative evaluations on individual components of the programme have already been presented. This section of the paper will deal primarily with summative evaluations of both a qualitative and quantitative nature.

All participants were asked to fill in evaluation forms asking questions about the content and delivery of the programme as well as the usefulness of such a programme. The evaluation form was based on those of Orlick (1982) and Gould *et al.* (1990). The first section asked participants to rate their current knowledge of each aspect of the programme, the importance to them, how often they intended using each technique (Likert Scale 1–5) and what aspect of the game they most hoped to improve. The second section asked participants to rate the overall effect of the programme (Likert –5 to +5) and a few open-ended questions regarding how the programme had helped them and how it might be improved upon. The same evaluation form was distributed after three months and again after six months (with the

Table 8.1   *Mean ratings for knowledge, importance and use of the six programme components*

Programme component	Knowledge			Importance			Use		
	Post	3 months	6 months	Post	3 months	6 months	Post	3 months	6 months
Self-awareness	4.00	3.56	3.16	4.20	4.20	4.10	4.00	2.90	2.30
Goal setting	3.30	3.30	2.50	4.20	3.50	3.80	3.60	2.50	2.60
Stress management	3.50	2.80	2.30	4.60	4.50	4.00	4.40	3.40	3.10
Imagery/visualization	3.60	3.20	2.80	3.90	4.40	4.40	4.10	4.20	3.30
Attention control	3.90	2.90	2.40	4.50	4.80	4.60	4.50	4.10	3.10
Theory to practice	3.50	2.80	2.50	4.50	4.40	4.30	4.30	3.10	2.40

necessary modifications to grammar). Eight (the same eight individuals) out of the ten participants responded on each occasion.

Table 8.1 presents the mean ratings of the three dimensions (knowledge, importance placed upon, and use of) for the six programme components (self-awareness, goal setting, stress management, attention control, imagery, theory to practice) assessed on three occasions (post programme, three months, six months). A three-factor repeated measures ANOVA revealed main effects for programme components ($F_{5, 162} = 5.12$, $P < 0.01$), dimension ($F_{2, 162} = 83.7$, $P < 0.01$) and time ($F_{2, 162} = 75.5$, $P < 0.01$. Tukey *post hoc* tests revealed that effects were caused by the goal setting component being rated significantly lower across all three dimensions, the importance dimension being rated significantly higher across components, and ratings for all components differed across all three occasions. Two two-way interactions achieved significance, programme components X dimension ($F_{10, 162} = 3.17$, $P < 0.05$) and programme components X time ($F_{4, 162} = 15.4$, $P < 0.01$). *Post hoc* tests of simple main effects revealed that the goal setting component was rated least in importance and used least and all components showed a significant decrease in ratings across the three occasions. The self-awareness component was rated significantly higher than the others on the knowledge dimension at both the three- and six-month evaluations. Both knowledge and use were rated significantly lower at both the three- and six-month evaluations.

It is surprising that the goal setting component emerged as being the psychological skill which was seen as being least important given the players' earlier acknowledgement of the necessity of planning for training. Perhaps these individuals found it difficult to apply goal setting to their golf and more emphasis on general time management may have been more beneficial given that these players are all amateurs fitting their sport around very busy lives, e.g. family, work and other sports commitments. The finding that both knowledge and use of psychological skills was rated lower at the three- and six-month evaluations was disappointing given the expressed intentions of the programme participants, but this result is similar to that found by Gould *et al.* (1990). This finding, in conjunction with some of the comments made regarding continuing the 'theory to practice' session throughout the season, may indicate that players actually need frequent reminders and advice regarding appropriate psychological skills training. Perhaps this programme suffered in being run over one intensive weekend, but this was the only feasible format given the participants' other commitments. The players were given very detailed handbooks with many suggestions for development and prac-tice of the psychological skills covered, but it would appear that some form of support system available after the initial programme would be a useful addition. It is also very reassuring that players consistently and unequivocally rated each element of the psychological skills programme as being very important across all three occasions. This result also reflects the findings of Gould *et al.* (1990) with wrestlers although, in contrast to Gould, this study showed that players' actual use of the psychological skills did not match their intended use. Again, participants' comments and general intuition would suggest that a support system available after the initial contact with the sport psychologists would greatly enhance players' commitment to practising and developing psychological skills. This need for a continued support system in relation to psychological skills has been discussed by many practising sport psychologists (Gould *et al.*, 1989; Orlick, 1989; Gould *et al.*, 1990) with recent suggestions focusing on the development of integrative models which would integrate psycho-logical skills as a natural part of performers' usual training programmes (Danish *et al.*, 1992; Sinclair and Sinclair, 1994). This latter suggestion seems a worthwhile one to explore and develop given the resource and financial constraints imposed on many sports when seeking sport science support.

Qualitative results showed that the majority of players (eight) believed that the psychological skills training programme had enabled them to develop an improved mental attitude. This belief was main-tained at each of the follow-up evaluations. Table 8.2 presents the breakdown of the numbers of players stating which game aspect they

Table 8.2   *Aspects of the game most improved through PSTP*

Game aspect	Number of players		
	Post	3 months	6 months
Mental attitude	8	8	8
Chipping/putting	6	2	2
Trouble shots	2	0	0
Driving	1	0	0
Fairway play	1	0	0
Tournament play	0	2	1

felt had benefited most from attending the psychological skills training programme (PSTP). Other factors which were believed to have improved as a direct result of being involved in the programme were chipping/putting and tournament play. Unfortunately, the improvement in various aspects of the game which were rated immediately after the programme did not generally hold across the follow-up evaluations. This finding may also reflect the previous results suggesting that both knowledge and use of programme components declined with time, and again findings such as this also emphasize the importance of practising and integrating psychological skills into everyday training/practice procedures. Despite the apparently limited effect of the programme on specific performance improvements the PSTP was consistently rated very highly in terms of overall effectiveness (see Table 8.3).

Table 8.3   *Mean rating of overall effectiveness of PSTP (on a scale −5 to +5)*

Post	3 months	6 months
4.25	4.00	4.00

In general, these results show that the immediate returns appear to be in changing attitudes rather than in terms of improved performance. This is noteworthy because so many studies investigating the effectiveness of mental skills rely solely on changes in performance measures; rarely do investigators explore the more subtle changes in attitudes and opinions, although a number of sport psychologists now acknowledge their importance (Vealey, 1988). Some insight into

---

Box 9: Participants' comments about PSTP benefits

Goal Setting

'Made me aware of how to practice instead of just going out and hitting balls.'

'Made me think and plan what I am capable of as a golfer and what I would hope to realistically achieve.'

Stress Management

'Increased my knowledge of how to handle various situations.'

'Helped me cope better with stress.'

Imagery

'Made me more aware of uses of imagery in golf.'

'Found imagery quite helpful on a lot of shots.'

Attention

'Made me more aware of need to pay attention in different ways.'

'Found my attention and concentration increased.'

Performance improvements

'Marked improvement on last year's performance in terms of ranking and enjoyment and satisfaction from game.'

'PST definitely helped me cope with recovery from injury ... my first championship for 1+ years, qualified to final eight out of 26 players.'

---

players' perceptions of programme benefits can be gained from Box 9 which outlines specific comments provided to the open-ended question, 'In what way, if any, did the programme help you?' The answers to this question were content analysed for coherent themes and the comments are provided in relation to the specific programme components to which they apply and in relation to perceived performance improvements. Most of these comments also support the notion that the programme assisted the golfers through changing their attitude towards preparation in their sport rather than through the provision of a 'bag of tricks' to improve performance. However, it must also be noted that although players believe that their attitudes have changed there was no manipulation check by tutors to assess whether attitudes or knowledge and practice had actually improved. This is definitely a worthwhile avenue for future research into programme effectiveness, particularly if long-term investigations are conducted into players' ability to integrate and consolidate material delivered in psychological skills training programmes.

The final section of the evaluation posed open-ended questions about programme improvements ('In what way, if any, do you think a programme like this could be better?' and 'Any other comments about the programme or its implementation?'). Once again, answers were content analysed for coherent themes with three predominant suggestions emerging which are presented in Box 10. The three suggestions for programme improvement are very much in line with suggestions already being made in the literature by reflective sport psychologists (for a review of sports psychology consultancy services see the special issue of *The Sport Psychologist*, Vol. 3, 1989). These suggestions also highlight the potential time demands to be made on consultant sport psychologists in terms of more individual work, additional follow-up sessions and more work on the golf course. Obviously, if each of these suggestions were to be taken on board then it would require a significant number of additional hours on the part of the practising sport psychologist. Therefore, a more economical and parsimonious alternative may be to explore ways of incorporating and integrating mental training programmes into existing physical training programmes so that coaches and players take more responsibilty for their own psychological skills training, treating it not as something which is separate from or in addition to practice but which is entirely integrated within it (see Sinclair and Sinclair, 1994).

Box 10: Suggested PST programme improvements

1. More time for individual work.
2. Follow-up sessions throughout season.
3. More practical work on the golf course.

Conclusions

This chapter has outlined the development, implementation and evaluation of a mental skills intervention programme for a group of elite golfers. Conclusions will be discussed in terms of the perceived advantages and disadvantages of the chosen educational-style model of psycho-behavioural intervention. One of the primary advantages of an educational approach is that it allows for fairly efficient dissemination of information to groups of individuals with a minimum of repetition. The concomitant disadvantage of this approach, which was highlighted by participants in this particular study, is the lack of time available to deal with individual concerns. A second advantage of a formal psychological skills training programme is that the components of the programme can be based on existing material(s), although considerable modification of such materials is usually necessary in order to ensure their applicability to the sport in question. This aspect of programme development points to the necessity for practising sport psychologists to constantly keep abreast not only of developments within the discipline of sports psychology but also to be familiar with the ever increasing numbers of 'handbooks' available for coaches and athletes, in order to make informed decisions when asked to provide such programmes. One disadvantage with this style of approach (currently being voiced in the literature by Hardy and Parfitt, 1994) is that it portrays the sport psychologist as 'the expert' who decides what needs to be learned rather than recognizing the equally valid experience and expertise which coaches and performers possess. The participant based evaluation procedures adopted in this case study (an advantage of the evaluative approach utilized) also highlighted the possibility for sport psychologists to learn from current practice in sport. It was suggested that rather than always seeking to apply psychology to sport we should be receptive to ways of informing theory through principles of good practice. A final point raised by the participant evaluations of this study is that intervention programmes like this serve an immediate short-term purpose of changing individual attitudes towards preparation (advantage) rather than effecting instantaneous performance changes (disadvantage). Suggestions for future intervention programme developments highlight the need to consider integrated models of psychological skills training which would involve coaches and players taking greater responsibility for their own mental training as an integral part of everday training procedures (see also Smith and Johnson, 1990; Hardy and Parfitt, 1994; Sinclair and Sinclair, 1994).

References

Albinson, J.G. and Bull, S. (1988) *A Mental Game Plan*. Ontario, Canada: Spodym Publishers.

Beggs, W.D.A. (1991) Goal setting in sport. In *Stress and Performance in Sport* (J.G. Jones and L. Hardy, eds) pp. 135–170. London: Academic Press.

Brewer, B.W. and Shillinglaw, R. (1993) Evaluation of a psychological skills training workshop for male intercollegiate lacrosse players. *The Sport Psychologist*, 6, 139–147.

Bump, L. (ed.) (1989) *American Coaching Effectiveness Programme, Level 2, Sport Psychology Study Guide (and Workbook)*. Champaign, IL: Human Kinetics.

Bunker, L. and Williams, J.M. (1986) Cognitive techniques for improving performance and building confidence. In *Applied Sport Psychology: Personal Growth to Peak Performance* (J. Williams, ed.) pp. 235–255. Palo Alto, CA: Mayfield.

Burton, D. (1992) 'The Jekyll/Hyde nature of goals: reconceptualizing goal setting in sport'. In *Advances in Sport Psychology* (T.S. Horn, ed.). Champaign, IL: Human Kinetics.

Cohn, P.J. (1990) Preperformance routines in sport: theoretical support and practical applications. *The Sport Psychologist*, 4, 301–312.

Danish, S.J., Petitpas, A.J. and Hale, B.D. (1992) A developmental-educational intervention model of sport psychology. *The Sport Psychologist*, 6, 403–415.

Daw, J. and Burton, D. (1994) Evaluation of a comprehensive psychological skills training program for collegiate tennis players, *The Sport Psychologist*, 8, 37–57.

Gallwey, T. (1978) *The Inner Game of Golf*. London: Cape.

Giddens, A. (1985) Jurgen Habermas. In *The Return of Grand Theory in the Human Sciences* (Q. Skinner, ed.) pp. 32–47. Cambridge: Cambridge University Press.

Gould, D. (1986) Goal setting for peak performance. In *Applied Sport Psychology* (J. Williams, ed.) pp. 133–147. Palo Alto, CA: Mayfield.

Gould, D., Murphy, S., Tammen, V. and May, J. (1989) An examination of U.S. Olympic sport psychology consultants and the services they provide, *The Sport Psychologist*, 3, 300–312.

Gould, D., Petlichkoff, L., Hodge, K. and Simons, J. (1990) Evaluating the effectiveness of a psychological skills educational workshop, *The Sport Psychologist*, 4, 249–260.

Habermas, J. (1970) Towards a theory of communicative competence, *Inquiry*, 13, 360–376.

Hardy, L. and Jones, G. (1994) Current issues and future directions for performance-related research in sport psychology. *Journal of Sports Sciences*, 12, 61–92.

Hardy, L. and Parfitt, G. (1994) The development of a model for the provision of psychological support to a National Squad. *The Sport Psychologist*, 8, 126–142.

Harris, D.V. and Harris, B.L. (1984) *The Athlete's Guide to Sport Psychology: Mental Skills for Physical People*. New York: Leisure Press.

Jones, J.G., Swain, A. and Hardy, L. (1993) Intensity and direction dimensions of competitive state anxiety and relationships with performance. *Journal of Sports Sciences*, 13, 1–15.

Kremer, J.M.D. and Scully, D.M. (1994) *Psychology in Sport*. London: Taylor and Francis.

Kubistant, T. (1988) *Mind Pump: The Psychology of Bodybuilding*. Champaign, IL: Human Kinetics.

Locke, E.A. (1991) Problems with goal-setting research in sports – and their solution. *Journal of Sport and Exercise Psychology*, 8, 311–316.

Locke, E.A. and Latham, G.P. (1990) *A Theory of Goal Setting and Task Performance*. Englewood Cliffs, NJ: Prentice Hall.

Martens, R. (1977) *Sport Competition Anxiety Test*. Champaign, IL: Human Kinetics.

Martens, R. (1987) *Coaches' Guide to Sport Psychology*. Champaign, IL: Human Kinetics.

Martens, R., Vealey, R.S. and Burton, D. (1990) *Competitive Anxiety in Sport*. Champaign, IL: Human Kinetics.

Murphy, S.M. and Jowdy, D. P. (1992) Imagery and mental practice. In *Advances in Sport Psychology* (T.S. Horn, ed.) pp. 221–250. Champaign, IL: Human Kinetics.

Nideffer, R.M. (1976a) Test of attentional and interpersonal style. *Journal of Personality and Social Psychology*, 34, 397–404.

Nideffer, R.M. (1976b) *The Inner Athlete: Mind Plus Muscle for Winning*. New York: Crowell.

Nideffer, R.M. (1985) *Athlete's Guide to Mental Training*. Champaign, IL: Human Kinetics.

Nideffer, R.M. (1986) Concentration and attention control training. In *Applied Sport Psychology: Personal Growth to Peak Performance* (J.M. Williams, ed.) pp. 257–269. Palo Alto, CA: Mayfield.

Orlick, T. (1982) *Coaches' Training Manual to Psyching for Sport*. Champaign, IL: Human Kinetics.

Orlick, T. (1989) Reflections on SportPsych consulting with individual and team sport athletes at summer and winter Olympic games. *The Sport Psychologist*, 3, 358–365.

Orlick, T. (1990) *In Pursuit of Excellence: How to Win in Sport and Life through Mental Training*. Champaign, IL: Human Kinetics.

Orlick, T. and Partington, G. (1988) Mental links to excellence. *The Sport Psychologist*, 2, 105–130.

Ostrow, A.C. (1990) *Directory of Psychological Test in the Sport and Exercise Sciences*, Morgantown, WV: Fitness Information Technology.

Ravizza, K. (1986) Increasing awareness for sport performance. In *Applied Sport Psychology* (J. Williams, ed.) pp. 149–162. Palo Alto, CA: Mayfield.

Rotella, R.J. and Bunker, L.K. (1981) *Mind Mastery for Winning Golf*. New York: Prentice Hall.

Rushall, B.S., Hall, M. and Rushall, A. (1988) Effects of three types of thought content instructions on skiing performance. *The Sport Psychologist*, 2, 283–297.

Salmela, J.H. (1989) Long-term intervention with the Canadian men's Olympic gymnastic team. *The Sport Psychologist*, 3, 340–349.

Savoy, C. (1993) A yearly mental training program for a college basketball player. *The Sport Psychologist*, 7, 173–190.

Sinclair, G.D. and Sinclair, D.A. (1994) Developing reflective performers by integrating mental management skills with the learning process. *The Sport Psychologist*, 8, 13–27.

Smith, R.E. and Johnson, J. (1990) An organizational empowerment approach to consultation in professional baseball. *The Sport Psychologist*, 4, 347–357.

Suinn, R.M. (1986) *Seven Steps to Peak Performance*. Toronto: Hans Huber Publishers.

Terry, P. (1989) *The Winning Mind*. Nottingham: Thorsons.

Vealey, R.S. (1986) Imagery training for performance enhancement. In *Applied Sport Psychology: Personal Growth to Peak Performance* (J.M. Williams, ed.) pp. 209–234. Palo Alto, CA: Mayfield.

Vealey, R.S. (1988) Future directions in psychological skills training. *The Sport Psychologist*, 2, 318–336.

Vealey, R.S. (1994) Current status and prominent issues in sport psychology interventions, *Medicine and Science in Sport and Exercise*, 26, 495–502.

Weinberg, R.S. (1988) *The Mental Advantage: Developing your Psychological Skills in Tennis*. Champaign, IL: Human Kinetics.

Weinberg, R. (1989) Applied sport psychology: issues and challenges. *Journal of Applied Sport Psychology*, 1, 181–195.

Williams, J. (1986) Integrating and implementing a psychological skills training program. In *Applied Sport Psychology: Personal Growth to Peak Performance* (J.M. Williams, ed.) pp. 301–324. Palo Alto, CA: Mayfield.

9
The immersion approach
Stephen J. Bull

Sport: Cricket

<u>Author's note</u>
In this chapter the term batsman has been used generically and should be read referring equally to women cricketers and men.

> 'When it comes to playing at the highest level I am a great believer in selecting people who can put their house in order mentally, even if they do not possess the pure cricketing ability of some others. There are a great many players – batsmen and bowlers alike – who look the part in the nets, in practice matches and out in the middle when the going is easy, but who crumble when the pressure is on.'
>
> John Snow (1976)

This quotation from former England fast bowler John Snow highlights the importance of appropriate psychological preparation in the game of cricket. Cricket is a sport requiring a unique blend of individual and team challenges. Players must work together as a team whilst also focusing on their own individual performance. As Glenn Turner (1975) explained, cricket is a great leveller where players will inevitably experience failures no matter how good they are. It is not uncommon for a player to score 100 one day and a duck the next. Maintaining a mentally tough attitude in these circumstances is difficult but essential if a player wishes to maintain optimal levels of performance. Indeed, as John Snow (1976b) also points out, '... all the help and encouragement in the world is wasted unless the mental attitude is correct. That, at all times, is of great importance and perhaps gets more so the higher the standard becomes.' The various skills of cricket require different forms of concentration and mental approach necessitating a finely developed sense of attentional control. As members of a team, cricketers must be able to communicate and work co-operatively with team-mates and be prepared, sometimes, to assume a playing style which conflicts with their preferred approach such as batting or bowling unusually defensively. Captaincy in cricket presents an additional set of challenges which are sometimes not met most effectively by those players with the best cricketing skills. Mike Brearley (1985) analysed the art of captaincy and discussed a range of important psychological factors such as charisma, aggression and decision-making.

The appropriate mental approach to match play will encompass many facets exemplified by well known players. Consider the confidence and positive attitude of Viv Richards, the determination and concentration of Geoff Boycott, the seemingly relaxed approach of Clive Lloyd, and the professional commitment and dedication of Richard Hadlee. Desmond Haynes explained how reading books on psychology helped him develop the skills of anxiety management, visualization and positive thinking (Steen, 1993). Ian Botham described how he could channel his concentration into just the few seconds before each ball is bowled and then switch off and relax in between deliveries (Botham, 1989). Joel Garner explained how he and Malcolm Marshall would psych each other up by using positive thinking (Garner, 1988). Contrast these players with the description provided by Glenn Turner (1975) of the club player who arrives at the ground no more than 15 minutes before the start of the game, who is madly rushing to get the pads on and then arrives in the middle without having had time to mentally prepare for the task in hand, and who, unsurprisingly, finds that he or she is soon back in the pavilion with the day's cricket virtually over.

Psychological skills training can help players to cope with stress, improve confidence and concentration, develop mental toughness and deal with injuries positively. Gordon (1989) suggests that cricket coaches and players who question the value of psychological skills training often provide accounts of 'legendary' players who were not taught psychological skills, nor appeared to need them. However, Gordon (1989) claims that all cricketers can improve their ability to concentrate and cope with stressful situations. He explains how psychological skills training can be taught to young players as a means of bypassing the extended process of acquiring mental skills by experience (the process usually taken by 'legendary' players). However, as pointed out by Shilbury (1989), psychological preparation for cricket is not a short-term process. It requires considerable time and a long-term approach to implementation.

In my experience as a sport psychologist working in cricket, I have developed a style of service delivery to which I refer as the *immersion approach*. By this I mean being a sport psychologist who operates as one of the coaching staff rather than as the isolated consultant who is drafted in for a special purpose and then departs. This is achieved by getting involved in other aspects of training, attending team meetings, being residential at some training camps and integrating as fully as possible with other members of the coaching team. I have found that being seen as a practitioner who has something tangible to offer in training and practice times is an effective means of gaining credibility amongst players. This credibility is important in building the necessary rapport for teaching psychological skills. The immersion approach has also enabled me to find out exactly which elements of psychological training have been well-received by players. I have managed to develop a relationship with players which has allowed open and frank discussion on the perceived usefulness of certain techniques. This feedback has subsequently informed my practice as a sport psychologist generally and been very influential in my decisions regarding the selection of appropriate psychological skills to teach other performers. This chapter provides a basic overview of the three elements of psychological training which I have found to be most useful in the years I have been employing the immersion approach in cricket – concentration, positive thinking and team building. The chapter also briefly describes my role as consultant for the England Women's Cricket Team who won the World Cup in 1993 for the first time in 20 years. This represents a case study of the immersion approach and includes a description of the role I played when providing an on-site sports psychology service during the actual World Cup competition. To conclude the chapter, I briefly review the advantages and disadvantages of the immersion approach and then present a series of recommendations for players, coaches, sports psychology consultants and other sports professionals working in cricket. Although the material throughout the chapter is cricket-specific, much of the content could be modified and adapted for use in other team, and to some extent individual, sports. I feel that the philosophy of the immersion approach is applicable in most (if not all) sports and that it is essential, not only for the sport psychologist to be seen as an integral part of the support staff, but for psychological training to be viewed as an integral part of an overall training programme.

Concentration skills

The most significant factor in cricket concentration is the necessity for switching on and off. It is not possible for a player to maintain a high level of concentration for a prolonged period of time. Therefore, it is necessary to intensify attentional focus at key times, such as the point of delivery, and then decrease the attentional intensity at other times. Glenn Turner (1975) reinforces this in the following quotation:

> 'Although you must look to your concentration, I feel it's also helpful to relax between deliveries, once you are established. So learn to switch yourself on and off; it's too tiring to try and concentrate for every minute of an innings.'

In discussing the theoretical aspects of concentration, Tenebaum and Bar-Eli (1993) explain that sport psychologists distinguish between two types of attention – focal and diffuse. Focal attention involves concentrating on a narrow element of the attentional field, whereas diffuse attention incorporates a wide span. Nideffer (1993), in reviewing his own attentional typology, makes the same distinction and also dichotomizes between internal and external styles of attention. Internal attention refers to feelings and/or thoughts, whereas external attention refers to concentrating on the field of play or the ball. Each of these different styles of attention is useful in cricket at certain times. The challenge for players is to maintain appropriate attentional focus at the right time. My experience has shown me that the use of concentration cues and performance protocols (Schmid and Peper, 1993) are particularly effective in this respect.

Use of concentration cues

Attentional skill can be developed by the use of 'triggers' or 'concentration cues' which assist the player in switching to high attentional intensity when necessary. Cues can also help players to focus on the key factors which contribute to anticipation such as, in batting – ball flight, bowler run up and bowler action at the crease (Barras, 1990). In Table 9.1 three types of cues are described – verbal, visual and physical. A combination of cues could be developed such as wiping the hand on the shirt at the same time as seeing the wicket-keeper crouch and silently saying 'focus'. Players may have different cues for the different elements of cricket performance. It is extremely

Table 9.1 *Examples of concentration cues. Reproduced with permission of Sports Dynamics from Bull* et al. *(1992)*

Verbal	'Focus' 'Ready' 'Cue in' 'Switch on' 'Now'
Visual	Seeing the bowler turn at top of run Seeing the wicket-keeper assume crouch position Looking at seam of ball Looking at the bails
Physical	Wiping hand on shirt Spinning ball in hand Tapping bat in front of crease Taking a deep breath

important, however, that the use of these cues is practised consistently so that the player becomes comfortable with their use to the point of using the cues almost automatically. Examples of cues used in other sports include the tennis player focusing on the strings of the racquet in between points (visual cue), the rugby player tugging at the shorts prior to taking a conversion kick (physical cue), and the golfer silently repeating 'head down' before swinging the club (verbal cue).

Developing concentration routines

The use of these personal cues can be extended into the development of pre-performance routines. Routines are commonly observed in sport and have acted as a useful concentration strategy for many successful performers. Cricketers are no exception, and the idiosyncratic behaviours of some players have become identifiable mannerisms. Between deliveries, for example, Chris Tavaré would stroll pensively in the direction of the square-leg fielding position. Alan Knott would engage in a series of stretching exercises, and on the way back to his mark Abdul Qadir would spin the ball from hand to hand (Bull *et al.*, 1992). These actions have some direct functional value – avoiding distraction, staying loose, and consolidating the wrist spinner's hand action – but they also contribute to a sequence of events designed to focus the concentration of all three players.

Table 9.2 provides examples of routines that could be used for batting, bowling and fielding. These examples could be adapted and modified to suit the needs of different players with different playing styles and personal preferences. Nevertheless, whatever the form, a pre-performance routine will act as a concentration-enhancing mechanism, particularly in the face of distractions and disturbances from on and off the field. Their use is also consistent with the recommendations arising from sports psychology research demonstrating that rehearsal strategies lead to improved performance in motor skills (Singer, 1988; Singer, *et al.*, 1989).

Table 9.2   *Routines for enhancing concentration. Reproduced with permission of Sports Dynamics from Bull* et al. *(1992)*

Batting	1. Take a deep breath
	2. 'Cue in' using personal trigger
	3. Feel the ball contact and leave the bat
	4. Repeat 'One ball at a time', 'Head down, head still'
Bowling	1. Take a deep breath
	2. 'Cue in' using personal trigger
	3. Imagine the ball to be bowled
	4. Check grip
	5. Repeat 'Hit the target', 'Follow through'
Fielding	1. Take a deep breath
	2. 'Cue in' using personal trigger
	3. Really focus and follow the ball
	4. Repeat 'This one's mine', 'Get down early'

A specific use of the pre-peformance routine was developed by Dr Sandy Gordon in his work with the Western Australian State Cricket Team (Gordon, 1990) and is shown in Table 9.3. He has successfully formulated a pre-delivery routine for bowlers which includes the use of breathing and self-talk as well as concentration cues.

Errors and distractions

Gordon (1992) also emphasizes the importance of having a plan to handle distractions which may occur during a game. He suggests that a plan reduces pressure as well as allowing players to maintain their focus of attention on relevant, rather than irrelevant, cues. Table 9.4

Table 9.3 *Examples of a pre/post delivery checklist and 'trigger' for bowlers. Reproduced from Gordon (1992) by permission of the Australian Coaching Council*

	Checklist	Behavioural and mental activities
	Pre-run up	Three release breaths, wipe hand on thigh, place ball in fingers
Pre-delivery	Top of run up Point of delivery	Affirmations – 'rhythm, smmoooth, relax' 'Trigger' – 'target, target, target'
Post delivery	Follow through	'Did I hit the spot?' 'Batsman's technique?'
	Walk back	Deep breaths, shadow action of desired delivery 'What do I have to do next time?'

provides an example of such a plan and suggests how a bowler can deal with the distraction of being hit all over the ground in a limited overs game.

Two further concentration skills which have been used successfully by high-performance athletes in various sports are *thought-stoppage* and *parking*. These are specific psychological strategies designed to remove a distracting thought from the conscious mind during a performance so that attention can be focused on task-relevant cues. In an article about concentration training for fielders in baseball, Grove (1991) describes a three step thought stoppage sequence which is equally applicable for cricketers. He uses an example of the fielder

Table 9.4 *An integrated coping response to deal with an external distractor. Reproduced from Gordon (1992) by permission of the Australian Coaching Council*

What if ... (external distractor)	Do this ... (integrated coping response)
I'm being hit all over the ground in a limited overs game	**Say:** 'Next ball ... in the block hole' 'Keep your rhythm and line' 'This is the ball ... c'mon'
	Do: Two release breaths, shoulder shrugs Visualize next bowl block hole Pre-delivery routine (checklist and trigger)

making an error during a routine play who is still thinking about the error as the pitcher is about to restart. The fielder is advised to first say 'Stop!' (either silently or aloud) and at the same time employ a physical mannerism such as tapping the thigh or slapping the pocket of the glove, then tell themself to take one or two deep breaths to facilitate refocusing, and finally, to use a word or short phrase to get the mind back on the task at hand. This process is clearly using a combination of verbal and physical cues and is similar to material covered earlier in the section on concentration cues.

In simple terms, when using the skill of parking, the athlete creates an image in the mind which successfully removes the distraction and *parks* it somewhere away from the athlete's attention in the here and now. Bull *et al.* (1996) provide examples of parking such as a rower seeing errors as stones which disappeared when dropped over the side, a golfer who imagined errors being put in a file and placed in a filing cabinet (so she could return to analyse them after completing the performance), a non-smoking Olympic wrestler who saw errors as cigarette butts to be fiercely stamped out by his foot. Gordon (1992) advocates the use of parking in cricket and describes how a bowler could use the skill to maintain appropriate focus of attention.

> 'Bowlers might therefore "park" a personal problem in their locker for future consideration, while they focus on the game. The bowler is effectively saying "I'm concerned about what happened at work yesterday – but I can't do anything about it right now – I'll 'park' it now and worry about it after the game". This strategy would help bowlers to prioritise concerns and switch-on to the most relevant cues.'

Bull *et al.* (1996) explain that with practice, the athlete establishes an automatic link between the image and attentional focus. For this to occur, the following steps must be taken:

- The player needs to establish an appropriate parking image which has personal meaning and can be comfortably used.
- The skill must be practised when in a relaxed state in order to develop a degree of competence.
- The skill must then be practised in training situations until the player becomes proficient.
- Then the skill can be used in game situations.

To recap, concentration is a key psychological skill in cricket. Frost (1993) suggests that, of the many psychological attributes required in cricket, it is the most significant and that 'developing control over concentration is fundamental for improvement of performance'. Frost (1993) also maintains that concentration in cricket can be learned and developed with practice in the same way technical and physical skills can.

Positive thinking skills

'All I know is that, when I'm batting, I believe I'm the best batsman in the world, that bowlers are second class, that I am in total control. If I feel negative at any point I stop the bowler and make him wait for me, just to reassert that control.'

Desmond Haynes in Steen (1993)

Research in sport psychology consistently demonstrates the positive relationship between self confidence and successful performance (Bunker *et al.*, 1993). Psychological skills training books invariably feature considerable sections on how to improve positive attitude. Cricketers should therefore be very aware of the content of their thinking and ensure that it is positively framed at all times. Fear of failure, self-doubt and negative thinking, however, are common in all sports, but medal winners and world champions are often characterized by their ability to override any niggling doubts and fear by replacing them with affirmations confirming their belief relating to performance potential in the big competitions. Table 9.5 shows how a cricketer can reframe negative thinking into positive thinking.

Enjoyment and mental toughness

Enjoyment is a crucial element in the maintenance of confidence and positive attitude. It's extremely difficult for cricketers to feel confident if they are not enjoying their game and if they do not enjoy competition generally. This is particularly the case when the competition is tough. Jim Loehr is an American sport psychologist specializing in tennis. He has worked with several top players in the world who have emerged from the Bollitieri Academy in Florida and has written extensively on mental toughness.

'When an athlete starts loving adversity, then s/he is becoming a competitor. The next time you encounter the impossible craziness, clench your fists, get a determined smile on your face and, with all the feeling and emotion you can muster, say to yourself – I LOVE IT!'

Loehr (1982)

Table 9.5 *Changing self-statements. Reproduced with permission of Sports Dynamics from Bull et al. (1992)*

Change from: negative self-talk	Change to: positive self-talk
'I'm worried about facing that opening bowler again.'	'I'll be okay against that opening bowler as long as I play off the front foot.'
'I just can't play spin bowling.'	'I *can* play spin if I'm prepared to work at it.'
'I can't seem to bowl a decent length today.'	'Relax and focus on the target area – the length will come.'
'I just can't get that dropped catch out of my mind.'	'Give me another chance – I'll make up for it next time.'
'That umpire has probably lost us the game.'	'Right, we'll just have to win this without any help from the umpires – but we can still do it.'

Loehr (1982) claims that competition in sport is a constant presentation of problems but that it is the athlete's emotional reaction to problems which will determine whether performance is negatively influenced. Problems must be seen as challenges rather than significant obstacles and the process of attempting to meet these challenges must be enjoyed.

Goal setting

Goal setting is a technique commonly used to promote enjoyment, as well as to enhance confidence and give purpose to training. Beggs (1990) suggested that goal setting can also provide coaches and athletes with a practical way of dealing with the negative results of anxiety on performance. Cricket is a sport which lends itself to the process of setting goals. Match statistics, run-rates and batting and bowling averages all present the opportunity for a natural form of target-setting which is intrinsic to performance on the field. However, in its wider sense, goal setting involves much more than merely setting targets for runs, wickets and catches over a season or tour. It involves ongoing monitoring and evaluation, the setting of different types of targets for different situations, the analysis of training techniques and match strategy, the documentation of short-term as well as medium and long-term targets, and the planning of specific practice schedules in accordance with the intended development and progress. Richard Hadlee is an excellent example of a totally motivated cricketer who used to set himself a variety of short-, medium and long-term goals. An extended discussion of the principles of goal setting, however, is beyond the scope of this chapter, but readers are directed to Bull *et al.* (1992) for an explanation of how goal setting can be used in cricket generally, and to Elliott *et al.* (1989) for a description of goal setting guidelines for the specific skill of fast bowling. The process of performance profiling, as detailed elsewhere in this book, is also a very useful tool in the goal setting process and can be used extensively in cricket.

Visualization

Finally, the skill of visualization can be used as a powerful tool in developing confidence as indicated by the two quotations below, by Desmond Haynes and Richard Hadlee. Most sports psychology text-books use the term imagery to describe this skill but I have found that visualization is more user-friendly in the practical world of sport.

> 'During practice for the second Test at Perth, I walked back from the nets to the dressing room with my bat raised as if I'd just made a hundred. I visualized it, then I lived it.'
>
> Steen (1993)

> 'I learned to play back successes in my mind, not as a spectator, but actually going through it all in the middle.'
>
> Hadlee (1985)

Murphy and Jowdy (1992) pointed out that many hundreds of studies have been conducted investigating the use of visualization in sport. The studies have generally shown that the technique can be very useful and theoretical explanations have been devised to explain how performance is enhanced. The two most commonly identified theories are the psychoneuromuscular theory and the symbolic learning theory. The psychoneuromuscular theory purports that when visualization takes place, the muscles involved in the movement being imagined are slightly innervated which enhances 'muscle memory' whereas the symbolic learning theory suggests that visualization helps performers to code their movements into symbolic components which helps make the movement more automatic (Vealey and Walter, 1993).

Cricketers could benefit by regularly putting aside five to ten minutes for a period of visualization when previous best performances are recalled such as a great innings, a successful bowling spell or some excellent fielding. During these times, players are encouraged to recall physical and emotional feelings associated with these performances as a means of reinforcing positive aspects which need to be repeated in future matches.

> 'Choose a positive and successful image of a desired bowling action and replay this image ten to twelve times vividly, "in colour", at the wicket or ground, and enjoy the sensations of confidence and success that are created.'
>
> Gordon (1989)

Another form of visualization which can be useful is to imagine how the ideal player would perform in a certain situation. Players can put themselves in this ideal player's boots and 'play his or her game'. A young cricketer could attempt to emulate the bowling accuracy and consistency of a top test player or the attacking batting of a favourite local county player. This technique can be used during an actual game situation as well as forming part of an overall mental training programme.

When using the skill of visualization, it's important to see successful performance and to feel the actions being imagined. For example, the feel of the seam of the ball, the sensation of swinging the bat or diving for a catch. It's also important to visualize the whole performance rather than snapshots and to run through the image at the correct speed rather than too quickly or in slow motion. These recommendations serve to make the visualization as realistic and life-like as possible, hence maximizing the chances of the confident feelings being transferred to a match situation.

Team building

Cricket is a team game and although it consists of a series of individual encounters, poor team spirit can have serious effects on the commitment, motivation and performance of individual team members. Different players are motivated in different ways and respond to different forms of encouragement. Contrast the personalities of Dominic Cork and Jack Russell. Compare the leadership styles of Michael Atherton and Graham Gooch. Some players are extrovert, abrasive and full of confidence, responding best to a forthright and authoritarian style of communication. Others are more reserved and sensitive, requiring a softer, more humanistic style. All players, and especially the captain, need to appreciate the different personalities within a team and interact accordingly. Prior to the England Women's Team winning the World Cup in 1993, a great deal of time had been spent on team building exercises designed to sensitize all members of the squad to how each player wanted to be treated on and off the field. Some wanted to be shouted at and verbally encouraged; others preferred to be left with their own thoughts.

Team cohesion

In psychological terms, team spirit is referred to as team cohesion and is characterized by social and task elements. Social cohesion refers to the extent to which players get on with each other on a social basis. High levels of social cohesion are exhibited by teams which spend time together off the field and enjoy each other's company in non-sport-related contexts. Task cohesion refers to the extent to which team members agree on the goals of the team and the strategies which are employed to achieve those goals. Widmeyer *et al.* (1993) provide a detailed discussion of the theoretical aspects of group cohesion. They review a conceptual model of cohesion in which two categories, Group Integration and Individual Attractions to the Group, are distinguished. Group Integration is described as concerning the beliefs and perceptions held by team members about the group as a whole. Individual Attractions to the Group concerns personal beliefs and perceptions held by each individual about why they joined, and why they remain in, the group. In an earlier publication, Widmeyer *et al.* (1985) identified factors related to the development of cohesion in sports teams. Three of these factors – individual roles, communication and codes of behaviour – are particularly relevant to cricket and are discussed below.

Individual roles

Carron (1988), in discussing group dynamics in sport, outlines the importance of role behaviours in the effectiveness of a sports team. He explains that as a team develops, strategic plans are established and individual members of the team are assigned certain roles within those plans. Team members are allocated formal roles pertaining to performance on the field, as well as informal roles such as team clown. Former test player John Snow explains how important these informal roles are by providing an example from his own playing experience.

> 'There is still another group – the jokers with a quip for every occasion who raise the spirits when the side is down, and crack the air of tension with a word or act when the feelings are aroused. The Robin Hobbs and 'Ollie' Milburns of the cricketing world are worth their place on any touring party as a mascot, irrespective of their cricketing ability. I've toured with them both, and drawn pleasure and comfort from their presence.'
>
> John Snow (1976)

Two crucial aspects of role behaviour in sport are role clarity and role acceptance. Role clarity refers to the extent to which players are clear about their role on the team. Are they expected to be a solid opening bat whose job it is to stay there and not worry about runs, or are they expected to go in early and set the innings off to a quick start by scoring rapidly? This type of role may well vary from match to match or indeed from one innings to another. Many players are expected to fulfil a different role depending on the side in which they are playing. For example, they may be an opening 'strike' bowler for the county side and yet for the national team they are expected to operate as a 'stock' first-change bowler. This can lead to difficulties and misunderstandings if the expected role is not made very clear to the player. As a team building strategy, I have always suggested that coaches should ensure that players are fully aware of what is expected of them and should not take this knowledge for granted.

Role acceptance refers to the extent to which players are satisfied with the role which has been allocated to them. Thus, a player may demonstrate a high degree of role clarity, i.e., he or she is fully aware of what is expected, but is not happy with this role, leading to a role conflict situation. Lack of role acceptance can have a serious effect on team cohesion, although with discussion and negotiation problems can often be resolved. I recommend that coaches and captains allow players to express their feelings if unhappy with a prescribed role and try to promote discussion relating to alternative roles. Group discussions are a very effective way of involving all members of a squad in the process of individual role allocation and the establishment of strategic plans. Players are able to express their own views, preferences and suggestions on how the skills of individual players can be best utilized. Bull *et al.* (1992) provide an example of how group discussions can have a positive influence on the attitude of an individual player in addition to improving the cohesion of the team as a whole.

> 'Some members of the England Women's Cricket Team were involved in a discussion prior to the European Cup in 1990. One player expressed her confusion and lack of confidence about her supposed role on the team. Four other players involved in the small group were surprised at her feelings, and proceeded to explain the value of her contribution to the team as a whole. It transpired that the player's role was different from that when she played for her club side, but she was encouraged and motivated by her teammates' open support and clarification. Afterwards she said, "I became a lot more confident as a team member. I have found it difficult to understand and establish the role I play, but after this discussion, I feel a lot more accepted by the squad".'

Team meetings and communication

Team meetings are an essential means of promoting open communication channels – an extremely important aspect of developing team cohesion. Carron (1988) suggests that team members should be given the opportunity to contribute their ideas for improving team functioning and that the provision of a changing room environment which is conducive to open communication clearly facilitates this process. However, Bull *et al.* (1992) point out that team meetings and increased communication must not become an excuse for criticism, back-biting and general moaning. There is certainly room for productive critical discussion but generally, and definitely in the early stages, the focus should be on positive aspects of team and individual performance.

Codes of behaviour

One important issue which needs addressing during team meetings is that of team rules and codes of behaviour. Psychologists refer to these elements of team functioning as group norms or standards. Examples would include not drinking alcohol the evening before a match, wearing smart clothing for away games, arriving at training sessions at least 15 minutes early, and the rotation of duties relating to pitch preparation. Whilst group norms can be a very effective means of developing team cohesion, they can also be an extremely detrimental force in breaking it down. If team members do not agree with certain behavioural expectations which are forced upon them by the management, then frustration develops. Cliques begin to form when players are frustrated and motivation can diminish leading to a decrease in performance levels. Players also become frustrated when individual members on a squad are observed not conforming to the team standards but are not sanctioned appropriately by management. This leads to a feeling of 'one rule for them and another for us', a statement frequently heard among players on teams with low levels of cohesion. Managers, coaches and captains should therefore take great care when establishing team standards and seek to involve the players in preliminary discussion relating to issues of implementation. Carron (1993) proposes that coaches should communicate clearly with team members the rationale behind the establishment and enforcement of group standards, explain how each individual member can contribute to the maintenance of standards, and develop effective methods of rewarding athletes who adhere and sanctioning those who do not.

Psychological training for the England Women's Cricket Team

'Enough people will realize that it (*psychological training*) was a positive help and one of the factors that helped us towards winning the World Cup.'

Member of England Women's Cricket Team (1993)

In 1988 I began working as sport psychologist for the England Women's Cricket Team as part of the Sports Council's Sports Science Support Programme. I delivered a five year programme of psychological training in preparation for the World Cup in 1993. In addition to employing the immersion approach, my style of consultancy was based, in part, on that used by Dr Jerry May in his work with the US Ski Team (May and Veach, 1987). To this end, I utilized a broad theoretical framework, attempted to fit into the existing programme, avoided being involved in team selection, assumed a low profile regarding the media and made constant attempts to ensure continuity of content. Additionally, I found the use of a flexible non-academic style to be most productive – a style also employed by Dr Sandy Gordon in his cricket sports psychology consultancy (Gordon, 1990).

Over the five year period, I met with the squad approximately five times per year, either at the University of Brighton (when the players were undergoing fitness testing) or during training camps at Lilleshall

National Sports Centre. I also attended several matches, including being present at the European Cup in 1990 and the World Cup in 1993. The consultancy service I provided took four basic forms. Firstly, workshop sessions for the squad as a whole during which the basic principles of psychological skills training were introduced. Secondly, one-to-one sessions with players were available on request. Thirdly, group meetings were held in which various team building exercises were employed in an attempt to foster communication, clarify roles and enhance both social and task aspects of team cohesion. Fourthly, regular meetings with the coach and manager for the purpose of planning training programmes, practice schedules and general management of the squad.

In the months leading up to the World Cup, the psychology programme became focused on two major areas, the development of confidence and the enhancement of team spirit through a further series of team building exercises. These two areas were selected on the basis of formal (and informal) feedback from players and coaching staff regarding the elements of my consultancy which were felt to be of most value. Key strategies reinforced for maintaining confidence were recalling previous excellent performances by using visualization, monitoring the nature of self-talk, consideration of how the ideal player would behave and the importance of setting regular targets and goals. Considerable time was also spent discussing the need to focus on *controlling the controllables* rather than getting frustrated and angry at things which could not be influenced. This is an important concept for athletes in all sports and is an issue of real practical relevance which must be addressed if positive attitudes are to be maintained in the face of adversity. I frequently used adaptations of rational emotive therapy (RET) (Ellis, 1982) in an attempt to encourage the players to keep sport-related problems in perspective. I use the term adaptation because I did not, at any time, engage in any type of formal therapy. Rather, I used the themes of RET in my presentations, in supplementary reading material I produced and when discussing various issues during informal interactions with the players. I suggested that they should be prepared for a variety of different problems which may arise throughout the competition and, in particular, acknowledge that matches would ebb and flow in terms of which side was dominating the match. I explained that the important factor would be to stay positive, committed and cohesive during periods of sub-par performance and misfortune. As a group, we explored this notion and worked towards team acceptance of the inevitability of ups and downs in performance. The following quote from one of the key players in the side illustrates this theme:

> 'When we were playing in the final nobody seemed to panic, even when New Zealand were taking quick singles and pushing the score along. I was just thinking what Steve was saying – just go with the flow and it will eventually come your way.'
>
> Member of England Women's Cricket Team (1993)

During the World Cup competition, my presence involved covering six broad roles. Each of these roles was facilitated by having an extremely supportive coaching and management team which regularly sought my advice and made great efforts to integrate me with the day to day running of the team.

- Involvement in pre- and post-match team talks.
- Counselling players who were *rested* or *dropped* for matches.
- Provision of advice to management on behavioural codes.
- Provision of advice on dealing with the media.
- Provision of positive reinforcement for the captain.
- General support and involvement in off-field activities such as videoing.

This general supportive role is, in my experience, an essential part of becoming accepted by the players and is an integral part of the immersion approach.

I evaluated my overall effectiveness as the team sport psychologist in three different ways. Firstly, I administered the Consultant Evaluation Form (Partington and Orlick, 1987) on two separate occasions during the five year programme. Secondly, I acquired ongoing informal feedback from coaches and players through discussions at mealtimes and general comments during training sessions. Thirdly, another member of the coaching staff conducted a formal evaluation interview after the World Cup competition. Aspects of the programme which were evaluated particularly positively included the work on team building and the training in positive thinking skills; hence their inclusion in the earlier parts of this chapter. Aspects evaluated negatively included the use of psychometric testing and orthodox relaxation training, both of which I removed completely from the programme at a fairly early stage. My general feeling (based on experience of consulting in other sports as well as cricket) is that relaxation training is an aspect of applied sports psychology which has perhaps been accorded too high a profile. My reservations about orthodox relaxation training concur with the views presented by Anshel (1991) who suggests that certain relaxation programmes may be over prescribed and incorrectly implemented. Although identifying the arguments in favour of relaxation training, he reviews the case against the use of relaxation techniques in sport, suggesting a number of potential problems. Anshel (1991) explains that, as yet, research has not clearly demonstrated a causal link between relaxation training and improved performance. He also suggests that some sports performers prefer to regulate emotion by techniques other than relaxation and some sports do not even require a relaxed state. He explains that there may indeed be advantages in ignoring fears and anxieties rather than focusing internally on them. Finally, he suggests that relaxation training tapes and videos have inherent problems such as their prescriptive pace and the possible distraction of external sources. In short, I think the England Women's Cricket Team felt relaxation training to be too far removed from the field of play. As team sport athletes, their gregarious personalities were also not conducive to the experience of deep relaxation in the context of their sport. Shorter versions of anxiety control such as centering (Miller, 1991), seem to be far more appropriate for this type of athlete and bear a much closer relevance to performance preparation.

As far as psychometric testing is concerned, I found that I used it merely as a means of generating discussion among the team on sport-related psychological skills. Although this may have its advantages, this is not the purpose for which the tests were developed, and is probably not the most productive use of time, a commodity which is often in short supply in sports psychology consultancy. I would advocate the use of performance profiling (a technique described elsewhere in this book) as a far better approach to pen and paper assessment of strengths and weaknesses.

The victory over New Zealand at Lord's in the World Cup Final was obviously an exciting day for everyone involved with the squad. One of my strongest memories is of warmly congratulating some of the players inside the Long Room, the famous part of the Lord's pavilion where the presence of women is not allowed (at the time of writing this chapter!). On the day of the final, the players were permitted to walk through the Long Room on their way from the changing rooms to the pitch and on their way to the post-match reception.

Conclusions and recommendations

'There is no crisis in cricket, there is only the next ball.'
W.G. Grace in Jarman (1990)

W.G. Grace made this statement in 1890. It is a maxim worth considerable attention in the game of cricket today and encapsulates many of the themes covered in this chapter. Concentration should be focused on the next ball at all times rather than what has gone before. Confidence should be maintained for future deliveries despite lack of success in previous efforts. Teams should remain cohesive and positive in the face of adversity and be patient throughout the ups and downs of a long match.

There are no miracles in the application of sports psychology to cricket. It will not transform a mediocre player into a test cricketer. However, it will maximize the chances of players reaching their potential and performing consistently in various types of pressure situation. Current research suggests, however, that athletes may not be particularly good at adhering to psychological training programmes despite acknowledging their value (Bull, 1991). It is therefore important that coaches and other sports professionals work with sport psychologists in encouraging athletes to use psychological training techniques regularly and to practise them on a consistent basis.

This chapter concludes with a brief discussion of the advantages and disadvantages of the immersion approach, followed by a series of recommendations for players, coaches, sport psychologists and other sports professionals designed to facilitate player use of psychological training in cricket. Each of these recommendations has arisen from my experience of employing the immersion approach in cricket, and in other sports.

Advantages of the immersion approach

I would note four major advantages of the immersion approach. Firstly, as mentioned earlier in the chapter, an immersion approach serves to enhance the consultant's credibility in the eyes of the athletes. They see the consultant as an integral member of the support team and as someone who can provide hands-on, practical advice. Secondly, a consistent active presence significantly contributes to the process of building a rapport with both the athletes and the coaching staff. Thirdly, the mere presence of the consultant can remind athletes about their psychological training and appropriate forms of competition preparation. This is a point also made by May and Brown (1989) concerning work in alpine skiing. Fourthly, it is far easier to gain extremely useful feedback about the sports psychology service if the immersion approach is employed. Mealtimes, evenings and times around physical training are excellent occasions in which to informally question athletes about the perceived effectiveness of the psychological services being provided.

Disadvantages of the immersion approach

I would note three potential disadvantages of the approach. Firstly, as Salmela (1989) points out, an immersion style can involve large periods of 'dead time' in which the consultant may feel very unproductive. Secondly, if the consultant is not careful, a dependency relationship may develop whereby the athletes are so accustomed to the consultant's presence that it becomes a necessary element of their training and competition environment. This must be avoided. I have always believed that the goal of sport psychologists is to make themselves redundant and therefore I would suggest that the degree of immersion should be monitored very carefully. Thirdly, some coaches and other members of the support staff may feel threatened by sport psychologists who completely immerse themselves in the culture of the sport, especially if they attempt to broaden their role to include assistance in physical training or being involved in competition preparation. This may be a particular problem in sports which have not yet fully accepted the contribution of sports psychology. However, carried out with discretion and subtlety, I believe an immersion approach is the ideal way in which to challenge the doubts and fears of sceptics.

Suggestions for the player

- Develop a number of concentration cues which work for you. Experiment with using them in the nets and in practice matches. When you feel comfortable with them, use them in a match situation.
- Develop pre-performance routines for batting, bowling and fielding. Again, practise using these before implementing them in a match situation.
- Use the skills of *parking* or *thought-stoppage* when you are distracted by an error. Again, practise these techniques first.

- Monitor your self-talk. Make sure you are thinking positively and learn how to reframe negative self statements into positive alternatives.
- Set yourself short-, medium and long-term goals. Discuss these with your coach or sport psychologist.
- Use visualization to recall previous good performances. Make visualization a part of your training and preparation programme.
- Enjoy the challenge of competition. When things don't go your way, stay committed and think about mental toughness. Remember, it's how you react to problems which affects your performance.
- Focus on controlling things that you can influence. Do not get unnecessarily angry and frustrated with factors over which you have no control. Accept them and get on with being competitive.
- Make sure you understand your role on a team. If you are unhappy with this role, talk to your captain or coach. Express your preferences, although accept that cricket is a team game and you may have to make sacrifices.
- Get to know your team-mates and understand their personalities so that you know how to motivate and encourage them appropriately. Accept that you may have to treat team-mates very differently in order to get the best out of them.

Suggestions for the coach

- Familiarize yourself with the psychological training techniques covered in this chapter so that you can advise and encourage your players in their use.
- Develop open communication channels within the team you coach. Encourage lots of small and large group discussion and allow players to express their views regarding codes of behaviour, identification of roles and training methods.
- Ensure that all players understand their role and if roles need to be modified for certain matches, communicate the specific details relating to the change.
- If you contemplate using a sport psychologist, ensure that he or she is accredited by the British Association of Sports and Exercise Sciences, and has the personal style to fit into the role of working with cricketers. Winter *et al.* (1990) suggest that a psychologist needs to be flexible and find ways to integrate with a team rather than a team having to accommodate the psychologist.

- To learn more about psychological training and working with teams, consider attending Advanced Workshops in these topics run by the National Coaching Foundation. Although based in Leeds, the NCF runs courses around the country. At the advanced level, there is a course on *Mental Training* and one on *Working With Teams*.

Suggestions for the sport psychologist

- Employ the immersion approach in your consultancy. Broaden your role so that you become accepted as a member of the coaching staff.
- Encourage the use of team discussions. Ensure that roles are reviewed and clarified on a regular basis.
- Be careful with the use of psychometric tests. They appear to be of limited use in applied settings and players are very sceptical. Performance profiling is a preferred method of eliciting relevant information relating to strengths and weaknesses.
- When introducing psychological training to players, be careful when utilizing orthodox approaches to skills such as relaxation and visualization. Make every effort to use cricket examples and demonstrate the real practical relevance of a specific technique.
- Create opportunities for the players to provide feedback on your work. Use different ways of generating this feedback such as a version of Partington and Orlick's (1987) evaluation form, group discussions and informal meetings at mealtimes.
- Read relevant publications documenting the work of other experienced professionals. Partington and Orlick's (1991) analysis of Olympic consultants' best ever consultancy experiences is particularly useful.

Suggestions for other sport scientists and physiotherapists

- Familiarize yourself with the basic principles of psychological training so that you can encourage players to use the techniques consistently.
- Learn as much as possible about the personality and interpersonal style of each player so that you treat them in an individual manner. Remember that a team will contain a blend of very different types of performer who have very different roles to play.
- Employ the immersion approach in your own work and try hard to become an accepted member of the coaching staff.

Finally, literature pertaining to the application of psychology to cricket is sparse. I have referenced the material of Dr Sandy Gordon throughout this chapter and would note that his applications of psychology have been very useful to me in my own consultancy work in cricket. If readers are interested in learning more about psychological training in cricket, and how it can be developed alongside other aspects of sports science, the books by Bull *et al.* (1992) and Elliot *et al.* (1989) are recommended.

References

Anshel, M.H. (1991) Relaxation training in sport: pros and cons. *Sport Health*, 9(4), 23–24.

Barras, N. (1990) Looking while batting in cricket. *Sports Coach*, 13, 3–7.

Beggs, W.D. (1990) Goal setting in sport. In *Stress and Performance in Sport* (J.G. Jones and L. Hardy, eds) pp. 135–170. Chichester, UK: Wiley.

Botham, I. (with Bannister, J.) (1989) *Cricket My Way*. London, UK: Willow Books.

Brearley, M. (1985) *The Art of Captaincy*. London, UK: Hodder and Stoughton.

Bull, S.J. (1991) Personal and situational influences on adherence to mental skills training. *Journal of Sport and Exercise Psychology*, 13, 121–132.

Bull, S.J., Fleming, S. and Doust, J. (1992) *Play Better Cricket: Using Sports Science to Improve Your Game*. Eastbourne, UK: Sports Dynamics.

Bull, S.J., Albinson, J.G. and Shambrook, C.J. (1996) *The Mental Game Plan: Getting Psyched for Sport*. Eastbourne, UK: Sports Dynamics.

Bunker, L., Williams, J.M. and Zinsser, N. (1993) Cognitive techniques for improving performance and building confidence. In *Applied Sports Psychology: Personal Growth to Peak Performance* (J.M. Williams, ed.) pp. 225–242. Mountain View, CA: Mayfield.

Carron, A.V. (1988) *Group Dynamics in Sport*. London, ON: Spodym Publishers.

Carron, A.V. (1993) The sport team as an effective group. In *Applied Sport Psychology: Personal Growth to Peak Performance* (J.M. Williams, ed.) pp. 110–121. Mountain View, CA: Mayfield.

Elliott, B., Foster, D. and Blanksby, B. (eds) (1989) *Send the Stumps Flying: The Science of Fast Bowling*. Nedlands, WA: University of Western Australia Press.

Ellis, A. (1982) Self direction in sport and life. In *Mental Training for Athletes and Coaches* (T. Orlick, J. Partington and J. Salmela, eds) pp. 10–18. Ottawa, ON: Sport in Perspective and Coaching Association of Canada.

Frost, J. (1993) Concentration and cricket. *Cricket Coach*, 23, 1254–1263.

Garner, J. (1988) *Big Bird Flying High*. London, UK: Arthur Barker.

Gordon, S. (1989) Psychology of fast bowling. In *Send the Stumps Flying: The Science of Fast Bowling* (B. Elliott, D. Foster and B. Blanskby, eds) pp. 43–53. Nedlands, WA: University of Western Australia.

Gordon, S. (1990) A mental skills training program for the Western Australian State Cricket Team. *The Sport Psychologist*, **4**, 386–399.
Gordon, S. (1992) Concentration skills for bowling in cricket. *Sports Coach*, **15**, 34–39.
Grove, J.R. (1991) Concentration training for infielders in baseball and softball. *Sports Coach*, **14**, 27–30.
Hadlee, R. (with Francis, T.) (1985) *At the Double: The Story of a Cricketer's Pacemaker*, p. 30. London, UK: Stanley Paul.
Jarman, C. (1990) *The Guinness Dictionary of Sports Quotations*. London, UK: Guiness Publishing.
Loehr, J. (1982) *Mental Toughness Training for Sports: Achieving Athletic Excellence*, p. 44. Lexington, MA: The Stephen Greene Press.
May, J.R. and Brown, L. (1989) Delivery of psychological services to the U.S. Alpine Ski Team prior to and during the Olympics in Calgary. *The Sport Psychologist*, **3**, 320–329.
May, J.R. and Veach, T.L. (1987) The U.S. Alpine Ski Team psychology program: a proposed consultancy model. In *Sport Psychology: The Psychological Health of the Athlete* (J.R. May and M.J. Asken, eds) pp. 19–39. New York, NY: PMA Publishing.
Miller, B. (1991) Mental preparation for competition. In *Sport Psychology: A Self-help Guide* (S.J. Bull, ed.) pp. 84–102. Ramsbury, UK: The Crowood Press.
Murphy, S.M. and Jowdy, D.P. (1992) Imagery and mental practice. In *Advances in Sport Psychology* (T.W. Horn, ed.) pp. 221–250. Champaign, IL: Human Kinetics.
Nideffer, R.N. (1993) Attention control training. In *Handbook of Research on Sport Psychology* (R.N. Singer, M. Murphey and L.K. Tennant, eds) pp. 542–556. New York, NY: Macmillan.
Partington, J. and Orlick, T. (1987) The sport psychology Consultant Evaluation Form. *The Sport Psychologist*, **1**, 309–317.
Partington, J. and Orlick, T. (1991) An analysis of Olympic sport psychology consultants' best-ever consulting experiences. *The Sport Psychologist*, **5**, 183–193.
Salmela, J.H. (1989) Long-term intervention with the Canadian Men's Olympic Gymnastic Team. *The Sport Psychologist*, **3**, 340–349.
Schmid, A. and Peper, E. (1993) Training strategies for concentration. In *Applied Sport Psychology: Personal Growth to Peak Performance* (J.M. Williams, ed.) pp. 262–273. Mountain View, CA: Mayfield.
Shilbury, D. (1989) Gaining the mental edge: a programme for club cricket. *Sports Coach*, **12**, 31–34.
Singer, R.N. (1988) Strategies and metastrategies in learning and performing self-paced athletic skills. *The Sport Psychologist*, **2**, 49–68.
Singer, R.N., Flora, L.A. and Abourezk, T. (1989) The effect of a five step cognitive learning strategy on the acquisition of a complex motor task. *Journal of Applied Sport Psychology*, **1**, 98–108.
Snow, J. (1976) *Cricket Rebel*. London, UK: Hamlyn.
Steen, R. (1993) *Desmond Haynes – Lion of Barbados*. London, UK: H.F. and G. Witherby.
Tenebaum, G. and Bar-Eli, M. (1993) Decision making in sport: A cognitive perspective. In *Handbook of Research on Sport Psychology* (R.N. Singer, M. Murphey and L.K. Tennant, eds) pp. 171–192. New York, NY: Macmillan.

Turner, G. (1975) *My Way*. Auckland, NZ: Hodder and Stoughton.

Vealey, R.S. and Walter, S.M. (1993) Imagery training for performance enhancement and personal development. In *Applied Sport Psychology: Personal Growth to Peak Performance* (J.M. Williams, ed.) pp. 200–224. Mountain View, CA: Mayfield.

Widmeyer, W.N., Brawley, L.R. and Carron, A.V. (1985) *The Measurement of Cohesion in Sport Teams: The Group Environment Questionnaire*. London, ON: Sports Dynamics.

Widmeyer, W.N., Carron, A.V. and Brawley, L.R. (1993) Group cohesion in sport and exercise. In *Handbook of Research on Sport Psychology* (R.N. Singer, M. Murphey and L.K. Tennant, eds) pp. 672–646. New York, NY: Macmillan.

Winter, G., Martin, C. and White, J. (1990) Sports psychology does work? Great! *Sports Coach*, **13**, 31–34.

10
Applying an organizational development model to a sports setting
Peter Galvin

Rationale

In recent years there has been a growing inclination among managers in industry and commerce to look to the sporting world for inspiration as to how they can get the best possible performance from their workforce. Some of the attraction associated with improving performance lies in the charisma of individual 'superstars' selling their own particular recipe for success. In other cases managers have been seduced by an increasing number of training courses which promise a greater understanding and improvement in areas such as 'how to motivate your team', 'how to develop long-lasting loyalty', 'how to develop your team's full potential', 'how to build a winning team' and so on. This chapter suggests that those working in sports organizations might benefit from looking at what commercial, industrial and educational settings have to offer by way of improving performance.

This chapter describes a model of organizational development actually used in educational settings but which is based upon many of the lessons learned from managing change in commercial settings. The model has been used by the author to improve the behaviour of pupils and the classroom performance of teachers. This model developed out of a considerable frustration for me in working with individual pupils in an attempt to improve their behaviour in school. It was clear that the success of this work was heavily (and usually negatively) dependent upon those group factors operating in the classroom – peer pressure, grouping of pupils, classroom organization, etc., and the 'performance' or behaviour of the teacher. These classroom or group factors and the teacher's behaviour were, in turn, directly affected by the prevailing 'atmosphere' or ethos of the school. For example, if the school held the view that trouble-makers should be dealt with very firmly then it was difficult for, me as the school psychologist, to successfully implement a programme of positive reinforcement of small behavioural changes. This view of the manner in which individual, group and organization interact led me to the conclusion that instead of trying to work with the individual pupil I should be working with the teachers and the school as a whole organization. In other words, working to improve the behaviour or performance of individuals in an organization often needed to be underpinned by trying to understand, manipulate and change the ethos or culture (I shall use the word culture in this chapter) of the organization itself such that it came to support rather than undermine the behavioural changes that the individual pupil needed to make.

This chapter proposes that schools and sports organizations have much in common given that the performance of the individual athlete is affected by and affects the team's performance and that the team's performance is influenced by the manner in which the organization as a whole operates. It is suggested, therefore, that the model of development used in schools could be applied to sports settings.

The process of development in sports organizations would be fundamentally concerned with developing a coherence or an integration of the organization, the teams (athletes and support teams) and individuals who are a part of it. This chapter argues that improved team and individual performance will result when all aspects of the organization are in harmony. This chapter proposes that clarity, consensus and consistency in the culture of an organization will improve the performance of athletes on the field.

Management gurus argue that understanding and manipulating an organization's culture will have a powerful and positive effect on the performance of those in the organization. Deal and Kennedy (1988) in their book *Corporate Cultures* state,

> 'Every organisation has a culture ... whether weak or strong, culture has a powerful influence throughout an organisation ... it affects practically everything ... because of this impact we think that culture also has a major effect on the success of the business.'
> Deal and Kennedy (1988)

If this is true, and many in the organizational development field feel strongly that it is, then it would seem vital that an organization defines its own culture clearly. The important point here is that if those within the organization do not commit themselves to defining its culture (and all that follows from it), then it will define itself quite randomly. The question is not whether sports organizations should or should not have to identify and develop their culture (the culture will exist); the question is whether this culture will be planned or accidental. The reason why it is so important to define the culture of a sports organization is because the culture of any organization defines the vision (a view of the future which informs actions) and values (a view of the present which informs actions) of the organization, which in turn make it possible to determine the long-term goals and short-term objectives of both the organization *and* the teams and individuals within it.

Writers in the management arena give high profile to the importance of organizational vision and values as a basis for informing day to day actions. Tom Peters in his book *Thriving on Chaos* states

> 'In a time of turbulence and uncertainty, we must be able to take instant action on the front line. But to support such action-taking at the front, everyone must have a clear understanding about what the organisation is trying to achieve.'
>
> Peters (1987)

Organizations must 'develop and live an enabling and empowering vision'. Other writers are equally enthusiastic about values. Deal and Kennedy (1988) write that values are

> 'the basic concepts and beliefs of an organisation; as such they form the heart of corporate culture. Values define "success" in concrete terms for employees – if you do this you too will be a success.'
>
> Deal and Kennedy (1988)

Success in commercial settings usually equates with improved financial performance. In a sporting context success would be measured in terms of an improvement in team and individual performance. This improvement would result from attention to a number of factors. Firstly, at the simplest level, the coherence that results from firming up the organization's culture will lead to a better run organization which increases the likelihood of better performance 'on the field'. A defined culture and the vision and values which come from it provides a basis for practical action-taking which leads to improved organizational efficiency. The key point here is that it becomes easier for sports organizations to identify and address organizational efficiency issues if the organization has coherence, a clear sense of where it is heading, with what kind of values and goals. Under these circumstances the organization has a better chance of answering questions of the kind, 'What organizational factors need to be addressed because by doing so it will help us achieve our goals? What organizational factors are making it less likely that we will achieve our goals? Is this practical decision about how the organization operates consistent with our values?'

Secondly, individuals and teams will improve their performance because they will have a clearer idea of how their goals and short-term objectives have a coherent link to the goals and values of the organization. Defining the culture, vision and values helps to identify the long-term goals of the organization which in turn inform an individual athlete's goals and short-term objectives. (This process can also happen in reverse where the organization begins by taking the goals of individual athletes and works these into a composite whole-organization view of the future.) To put it another way, it helps those in the organization to better understand the complex nature of the relationship between the goals of an individual athlete, the team and the organization.

The third area is more difficult to define but is about the 'feel good' factor that results from being part of a team and an organization that is pulling together, is in harmony, has synergy (i.e. is greater than the sum of its parts). In the sports psychology literature this notion of team cohesion and synergy is a well-accepted phenomenon. This chapter suggests that this synergy and the resulting improvements in performance can be greater if it applies at the level of the whole organization rather than simply at the level of the team of athletes who constitute only a part (albeit an important part) of the organization. It is important to remember that the team of athletes is only one team within the organization; management teams, support teams and administrative teams also need to feel a part of the organization, they also need to function efficiently and in harmony if the organization is to maximize its full potential and if performance on the field is to be the best it can be.

Finally it is suggested that performance will improve because the athletes and support staff play a part in the process of defining the organization's culture. Lessons learned in industry and education suggest that when members of the organization are involved in determining the direction of the organization they show more commitment, have higher self-esteem and that these 'intangible' factors positively affect performance.

The principles behind the process of development

The model of development is simple and robust. In brief the model supports the development of systems and structures at three levels

- the whole organization
- the team(s) within the organization
- the individual sportspersons within the team(s)

Improvement in performance is based upon *six key principles* within this three tier model. Those involved in the development process need to feel comfortable with these basic principles of changing behaviour at the three levels described. The organization needs to act as follows:

1. Identify and develop a culture for the organization

This culture is a composite of the vision and values of the organization which, in turn, help identify clear organizational goals which then inform team objectives which in turn inform individual performance targets. Vision and values cannot be imported; organizations must develop their own. An organization and the people within it need ownership if the values are going to influence behaviour through times thick and thin. One organization cannot simply copy the values of another no matter how successful they appear to have been for the other organization. This runs the risk of the 'not invented here' syndrome operating.

NB: Having identified a guiding vision does not mean that this vision cannot be changed or modified as the process develops; indeed it is likely that it will be altered.

2. Make sure that the culture, vision, values and the goals and objectives that follow have been developed by all members of the organization

Involvement of all members of the organization in developing vision and values is a key part of the process. 'Outsiders' can guide and indeed should play a vital role in the development process, but visions, values and practice come from within not from outside. Within this process team-building is achieved because team members have played a part in developing and are clear about the team goals and their part in accomplishing these goals.

Once agreed, vision and values should be communicated frequently and clearly. This would normally result in, at one level, a mission statement, policy document or charter for the organization. At other levels it might result in the production of operating procedures that define 'the way we do things around here'.

3. Notice, encourage and reinforce behaviour which meets these goals or is directed by them

The basis of this approach is that there should be positive reinforcement of all behaviour that is consistent with the organization's goals. As a culture and a country we are not always very good at telling people when they have done well. The very simple principle is that if people perform 'the required behaviour' they are more likely to repeat the behaviour if they feel positively reinforced or rewarded for doing so. Often this reinforcement will be intrinsic or will result from improved performance; at other times it will need to be externally delivered. Not all members need reinforcement of the same type or at the same level. The policy of the organization will identify the broad principles of reinforcement, but the management of individuals will continue to require the discretion of coaches and managers as to what works and what does not.

4. Identify the limits of behaviour which do not meet the goals and the organization's responses to them

Behaviour can be positively developed by ensuring that there is clarity and consistency about how the organization handles situations when something goes wrong. Fundamentally a positive approach uses a supportive method to achieve the identified behaviour or goals; however, there is also a need for an organization to have identified disciplinary procedures when agreed principles are contravened. These procedures should be consensus-based, fair and *reasonably* consistently applied. The devil is in the word 'reasonably'; just as individuals respond to different kinds of reinforcement, so too they respond to different forms of sanctions or punishments. It is usually false comfort to imagine that an organization can identify a disciplinary procedure that determines that misdemeanour x irrevocably and inevitably leads to punishment y. The organization's policy statement should again identify the broad parameters for action but allow flexibility and the discretion of coaches and managers. That flexibility will apply is what needs to be made clear; the consistency lies in the flexibility, i.e. we will be consistently flexible.

5. Find supportive structures for those who find success difficult

As was suggested in point 4, rather than relying on punishment as a method of controlling behaviour it is usually more productive to look for ways of helping the person with a problem solve that problem. Punishment unless it is extreme is, by and large, a poor modifier of human behaviour. The programmes of support should be designed to help all athletes and support staff fulfil their part in achieving the organization's goals. The 'right' culture will increase the likelihood of programmes of support for individual sportspersons being successful. Sport psychologists working with the individual athlete using relaxation or cognitive restructuring programmes, for example, are likely to find these more effective in a context where these programmes are seen as necessary to achieve team and organization objectives.

6. Make sure that in managing better performance the organization uses the 'lightest possible touch' and the least restrictive systems and structures of managing behaviour

One goal of this system is to develop independent, self-motivated athletes. In order to achieve this goal it is vital that the organization offer the 'right' level of support. If the system is too restrictive it will not meet athletes' needs nor will it if the system is too 'flabby'. Treating athletes like children when they do not need that level of structure will inhibit performance; giving too much freedom at a time when athletes need support and guidance will have a similarly damaging effect. The trick, as good managers and coaches know, is to match their level of support to that required by the athlete (and other members of the organization) at different times and under different circumstances.

The development process

The principles of managing behaviour or improving performance are translated into a developmental process that will usually include the following components and events:

1. The management team meet to consider the implications of getting involved in the development process

They will need to get a sense of the long-term goals of the work and the likely demands on resources and personnel; they will need an idea of the likely timescale for development. This group will also need to decide on how this work will be evaluated. Generally, evaluation will involve some form of pre- and post-intervention measures. This evaluation should consider changes in the way the organization operates, changes in team and individual performance and changes in people's perceptions of change – how the organization was then and how it is now. The team should discuss the implications of using an 'outside consultant' to facilitate the work; if it is decided to use a consultant they should meet the management team to establish the kind of problems being experienced and the areas which it is felt could be improved. If an outside consultant is used they can play a central role in carrying out step two of the process.

2. Conducting a review or 'audit' of the situation in the organization, its strength and weaknesses

If possible and practical this should involve getting opinions from all members of the organization. If a rating scale is used this can be repeated at the end of the process to see what changes people perceive have happened. If it is not practically possible to interview or questionnaire everybody a carefully selected section of the organization should be 'reviewed'. The review can take a number of forms; questionnaire, structured interviews and observation are the most commonly used. The review will seek to highlight positive aspects of the organization as well as areas for development. It will also look at how the unwritten rules and values that people have, fit with the written policy and/or operating procedures.

3. The data are collated such that patterns and commonly held views begin to emerge; this collated data provide the raw material for discussion at a number of workshops or discussions involving all members

These 'meetings' will probably take up one, or perhaps two days. The broad purpose of the meetings is to look at 'where are we now?' and 'where do we want to be in the future?' Specifically, through a process of discussion and problem-solving, members working in small groups will seek to identify key values and to define the culture of the organization. From this will flow agreement about other more specific areas of the organization's operations. The discussion groups will address and reach agreement about those areas already referred to, namely developing long-term goals, team and individual expectations of performance, positive systems of encouragement, responses to inappropriate levels of performance, organizational factors which need attention because they are inhibiting performance, e.g. state of training facilities, team kit, relationships with the press, etc. Evaluation criteria will be identified in order that managers, coaches, athletes and support staff will know when they have achieved their goals. Performance criteria will not always be performance related.

4. Information from this meeting is synthesized, usually by a small, cross-sectional working group and written into the organization's mission statement, policy or charter

This document will also describe any operating procedures which have been agreed by the group. This document should remain in draft stage at this time because it may be modified as the rest of the process unfolds. In addition action plans will be completed that detail the 'what', 'who', 'how', 'where' and 'when' of the agreed changes.

5. This group along with the senior management team will decide how this mission statement is 'kept alive' through written and verbal communications

Other ways of firming up or representing the organization's culture will also be agreed (logos, team kit, etc.).

6. Teams (athletes and support) within the organization then meet together to identify with managers and coaches those team performance goals that are consistent with the policy/charter of the organization

What happens in effect is that the organization's goals are 'differentiated' for the team in question and appropriately specified in terms of team goals. At this stage goals for the 'first team' might be quite different to 'second or third' team goals. Again 'incentives' and 'sanctions' systems are identified at this level. Any organizational details or 'blocks' to required performance which have not been raised yet and which need attention at the team level, e.g. state of team kit, captaincy of team, are identified at this point.

7. Any team training needs which have not already been identified are agreed

For example, specific training routines or team building exercises may be agreed. Measures of success within the broad evaluation criteria identified at the organization level are agreed. At this level performance criteria might include measures of organizational efficacy at the team level and group cohesion, as well as any performance team goals.

If an outside consultant is being used then this would be an appropriate time to meet again with the management team to get a view of how the development process is going and if changes need to be made.

8. The next task is for coaches to sit down with individual athletes and to agree those individual performance targets which will need to be met in the context of what the team needs to achieve

It may be at this stage that, as individuals identify their performance targets, some of the team goals may be found to be unrealistic (perhaps too ambitious or perhaps not ambitious enough) and so may need to be redefined. *Individuals must be motivated by their targets because it is these targets for these individuals that represent the reality of this process of development; without these targets the process will not come alive.* It may be at this stage that the team's and even the organization's visions and goals need to be redefined. If this happens this should be seen as a positive step, inevitable in a living organization, and not cause for recrimination. What this means is that the process is in reality cyclic – the mission statement and the vision of the organization set the context for team and individual goals but this vision is redefined as athletes ask themselves 'What does this mean for me?'

As well as targets for performance, the coach and athlete will need to identify those levels of positive reinforcement and negative consequences which are seen as necessary for the achievement of these targets. As in step 6 any organizational changes necessary to support the individual programmes are also identified. Again appropriate individual evaluation criteria are identified.

9. Individual support, training programmes are set up

This may be the level at which the sport psychologist will offer individual performers support.

10. Date set for a whole-organization review

This might take place about three months after the initial meeting. The purpose of this meeting is to check on progress (not all of which will have been successful) and pull the organization together again by reaffirming vision and values. New goals can be set if necessary.

Summary

The notion of team culture and the effect that this can have on performance is not a new idea in sport. What is different about this approach is the suggestion that benefits to performance will accrue when the organization, the team or teams and the individual are all working in harmony. The key positive features of this model of developing a better performing organization are as follows:

- The members (athletes and support staff) of the organization have a say in developing the culture, and hence goals and values, of the organization. This motivates better performance at all levels of the organization.
- The developmental process is positive, supportive and non-threatening.
- The goals and values of the organization are set down and communicated to all in a written policy or charter.
- These organizational goals give the management team a clearer mandate to manage an agreed framework within which management tasks are identified.
- Individuals, teams and support staff are clearer about their 'performance objectives' and how these objectives fit into the overall goals for the organization.
- Support structures within the organization are more effectively directed.

- The organization can more easily determine whether it is operating in a manner which supports the organization's goals.
- How effectively the organization is performing is determined by measuring those changes, consistent with the organization's mission statement, in the performance of the organization, the teams, the individual athletes and the support staff.

References

Deal, T.E. and Kennedy, A.A. (1988) *Corporate Cultures*. Harmondsworth: Penguin.

Peters, T. (1987) *Thriving on Chaos*. London: Pan Books.

Part Four

Freud on fencing: the role of unconscious psychological defences

Carole Seheult

Sport: Fencing

Prologue

Fencer A vs Romanian champion (Final score 5–4)

Very intimidating because of his size – he almost makes you freeze over what you're going to do. He makes a lot of attacks. When I got my last perfect hit it was the one I was after – that flick on the wrist. I was waiting for that, but I missed it a couple of times, and this time, I thought 'This is it, I'm going to get it; if I don't, that's it. I'd be in big trouble then'. It's being consistent, just going together. The first I took – I drew a counter attack, a high prime riposte to his leg, which he didn't like, but that's the way it goes y'know. It was double, double, then he got the nice one on me. Then I thought he had another on me and I was down; then I had to hang in but I daren't attack him, as he was so well covered and he's got such a bloody good reach. I can't get through so I waited for the outside and he did exactly what I wanted him to do, I was just waiting for it. Then it was four all and I knew if it came to a scuffle it was anyone's. Then I saw one of us had got a light on ... The last one (hit) was a bit funny really. That's the way it goes – that's the luck you really need.

... and 15 minutes later

Fencer A vs Canadian champion (Final score 3–5)

I knew I was going to miss sometime and I missed at the end unfortunately. The thing was, when I lost the fight was when he did that hit to my toe. I didn't think he was going to do it. If I'd really taken it seriously I'd have just gone on and hit him but I didn't do that and it's really what cost me the fight. That's the turning point – the hit to the toe. That was a gift actually; all I needed to do was to hit him – he was totally open y'know. It was stupid. I didn't react then. It's still a good sort of fight but it's still disappointing. I still can't get the distance right to quite get through at the end. I should have made another double and another double until something went wrong, but it's difficult. I didn't know how to fight him. I went on the piste not having a clue what to do. He's got an awkward style; I'd not faced anyone like that for a while.

Introduction

The aims of this chapter are twofold: firstly to introduce and discuss the potential for the use of the Defence Mechanisms Test (DMT) (Kragh, 1969) in the assessment of the personalities of competitive athletes, and secondly to report on a study of the profiles of unconscious defence mechanisms, as identified by the DMT, in a group of competitive fencers.

As its name suggests, the DMT claims to measure subconscious psychological defence processes, which, according to the psychodynamic model of personality upon which this test is based, are activated within the individual whenever confronted by a situation perceived as either threatening or anxiety provoking. Under such circumstances automatic patterns of behaviour, triggered by these subconscious processes, may come to form major and influential components in an individual's repertoire of responses to which he or she will typically resort as a means of coping and retaining mental equilibrium when coming up against situations which might otherwise prove overwhelming.

The DMT was originally constructed by Kragh in 1957 with the 'practical motive' of being used as a personality test in the selection of pilots for the Swedish Air Force. In this context it was considered to go beyond the usual personality questionnaires and interviews which, along with tests such as the Rorschach, had proved to be of little or no value in diminishing the failure rate at the basic training school (Kragh, 1991).

Since that time the DMT has been applied in a number of different contexts including personnel selection and to predict performance in a wide variety of what are considered as potentially stressful occupations. These include the selection of naval divers (Ursin *et al.*, 1978;

Vaernes, 1982), parachutists (Baade *et al.*, 1978) and public service vehicle drivers (Svensson and Trygg, 1994); to predict accident proneness (Neuman, 1978; Svensson and Trygg, 1994); and in clinical settings as a means of differential diagnosis (Rubino *et al.*, 1991).

Given this description, the DMT would appear, at least on the face of things, to have distinct possibilities as a way of understanding some of the individual differences which are recognized as existing in the way in which athletes and players respond to the high levels of stress considered as inherent in competitive sport. The technique might also offer a useful approach to furthering research into some of the underlying processes which mediate the individual experiences of stress, the complexities of which have yet to be completely understood (Jones and Hardy, 1990).

So far only one empirical study (that of Apitzsch and Berggren (1993)) has been published which has used the DMT in the area of sport. In a large scale descriptive study of the personality of elite soccer players the authors investigated various psychological factors which might affect the performance. Amongst a number of interesting findings, significant differences were indicated in the patterns of psychological defences between 'more' and 'less' successful players. 'More' successful players showed significantly more occurrences of two specific signs of defence, namely Repression and Introjection of the Opposite Sex. These are manifested behaviourally by the 'more' successful players showing characteristically higher levels of energy and possessing the ability to turn potentially challenging situations to their own advantage.

For the purposes of this chapter Apitzsch and Berggren's (1993) study is used as a starting point; however, the focus in this case will be on the application of their model in the sport of fencing. Subjects for the empirical study were all British fencers, a number of whom have represented their country in epee, foil or sabre, weapons used at Olympic and World Championship level.

Defence mechanisms and how they operate

Before embarking upon a detailed description of the DMT and discussing how it might be used in applied sports psychology, it is probably worthwhile reviewing those aspects of the psychoanalytic model from which these particular psychological constructs are derived.

Understanding the way in which people perceive and then deal with pressurizing or stressful experiences in their lives is a key concept in most of the theories of personality which have been developed over the past century. The observation that individuals will protect themselves by either failing to recognize or by distorting otherwise painful perceptions of pressures, threats or personal inadequacies is both a familiar and accepted aspect of human behaviour. However, the psychological processes which trigger off these defensive strategies and manoeuvres are, by their very nature, not available to consciousness nor accessible to individual awareness (Cramer, 1991).

The concept of unconscious psychological defence mechanisms was originally put forward by Freud in 1894 in his study entitled *The Neuro-Psychoses of Defence*. Freud saw these processes as playing a vital role in his psychoanalytic theory of personality where they were employed by the ego in its 'struggle against painful or unendurable ideas or affects' (Freud, 1937).

In a further discussion of this concept in the *Ego and the Id* (1923), Freud argued that the ego and the id exist in a state of constant conflict resulting in unpleasant instinctual impulses, such as anxiety or guilt, which seek to find expression via the ego and its various functions. To protect itself against these potentially overwhelming feelings it is hypothesized that the ego seeks to bar such impulses by the employment of what is termed in psychoanalytic theory as mechanisms of defence. These processes, which are unconscious and therefore inaccessible to awareness, trigger off behaviours which are observable and serve the function of modifying the individual's experience of anxiety or may, as in the case of Repression, eliminate it completely.

Further work by Anna Freud published in 1937 elaborates upon the workings of defensive strategies and illustrates ways in which they may be observed to operate, citing numerous clinical examples. She defined the role of defence mechanisms as ways by which painful and unwanted feelings are kept at bay or made more bearable. She also provided an initial classification of the major defence mechanisms based upon the nature of the processes which are assumed to be taking place at the unconscious level. These, she suggests, include Repression, Denial, Reaction Formation, Regression, Identification with the Aggressor, Projection, Isolation and different forms of Introjection (Freud, 1937).

Fenichel (1945) divides ego defences into two categories which he terms *successful* and *unsuccessful*. Successful defences are those which bring about a cessation of that which is being warded off, usually assumed to be unpleasant feelings such as anxiety or guilt, and unsuccessful defences, those which necessitate continual repetition of the warding off process 'to prevent the eruption of the warded-off impulses'.

Successful defences are usually considered as coming under the category of sublimation. These are defences whose common factor is that they allow an acceptable expression and discharge by the ego of so-called undesirable impulses. Frequently quoted examples of sublimation are artists, potters and bread-makers who are considered to sublimate their desire to handle faeces by painting, working with clay or kneading dough. The playing of contact sports such as rugby or ice-hockey has also been suggested by some writers as the sublimation of aggression (Kline, 1984).

The second category of defences, those classified as unsuccessful, include the pathogenic responses which are considered by Fenichel (1945) to be the basis of neuroses.

Psychological defences and sport

The area of competitive sport, particularly at the elite level, is likely to provide ample opportunity for the exercise of an individual's defence mechanisms. Head-to-head competition or involvement in major championships where an athlete or player has to be prepared to put him or herself on the line, to ask of themselves testing questions regarding levels of skill and commitment, and to extend limits of performance, will undoubtedly trigger instinctual feelings of anxiety against which the ego will need to protect itself. Further pressures may also come from external sources such as relationships with significant others, for example, coaches, sponsors, officials and family, as well as internal feelings regarding rivals and opponents.

So far in this chapter most of the discussion regarding the role and nature of defence mechanisms has been centred on their relationship to seemingly negative aspects of the processes. Freud's original writings associated defences with a variety of psychological problems while Anna Freud (1937) and Fenichel (1945) both support the view that the operation of defence mechanisms is the major cause of neurotic psychopathology.

Most of the early users of the DMT, notably Kragh (1969),

Neuman (1978), Vaernes *et al.* (1988a) and Svensson and Trygg (1994) used the test for negative selection purposes. All suggested that high levels of defensiveness were possible contraindications for the training of individuals such as pilots, divers and public service vehicle drivers from whom consistent levels of performance in terms of reality testing and decision making are demanded.

However, despite this apparent thumbs down for defensiveness not everyone has been equally critical and there have been a number of suggestions that employing defences may allow an increased tolerance of stress by making unpleasant instinctual impulses more bearable (Freud, 1937). This view has also been supported by Cramer (1991) who suggests that defences are part of the normal developmental processes and play an adaptive role in the lives of everyone, children, adolescents and adults.

In their pioneering monograph on the personalities of elite soccer players Apitzsch and Berggren (1993) marshall the arguments and evidence for a more adaptive role for these processes within the overall organization of the personality. In line with other writers in this area they suggest a less uncompromising, dualistic function for the defences which allows for both interaction and responsiveness to changes in the individual's internal and external environment.

Continuing with this more flexible stance, the writers put forward a model suggesting that the conscious behavioural manifestations of the defences may be experienced and subsequently emerge at a point along a continuum designated at one end as being 'highly adaptive' and at the other end as 'highly maladaptive'. At the adaptive end of the continuum behaviours will occur which may be useful and beneficial to the player and at the maladaptive end behaviours will occur which are considered to be potentially deleterious to performance and mental equilibrium.

In any given circumstance the level of adaptation accorded to the behaviour and the point on the continuum at which it emerges, will be determined not only by the context in which the stressor occurs but also by the number of factors which, according to the authors, include the individual's ego strength, the intensity of the threat, previous experience of the threat, and the interaction between and/or simultaneous use of, different mechanisms (Apitzsch and Berggren, 1993).

This formalization of a dualistic model relating the activation of defence mechanisms to typical patterns of overt behaviour which vary in their level of adaptiveness with regard to the individual's function, is a unique feature of Apitzsch and Berggren's (1993) study. However, although not previously put forward in precisely this fashion, the ideas that it incorporates are supported by numerous workers in the area beginning with Freud himself.

Example of a psychological defence

To serve as an example of how this model might operate in practice and in the context of fencing, the sport on which the latter part of this paper will focus, consider the behaviour of a fencer who habitually uses the defence of Denial, the direct negation of a threat. In a competitive situation such a fencer may refuse to be cowed by the 'unbeatable' reputation of his opponent. This is undoubtedly an adaptive response. However, in the same circumstances, despite refusing to be overwhelmed by his opponent's reputation, the fencer would be ill-advised to deny the reality of the same opponent's depth of experience, level of technical skill or standard of mental or physical toughness.

Building on their dualistic model of defences, Apitzsch and Berggren (1993) develop this further formulating descriptions of the classical defence mechanisms, following each with their hypotheses as to how that particular defence might be manifested behaviourally, both in general as well as in the context of soccer. Their list of descriptions is restricted to the ten defence mechanisms identified by the DMT (Kragh, 1985) and is coupled with a descriptor which summarizes the respective adaptive and maladaptive endpoints. For example, the adaptive endpoint associated with Repression is described as 'energetic' and the maladaptive descriptor as 'conversion'; and for the defence of Isolation, 'stability' and 'inflexibility' respectively.

Defences and their behavioural manifestations

In order to make this meaningful with regard to fencing, the descriptions of the ten defences, as identified by the DMT, and the adaptive/maladaptive endpoint descriptors, as suggested by Apitzsch and Berggren (1993) have been taken and the descriptions of behavioural manifestations modified to fit the specific context of fencing. These are listed in the section below.

Repression

Repression takes place when the ego finds itself struggling with instinctual stimuli (Freud, 1937). The defence of Repression has been described as consisting of an 'unconsciously, purposeful forgetting' or a denial of entry to the conscious awareness of the threatening or anxiety provoking perception (Fenichel, 1945). Gaps in reactions, 'tip of the tongue' phenomena and, in the extreme, hysterical reactions have all been described as associated with the use of this defence (Fenichel, 1945; Kragh, 1969).

Apitzsch and Berggren (1993) suggest adaptive and maladaptive endpoints as being 'Energetic' and 'Conversion' respectively. The suggested adaptive endpoint on the behavioural continuum results from what the writers describe as the antithesis of hysterical conversion which can be observed in the individual as highly energetic behaviour, nervous ticks, vivid daydreaming and a 'dramatizing appealing attitude'. The descriptors of the two endpoints characteristic of this defence are as follows.

Adaptive (Energetic)

The fencer acts instantaneously and without hesitation. He or she responds flexibly both mentally and physically and has the capacity to operate simultaneously on a number of tracks. The fencer meets the demands of the situation vigorously delivering fast attacks, defending and responding in a decisive manner.

Maladaptive (Conversion)

The athlete becomes paralysed or frozen to the spot not knowing what to do next or completely losing track of the ongoing situation. He or she may 'forget' how to do things which in normal circumstances would be automatic or second nature.

Isolation

Isolation is a defence mechanism which has been associated with compulsion neuroris. In using this defence the individual separates and breaks the connections between the emotional and cognitive aspects of a situation and is resistant to any demonstration of their existence (Fenichel, 1945). He or she erects a 'mental wall' to keep the affect and emotion out of awareness. By doing this the person strives to keep a clear mind, often intellectualizing situations and distancing themself from emotional upsets created by negative impulses. The descriptors of the two endpoints characteristic of this defence are as follows.

Adaptive (Stability)

The fencer performs reliably and consistently meeting expectations even when he or she has to change their approach or make adjustments to the 'game plan'. This consistency will be maintained regardless of the level of competition.

Maladaptive (Inflexibility)

The fencer is unchangeable and become stuck in his or her ways, continually ruminating over small difficulties and finding it difficult to start new tasks or meet new challenges. The athlete cannot change strategy or come up with new ideas. He or she will execute the same kind of moves even though they are not successful and have the same kind of thoughts which go round and round in their head.

Denial

Threats of disturbing stresses are negated. Denial is considered as a primitive defence associated by a number of writers with a view that its users have dishonest or psychopathic personalities. Sjoback (1991) calls denial 'the last line of defence' and is a reaction to and directed against unpleasant and upsetting external events (Freud, 1937; Fenichel, 1945). The descriptors of the two endpoints characteristic of this defence are the following.

Adaptive (Ignorance of adversity)

The fencer's level of performance is maintained however difficult the challenges being faced and even when realistically the chances of winning are very slim. As the fencer does not perceive any danger the possibility of losing does not cross their mind even if they are trailing by six or seven points and only fifteen seconds remain on the clock.

Maladaptive (Ignorance of reality)

The athlete does not understand the extent of the challenge they are being called upon to face. They therefore misjudge their own behaviour in relation to the situation. For example, a fencer may totally underestimate the strength of an opponent and fail to make the required effort and win the fight.

Reaction formation

This defence operates by reversing affect to manifest itself as the opposite and is said to originate from the infantile strategy of concealing unpleasant or dangerous impulses; for example, the ardent pacifist who reacts against his aggression or the rugby player whose emphasis on heterosexual virility is really a reaction formation to latent homosexuality (Kline, 1984). It is seen as bearing similarities to Denial and as being linked with the occurrence of aggression inhibition and psychosomatic symptoms such as stomach ulcer (Kragh, 1969). Reactions thus elicited from the subject and whose goal may be to conceal the original impulse, often turn out to be both exaggerated and ambiguous (Apitzsch and Berggren, 1993). The descriptors of the two endpoints characteristic of this defence are as follows.

Adaptive (Benign interpersonal relationships)

This may be a particularly adaptive defence for a fencer in that aggressive impulses may be expressed as kindly, social intentions! As a member of a squad or a team this person will be seen as maintaining good positive relationships and as helpful to others.

Maladaptive (Ambiguous interpersonal relationships and behaviour)

Used maladaptively this defence manifests itself in communications which are not straightforward and the misjudgement of other people's emotional signals or attempts to make contact. It has also been suggested that an athlete or player using this defence maladaptively may not exert all efforts in a fight but back off and give away a victory. Such fencers might be expected to lack the 'killer instinct' when finding themselves in a closely fought encounter.

Identification with the aggressor

According to Anna Freud (1937) this defence comes about through the introjection of some characteristic of the object which has created anxiety and by manifesting that characteristic by imitation. Thus it is considered that people who use this rather more rare type of defence do so as a reaction to having experienced aggression directed towards themselves during childhood. The descriptors of the two endpoints characteristic of this defence are the following.

Adaptive (Assertiveness)

The fencer with this defence in his or her repertoire would be likely to perform powerfully and with determination. He or she would be a forceful but fairminded fighter with no intention of harming an opponent. He or she would show no hesitation in taking on the toughest opposition.

Maladaptive (Aggressiveness)

Used maladaptively this defence may cause a fencer to lose control of their aggressiveness hitting their opponent far harder than necessary and running the risk of incurring penalties for unfair play.

Introaggression

In this defence aggressive impulses, originally directed outward, come to be turned inwards against the self. This is said to make the person vulnerable to passive and depressive moods. Freud (1937) gives a case example of the development of this reaction corresponding with the latency period and following jealousy of older and younger male siblings. Fenichel (1945) makes connections between inwardly directed hostility and masochism. The descriptors of the two endpoints characteristic of this defence are the following.

Adaptive (Ability to withstand pain)

Apitzsch and Berggren (1993) suggest mental and physical tolerance for pain as being the adaptive modality for expression of this defence. This would be particularly useful to epeeists for whom it would be advantageous to withstand the pressure of hard hitting opponents without flinching or backing off.

Maladaptive (Pain seeking)

Becoming actively involved in or exposing oneself to potentially painful situations could lead to a detrimental outcome for a fencer. It could also lead to a higher risk of injury. It is hypothesized that athletes or players with a tendency to push themselves beyond their mental and physical limits or 'over-train' could exemplify the maladaptive operation of this defence.

Introjection (identification with the opposite sex)

Fenichel (1945) describes the defence of Introjection as 'an example of how primitive automatic mechanisms are tamed and used by the ego for its purposes'. By taking in (introjecting) and incorporating attributes of the opposite sex the ego defends itself against external threats but at the same time may become confused by the alien introject. The descriptors of the two endpoints characteristic of this defence are as follows.

Adaptive (Immediate adaptiveness)

Used adaptively this defence enables the athlete or player to accommodate rapidly to new situations and to settle into new regimes. In competition the fencer will adapt quickly to his opponent's changing tactics and modify his or her own strategies accordingly.

Maladaptive (Softness)

Rather than adaptive, the fencer's behaviour is seen as too malleable or even 'wimpish'. He or she may also fail to attack when offered the opportunity and be reluctant to use their full physical capacity.

Polymorphous introjection

In this defence a number of external objects may be incorporated or internalized to confer 'omnipotence' of function and satisfy the individual's need for an auxiliary ego. Kragh (1985) suggests that the need for Introjection comes about to fill in voids in the individual's self-perception, for example, problems with self-esteem created by the undermining of the individual's self-confidence. The descriptors of the two endpoints characteristic of this defence are as follows.

Adaptive (Ability to thrive on others)

An individual who characteristically employs this defence does so to gain the approval of others. This has the effect of making him or her a loyal group member as long as these efforts are appreciated by others. The same goes for performance; the athlete will maintain a high level of performance as long as he or she is being encouraged by team-mates.

Maladaptive (Dependency)

The athlete continually demands support and approval from team-mates, coaches and officials. They also become dependent on others, are unable to take the initiative or make their own decision.

Projection

According to Fenichel (1945) Projection as a defence is the ego's rejection or 'spitting out' of painful or unpleasant impulses. Threats from the inside are avoided by projecting these feelings onto other external objects. Not only hostile feelings but loving and erotic feelings can be projected. It is suggested by Apitzsch and Berggren (1993) that people who use Projection tend to be observant individuals, who are both mentally alert and physiologically aroused. The descriptors of the two endpoints characteristic of this defence are the following.

Adaptive (Sensibility)

This defence would see to be one which would be highly desirable for a competitive fencer. Individuals with this defence are described as being able to sense what is happening and going on in the minds of others. They would probably be endowed with good 'game-reading' skills, quickly becoming aware of their opponent's strengths and weaknesses and able to capitalize on this information.

Maladaptive (Suspiciousness)

Maladaptive Projection is manifested in behaviour suggesting suspiciousness and distrust of others. Within the team such a person may be seen as a bit of a 'wet blanket', imagining that other people are conspiring against him or her.

Regression

Regression is a means of defence employed by the ego when meeting with frustration. In Regression the individual may return to a more infantile level of function when their wishes were not frustrated, or alternatively to a state of primary narcissism (Fenichel, 1945). The main reasons for this psychological return are the feelings of relative security which might be encountered and the enjoyment of childish 'wish-fulfilment' rather than having to confront adult reality. The descriptors of the two endpoints characteristic of this defence are the following.

Adaptive (Creativity)

Again the adaptive use of this defence might be seen as highly advantageous to a competitive fencer, its main characteristics being the ability to be creative and find new solutions to old problems. A fencer using this defence would be unlikely to fall into old routines and be regarded as innovative and unpredictable with an ability to vary tactics and strategies.

Maladaptive (Fragmentation)

Apitzsch and Berggren (1993) suggest that maladaptive Regression will create a temporary breakdown in mental function resulting in a loss of reality-testing. It may also precipitate irrational and inappropriate behaviour perceived as bizarre by others around.

Defences and sport

So where does this leave the relationship between defences and sport? How might knowing about the psychological defences operating within an individual athlete or player prove useful or helpful in the enhancement of sporting performance?

One important connection here is the relationship which exists between stress and performance in competition. It is now well established that a performer's experience of stress and anxiety can have a critical effect upon the outcome of competition, particularly where individual differences in ability to remain focused, self-confident and composed under pressure could be the decisive factor. Thus the role of defences in mediating the experience of threat or anxiety becomes crucial, and a better understanding of the way an individual athlete is likely to respond in situations such as selections trials, qualifying competitions for major championships or even Olympic finals, can only be regarded as useful.

The Defence Mechanisms Test

Background to Test

As already discussed, the DMT was constructed some 35 years ago by Swedish psychologists working at Lund University. Since then, although considerable research and development has taken place resulting in a substantial literature, awareness and application of the DMT has remained restricted to the Scandinavian countries and a small number of other centres in Western Europe. An updated review of available methods, including the DMT, and results of studies aimed at measuring and quantifying defence mechanisms can be found in Olff *et al.* (1991).

Within the UK there are less than ten psychologists trained and experienced in the use of the DMT and only two British psychologists (Kline and Cooper) have contributed to the scientific discussion in this area (Cooper and Kline, 1986; Kline, 1987, 1991, 1993).

An evaluation of the DMT was carried out by Cooper and Kline (1986) and a further discussion of the scientific status of the test was given by Kline in 1987. Kline also reviewed the test with regard to its value as a psychometric instrument (Kline, 1993). His overall conclusions regarding the DMT are that despite his feeling that some of the more striking claims made for the test should be viewed with caution, the data regarding the clinical uses and also data derived from the application of the test in military selection, are more convincing. This being the case, he supports the view of the DMT as being 'a most useful personality test' in clinical and other applied contexts.

Instructions for the administration of the test and a description of the tachistoscope can be found in the DMT Manual which was published in English in 1985 (Kragh, 1985). However, the mechanics of administering the DMT are one thing and, although they could probably be acquired in a relatively short amount of time, the scoring and interpretation are a different matter, requiring a much longer period of supervised experience before an acceptable level of competency and reliability can be attained. For this reason a detailed description of the methodology will not be presented.

The basic framework of the DMT rests in three areas, perceptgenetics, psychoanalytic theory and projective tests, all of which tend to be controversial in their own right amongst mainstream British psychologists.

Perceptgenetics refers to both a theory and a set of techniques, an account of which appears in Kragh and Smith's book *Perceptgenetic Analysis* (Kragh and Smith, 1970). As well as the DMT, other techniques included in this category are the Spiral After-Effect Test, the Stroop Word-Colour Test and the Meta-Contrast Test. Like the DMT, these procedures claim to allow the identification of the unconscious psychological mechanisms which underlie perceptual processes, thus directly affecting perception and in turn, overt behaviour.

In the case of the DMT the perceptual processes which are revealed resemble what in psychoanalytic terms are called defence mechanisms, the psychological strategies which are activated within the individual's unconscious to deal with stress or threat. The nature, function and behavioural manifestations of defence mechanisms have already been discussed.

As in other perceptgenetic techniques the methodology of the DMT is characterized by the employment of serial presentations of visual stimuli. In the case of the DMT the visual stimuli are presented tachistoscopically, first below the threshold of perception and then, gradually, at decreasing speeds. These progress from an initial exposure of 100 ms to a final exposure time of 2 s (full time).

After each presentation subjects are required both to describe verbally and to draw what they have seen. Distortions and changes in the descriptions of the stimuli are held to reflect the inner conflicts and experiences of the individual. These deviations are known as 'signs' and correspond with the classic defences described by Anna Freud (1937), namely Repression, Isolation, Denial, Reaction formation, Identification with the Aggressor, Introaggression, Introjection, Projection and Regression.

The pictures used as visual stimuli in the DMT are composed of three elements; a young person of the same gender as the subject taking the DMT, designated the Hero; the Hero's attribute, a gender-appropriate object known as the Instrument, and an ugly looking adult the same gender as subject who appears in the picture to be threatening the Hero and referred to as the peripheral person or Pp. For a detailed discussion of the development of the test including the visual stimuli, readers are referred to the test manual (Kragh, 1985, 1991).

Scoring and interpretation

Following presentation of the pictures, the drawings and verbal reports (test protocols) are examined and all distortions or deviations from reality are recorded and coded according to the specific criteria for each sign and its variants (Kragh, 1985). These signs correspond with the ten major defences described previously. As an example of this, the sign for Repression is coded if either the Hero (H) or Peripheral person (Pp) is drawn or reported as being inanimate, an animal or an object. The main criteria for scoring the presence of a defence are listed below.

- *Repression.* Hero and Pp have quality of rigidity or are inanimate, masked or seen as animals.
- *Isolation.* Hero and Pp are separated from each other, parts of the picture are excluded or are whitened.
- *Denial.* Existence of threat is denied or made light of.
- *Reaction formation.* The threat is turned into its opposite.
- *Identification with the Aggressor.* Hero is person attacking or threatening.
- *Introaggression (turning against self).* Hero or instrument are hurt or worthless; instrument is a threat to hero.
- *Introjection of the opposite sex.* Hero's sex is not that of subject.
- *Introjection of another object.* Hero is duplicated or multiplied; the identity of the central figure is drastically changed.
- *Projection.* Successive and specific changes to Hero before Pp becomes threatening; secondary change to Pp via Hero.
- *Regression.* The structural content of the picture breaks down to a structure belonging to an earlier stage of perceptgenesis.

An accurate and useful interpretation of a subject's protocols requires considerable practice and experience. As well as identifying the various sign variants according to the criteria set down in the test manual, the tester also needs to take cognizance of the perceptgenetic series as a whole, noting the development of the signs through a number of phases, the appearance (and disappearance) of the threat and the emergence of all elements as a correct, undistorted visual percept.

Fencing

Fencing or swordsmanship has existed from the earliest times. Doubtless it had its beginnings with the ancient hunter-gatherers who used primitive swords and spears to hunt and kill animals for food and who also used the same weapons to defend themselves against their enemies or to conduct the occasional raiding party against a neighbouring tribe.

Today's Olympic fencer has come a long way since then. The modern sport comprises three weapons, foil, epee and sabre, with both men and women competing up to Olympic and World Championship level. The sport is regulated by its own international governing body, the Federation Internationale d'Escrime (FIE), who lay down all rules with regard to standards of equipment and safety and for competition worldwide.

Each of the three weapons is distinct with different rules and conventions for each weapon regarding the conduct of fights. Foil is descended from court sword fighting of the seventeenth and eighteenth centuries. The foil has a thin flexible blade and hits are scored with the point of the foil on the torso of the opponent. Foil technique emphasizes strong defence and a hard hitting attack to the body.

Epee fighting developed directly from the nineteenth century duelling. The target area for epee is anywhere on the opponent's body. Epee technique emphasizes timing, point control and a good counter attack. Double hits are allowed in epee fighting and as such have an influence on strategy.

Sabre fighting comes from the cavalry tradition and in keeping with its history the target area is anywhere above the opponent's waist. Here the emphasis of technique is on speed, feints and running attacks.

With all three weapons the aim of the fencer is the same, to score hits on his or her opponent within the designated target area and within the given time constraints. At the same time as attacking and scoring hits, there is the obvious requirement for the fencer to defend and avoid being hit. Each bout is refereed by a 'president' (now called a referee) whose job it is to conduct the fighting, decide the score, ensure safety and arbitrate in any dispute.

Notwithstanding the three different weapons and their separate emphases regarding technique, the requirements of competitive fencing are very similar. According to Pitman (1988) these include athleticism, mental and physical agility, and a high degree of technical skill. Within the bout great concentration is needed to both bluff and counter-bluff the opponent, feeding false information but at the same time trying to anticipate the opponent's next move. Other psychological skills considered necessary include stress management, visualization and relaxation, plus the ability to maintain focus, concentration and emotional composure under intense conditions of combat. However, these skills would not be considered specific to fencing, but would be applicable in almost every sport in the competitive situation. The flow of cognitions (both positive and negative), problem solving, planning and decision-making that may go on in the fencer's mind during competition is exemplified by the first-hand feedback recorded from a fencer (fencer A) immediately after the completion of two fights in a World Cup competition and presented in the Prologue at the beginning of the chapter. This quotation also demonstrates demand upon the fencer to develop a coherent game plan plus the ability to size up one's opponent's tactics and strategies rapidly and realistically.

Fencing is classified as a direct, individual sport and as such fencers might be expected to demonstrate distinct differences in the way each will approach competition and in the tactical styles they will employ in so doing. One system of classifying these different tactical styles is that cited by Wojciechowski (1993). This system was originally developed in the USSR and is based upon what the Russian coaches refer to as the coefficient of fencer activation (K_{act}) (Turecki, 1985). This factor is defined as the ratio of the number of attacks to the average time between the president's command 'Allez' and 'Halt'

$$K_{act} = N_{at}/t_f$$

where K_{act} is the coefficient of fencer's activation, N_{at} is the number of actual attacks, and t_f is the average time between the president's commands 'Allez' and 'Halt'. The higher the coefficient of fencers' activation the more attacks the fencer makes and the less time is spent on preparation.

Based upon this calculation four tactical styles have been proposed. These are

- permanently pressing
- manoeuvring/attacking
- manoeuvring/defending
- permanently defending.

Permanently pressing

This tactical style is more frequently seen amongst foilists. The fencer tends to attack constantly, either pushing forward attempting to make a premeditated attack or making false attacks which eventually end in real ones. When they do not succeed with this strategy these fencers try to increase the speed and intensity of their attacks rather than change to an alternative approach.

Manoeuvring/attacking

These fencers score hits by making attacks, varying distance and direction and making many preparatory actions. They tend to be active and take the initiative in distance and movement. These fencers are described as flexible and find it easy to change to a defensive strategy when required. They tend to be quick thinking.

Manoeuvring/defending

Wojciechowski (1993) describes those using this style as 'the most complete fencers'. They are tacticians who blend equally both defensive and attacking strokes and at the same time like to manoeuvre themselves on the piste to feel out the opponent. They make the most difficult opponents to fence.

Permanently/defending

Fencers in this group score mainly from ripostes and counter attacks and rarely make premeditated attacks. However, they may get forced into a situation where they have to attack either when running out of time or finding themselves backed up against the end of the piste. Wojciechowski (1993) describes them as different from other fencers by being more realistic in their assessment of events, more emotionally stable and by being in permanent control of the situation.

Taken from the psychodynamic point of view these four tactical styles and their associated behaviour can be said to be the overt manifestations of patterns of underlying psychodynamic processes, including defence mechanisms, which motivate and influence the individual fencer during competition. The next step therefore in better understanding these responses and influences in performance would be to consider which particular defences might be operating in fencers categorized as showing a specific tactical style. Based on the behavioural descriptions given by Wojciechowski (1993) the following defence mechanisms are hypothesized as being associated with the four different styles.

Permanently pressing

There is a suggestion here of assertiveness as well as that of inflexibility of the type associated by Apitzsch and Berggren (1993) with Identification with the aggressor and also with Isolation. Individuals showing Isolation are often said to be realistic but not creative.

Manoeuvring/attacking

Psychological characteristics mentioned here include energetic activity and quick thinking, both of which are associated with the adaptive endpoint of the defence of Repression. Tactical flexibility and adaptability are also mentioned, both of which are associated with Introjection of the opposite sex.

Manoeuvring/defending

This tactical style is described as that of the 'complete fencer'. Tactical characteristics include flexibility of approach and the skills of 'game reading', an awareness of what the opponent is trying to do. The defence mechanisms associated with these behaviours are Introjection of the opposite sex and Projection.

Permanently/defending

Fencers in the fourth category of tactical styles are described as realistic, emotionally stable and as being in good control of the situation on the piste. In terms of defences what is being described seems to be Isolation and Reaction formation (see Table 11.1).

The psychodynamics of fencing: tactics and defences

Empirical study

This study explores the nature and occurrence of psychodynamic factors as they occur in fencers and other individual sports performers and their possible influence upon performance in competition.

The study addresses three questions:

- What kind of unconscious psychological defences occur in the personalities of competitive fencers?

Table 11.1 *Tactical styles and psychological defences*

Tactical style	Defences (adaptive – maladaptive)
Permanently pressing	*Isolation* Stability – Inflexibility (realistic but not creative)
	Identification with the aggressor (Assertiveness – Aggressiveness)
Manoeuvring/attacking	*Repression* (Energetic – Conversion)
	Introjection of opposite sex (Immediate adaptiveness – Softness)
Manoeuvring/defending	*Introjection of opposite sex* (Immediate adaptiveness – Softness)
	Projection (Sensitivity – Suspiciousness)
Permanently defending	*Isolation* (Stability – Inflexibility)
	Reaction formation (Benign interpersonal relationships – Ambiguous relationships/inhibited aggression)

- How do these processes in fencers compare with those operating within elite performers in other sports, in particular individual performers in target sports?
- In terms of the individual's profile of psychological defences, how do the defences manifest both individually and interactively?

Procedure

The DMT was used to identify subconscious defence mechanisms operating in a group of 36 elite sports people, comprising 16 fencers and 20 elite competitors in target sports, including field archers, rifle and pistol shooters. Eight of the fencers and all of the shooters and archers competed at national or international level. The remaining fencers performed at regional level.

All subjects were volunteers and were administered the DMT by the author at some time during the period between January 1993 and February 1995. All test protocols (drawings and verbal reports) were scored and interpreted by the author, and a sample of eight were further cross checked by experienced DMT users for the purposes of reliability of scoring.

The occurrence of the ten main signs of defence and their variants was recorded from each of the test protocols for all 36 subjects and this information was collated for further analysis.

As well as this psychometric data, further information collected from each subject included age, details of the subject's experience in his or her sport and information as to what each subject considered to have been their two 'most satisfying' competitive performances. Based on this information each subject was also classified on a four-point scale regarding their performance level within their sport, i.e. international, national, regional and club level.

Defences in fencers

Within the group of sixteen fencers signs of all ten psychological defence mechanisms, as identified by the DMT, were recorded by at least one subject. The number of fencers showing each sign and its variants appears in Table 11.2. Sign variants of Isolation and

Table 11.2 *Numbers of fencers with sign-variants for ten defence mechanisms as identified by the DMT (Kragh, 1985)*

Defence mechanism	Numbers of sign-variants								
	0	1	2	3	4	5	6	6+	Totals
Repression	1	5	3	4	2	1			15
Isolation	0	0	2	2	3	4	2	3	16
Denial	12	4							4
Reaction formation	9	1	6						7
Identification with the aggressor	13	3							3
Introaggression	4	6	5	1					12
Introjection of opposite sex	0	4	7	3	2				16
Polymorphous introjection	12	1	2	1					4
Projection	8	6	2						8
Regression	12	4							4

Introjection of the opposite sex were identified in all sixteen fencers and sign-variants of Repression in fifteen. Identification with the Aggressor was shown by three of the sixteen and Denial, Polymorphous introjection and Regression by four subjects each.

This representation in all or the majority of fencers of Isolation, Repression and Introjection with their hypothesized behavioural manifestations of stability, energy and adaptability would seem particularly useful for athletes in an open skilled sport such as fencing. It is also interesting to note that these findings are in line with those of Apitzsch and Berggren (1993) that the group of footballers in their study categorized as more successful showed significantly higher scores for particular variants of Repression and Introjection of the opposite sex in their DMT protocols.

Fencing and Target Sports

Comparisons between the occurrence of signs of defence in fencers and target sportsmen revealed a number of significant differences between the two groups. Amongst the shooters and archers only nine of the ten major signs were indicated. Identification with the Aggressor was not revealed by any of the test protocols. As with the fencers, all subjects showed Isolation in their protocols and eighteen out of twenty showed Introjection of the opposite sex.

Seventeen of the group of twenty target sportsmen and women showed Reaction formation in their profiles. This is a significantly higher level of occurrence than amongst the fencers, only seven of whom had this defence identified in their profiles.

Statistically significant differences in frequencies were found between the two subject groups for a total of five defences, Repression, Reaction formation, Identification with the Aggressor, Projection and Regression (see Table 11.3). Further comparisons between the two groups of subjects were made using principal component modelling (PC modelling), a methodology originally suggested by Armelius and Sundbom (1991) as a way of constructing a soft model of personality organization (PO).

Principal component analysis was carried out on a set of ten variables for each of the thirty-six subjects. These variables comprised the individual scores for the occurrence of different variants for each sign of defence. For example, if a subject indicated the presence of four variants of Repression in their protocol they were given a score of four for Repression.

Table 11.3   *Occurrence of ten main signs of defence mechanisms in fencers (n = 16) and shooters and archers (n = 20)*

Defence mechanism	No. of fencers with sign (*n* = 16)	No. of shooters and archers with sign (*n* = 20)[a]
Repression	15	9*
Isolation	16	20
Denial	4	4
Reaction formation	7	17*
Identification with the aggressor	3	0*
Introaggression	12	13
Introjection of opposite sex	16	18
Polymorphous introjection	13	15
Projection	8	4*
Regression	4	1*

[a]Frequencies statistically different from those of fencers are indicated with an asterisk.

Principal component analysis yielded a set of principal components, the first three of which accounted for 53 per cent of the total variance. Examination of the coefficients for the first two PCs revealed that the highest loadings on PC1 were for the defences of Polymorphous introjection and Reaction formation and on PC2 for Repression and Introjection of the opposite sex (Figure 11.1). Plotting of individual scores against the XY axes of PC1 and PC2 revealed a general tendency for fencers to be discriminated from shooters and archers by their score on these four variables, fencers scoring higher on PC2 (Repression and Introjection of the opposite sex) and target sportsmen on PC1 (Polymorphous introjection and Reaction formation) (Figure 11.2).

A further finding revealed by these data is that in comparison with the shooters and archers, the fencers show much wider variation in their personalities as measured by their profiles of defences. Whereas the shooters and archers tend to cluster together, the fencers represent a much more disparate group with much greater variation in personality as measured by the presence and nature of defences.

Various reasons could be hypothesized for this, one being the difference between the two groups in terms of their level of performance and achievement, and another alternative being the reflection of very real intersport differences. In a study of hockey players Williams and

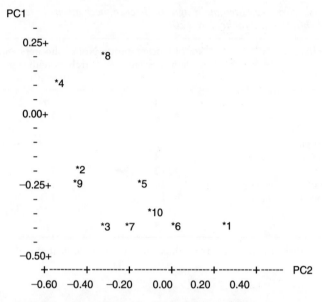

1 = Repression, 2 = Isolation, 3 = Denial, 4 = Reaction formation,
5 = Identification with the aggressor, 6 = Introaggression,
7 = Introjection of the opposite sex, 8 = Polymorphous introjection,
9 = Projection, 10 = Regression.

Figure 11.1   *Defence mechanisms plotted against first two PCs of Principal Component analysis of scores for each defensive sign*

Parkin (1980) compared personality profiles between different levels of players. Results indicated the international level hockey players exhibited personality profiles that differed from those of club level players but not national level players. In explanation of this phenomena Silva (1984) suggested that as the prospective elite athlete moves up through the levels of the sport, athletes become more similar in their personalities and psychological traits through a process of 'natural selection', certain personality traits predisposing the athlete or player to be able to ascend the next rung of the ladder. He goes on to suggest that this artefact of sampling may be responsible for some of the lack of success for this type of research. In the case of this current study it might well be that the discrepancy between the levels of ability and achievement between the two groups could be the cause of the intergroup differences.

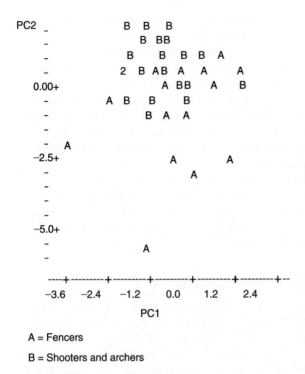

A = Fencers

B = Shooters and archers

Figure 11.2 *Subjects plotted against first two PCs of Principal Component analysis of scores for each defensive sign*

The alternative explanation that the discrepancy may reflect real differences between the personalities of athletes in different types of sport is, however, equally tenable. Classic work by Schurr *et al.* (1977) clearly demonstrated differences between the personality profiles of participants in team and individual sports and between direct and parallel sports, which fencing and target sports respectively represent. In the study of Schurr *et al.* (1977) direct sport athletes were observed to be more independent and to have lower ego strength than parallel sport athletes. In the study report here, which deals with unconscious processes rather than those traditionally measured by self report or questionnaire methods, it is difficult to assess whether or not the findings of Schurr *et al.* (1977) would be supported as there are no direct equivalents in the DMT to the measures which they report.

Another factor to be taken into consideration is the common-sense view that there will be very little variation in the way that one executes a perfect shot in shooting, whereas the perfect hit in fencing may materialize in a myriad of different ways.

So far there have been few empirical studies which have explicitly investigated the specific personality profiles of fencers. An exception to this is a study of female fencers carried out by Williams *et al.* (1970). Utilizing the Cattell 16PF and the Edwards Personal Preference Schedule, Williams *et al.* (1970) demonstrated female fencers to be very reserved, self-sufficient, aggressive, dominant and independent, with a below average desire for affiliation and nurturance. They also showed a need to be the very best, and to be intelligent, creative, experimenting and imaginative. However, such characteristics do not seem to be entirely specific to athletes in fencing; almost identical results were also revealed in the personalities of female college ice hockey players and champion female race car drivers (Bird, 1968; Tutko, 1978).

Patterns of individual response amongst fencers

Information additional to that provided by the DMT was available for only one subject in the study. This is the fencer whose first-hand feedback is presented in the Prologue of this chapter. In terms of level of performance, this fencer had been ranked nationally within the top eight on results from both domestic and international competition.

Protocols from this fencer's DMT demonstrated the presence of nine out of ten possible defence mechanisms; only that of Polymorphous introjection is absent. In relation to the number of defences found in other protocols this was the highest number of defences recorded from any of the 36 subjects in the study.

When examined in terms of the nature of the sign-variants represented, those of Repression, Isolation and Introjection of the opposite sex were predominant. According to Wojciechowski's (1993) classification of tactical styles this would suggest placing him in the attacking/manoeuvring category. A more detailed examination of the pieces of feedback quoted in the Prologue reveals some evidence in support of this suggested classification.

For example, in the first piece of feedback describing the fight which the fencer won the main emphasis is placed on attacking and manoeuvring in order to make particular premeditated attacking moves. Despite the winning performance, there is some evidence of maladaptive Repression, 'He almost makes you freeze over what you are going to do,' and indeed other examples of feedback from the same fencer, including the second piece quoted in the Prologue, refer to instances when the fencer either did not know what to do or described himself as being 'Frozen to the spot'.

Evidence of the immediate adaptability associated with Introjection of the opposite sex comes from the first piece of feedback where the fencer both plans an attack but is also adapting his moves to such aspects of his opponent as his size and reach. This is in line with Apitzsch and Berggren's (1993) hypothesized adaptive endpoint for this defence.

In the second piece of feedback quoted in the Prologue and which followed a losing fight, there is some suggestion that Denial might play a part when the fencer reports, 'I didn't think he was going to do it' (toe hit). 'If I'd really taken it seriously I'd have just gone on and hit him, but I didn't do that and it's really what cost me the fight.' There are hints here also of the self-blame associated with the maladaptive end of another sign of defence, Introaggression.

While it is recognized that there are inherent dangers in over-analysing and reading too much into isolated pieces of information such as the above, it is still interesting to use these more qualitative approaches in trying to gain more understanding of at least some of the processes which might be in operation at the conscious or subconscious level.

Apitzsch and Berggren (1993) have pointed out that these processes are complex in their interactions. Manifestations of a particular defence in an adaptive or maladaptive way are probably determined by several factors, not the least being the interaction with other defences.

The stress of competition is another factor which must be taken into account; however, the extent to which such pressure in any given situation will be perceived by the individual as anxiety provoking or negative will be determined not only by internal factors such as previous experiences and unconscious processes but also by external variables which will act systemically to modify and influence the individual's response.

The DMT offers an innovative approach in starting to tease out and understand these complex and powerful intrapersonal processes.

References

Armelius, B. and Sundom, E. (1991) Hard and soft models for the assessment of personality organisation by DMT. In *Quantification of Human Defence Mechanisms* (M. Olff, G. Godaert and H. Ursin, eds). London: Springer-Verlag.

Apitzsch, E. and Berggren, B. (1993) *The Personality of the Elite Soccer Player*. Sweden: Lund University.

Baade, E., Halse, K., Stenhammer, P.E., Ellertsen, B., Johnsen, T.B., Vollmer, F. and Ursin, H. (1978) In *Psychobiology of Stress: A Study of Coping Men* (H. Ursin, E. Baade and S. Levine, eds) pp. 125–160. London: Academic Press.

Bird, E.I. (1968) Personality structure of Canadian inter-collegiate ice hockey players. In *Contemporary Psychology of Sport: Proceedings of the Second International Congress of Sport Psychology* (G. Kenyon, ed.). Washington, D.C.: International Society of Sports Psychology.

Cooper, C. and Kline, P. (1986) An evaluation of the Defence Mechanisms Test. *British Journal of Psychology*, 77, 19–31.

Cramer, P. (1991) *The Development of Defense Mechanisms: Theory, Research and Assessment*. London: Springer-Verlag.

Fenichel, O. (1945) *The Psychoanalytic Theory of Neurosis*. London: Routledge and Kegan Paul.

Freud, A. (1937/1946) *The Ego and the Mechanisms of Defence*. Hogarth Press and the Institute of Psycho-analysis.

Freud, S. (1894) *The Neuro-psychoses of Defence*. Standard Edition, Vol. 3, pp. 45–61. London: Hogarth Press.

Freud, S. (1923) *The Ego and the Id*. Standard Edition, Vol. 19, pp. 12–66. London: Hogarth Press.

Jones, G.J. and Hardy, L. (eds) (1990) *Stress and Performance in Sport* pp. 281–296. Chichester: Wiley.

Kline, P. (1984) *Psychology and Freudian Theory: An Introduction*. London: Routledge.

Kline, P. (1987) The scientific status of the DMT. *British Journal of Medical Psychology*, 60, 53–59.

Kline, P. (1991) The relationship between objective measures of defences. In *Quantification of Human Defence Mechanisms* (M. Olff, G. Godaert and H. Ursin, eds). Berlin: Springer-Verlag.

Kline, P. (1993) *Personality: The Psychometric View*. London: Routledge.

Kragh, U. (1969) *Manual till DMT. Defence Mechanisms Test*. Stockholm: Skandinaviska Testforlaget.

Kragh, U. (1991) Notes on the development of the DMT. In *Quantification of Human Defence Mechanisms* (M. Olff, G. Godaert and H. Ursin, eds). London: Springer-Verlag.

Kragh, U. (1985) *Defence Mechanisms Test. DMT Manual*. Stockholm: Persona.

Kragh, U. and Smith, G.J.W. (eds) (1970) *Perceptgenetic Analysis*. Lund: CWK Gleerup.

Neuman, T. (1978) Dimensionering och validering av percept-genesens forsvarsmekanismer. En hierarkisk analys mot pilotens stressbeteende. *FOA rapport C 55020–H6*. Stockholm: Forsvarets forskningsanstalt.

Olff, M., Godaert, G. and Ursin, H. (eds) (1991) *Quantification of Human Defence Mechanisms*. London: Springer-Verlag.

Pitman, B. (1988) *Fencing: Techniques of Foil, Epee and Sabre*. Swindon: Crowood Press.

Rubino, A., Pezzarossa, B. and Grasso, S. (1991) DMT defences in neurotic and somatically ill patients. In *Quantification of Human Defence Mechanisms* (M. Olff, G. Godaert and H. Ursin, eds). London: Springer-Verlag.

Schurr, K.T., Ashley, M.A. and Joy, K.L. (1977) A multivariate analysis of male athletic characteristics: sport type and success. *Multivariate Experimental Clinical Research*, **3**, 53–68.

Silva III, J.M. (1984) Personality and Sport Performance: Controversy and Challenge. In *Psychological Foundations of Sport* (J.M. Silva III and R. Weinberg, eds). Champaign, IL: Human Kinetics.

Sjoback, H. (1991) Defence, defence, defence: How do we measure defence? In *Quantification of Human Defence Mechanisms* (M. Olff, G. Godaert and H. Ursin, eds). Berlin: Springer-Verlag.

Svensson, B. and Trygg, L. (1994) *Personlighet, olycksbenagenhet i trafiken och yrkesanpassning. Tre perceptgenetiska studier (Personality, accident-proneness in traffic and professional adaptation. Three percept-genetic studies)*. Stockholm: Alqvist and Wiksell International.

Turecki, B. (1985) *Duel of Fencers*. Referred to in *Theory, Methods and Exercises in Fencing* (Z. Wojciechowski, ed.) (1993). London: Amateur Fencing Association.

Tutko, P. (1978) Personal communication in Williams J., Personality characteristics of the successful female athlete. In *Sport Psychology: An Analysis of Athlete Behaviour* (W. Straub, ed.). Mouvement, Syracuse.

Ursin, H., Baade, E. and Levine, S. (1978) *Psychobiology of Stress: A Study of Coping Men*. New York: Academic Press.

Vaernes, R.J. (1982) Three DMT predicts inadequate performance under stress. *Scandinavian Journal of Psychology*, **23**, 37–43.

Vaernes, R.J., Warncke, M., Myhre, G. and Aakvaag, A. (1988) Stress and performance during simulated flight in a F-16 simulator. *Proceedings of the NATO Advisory Group for Aerospace Research and Development (AGARD)*, **11**, 1–9.

Williams, L.R.T. and Parkin, W.A. (1980) Personality profiles of three hockey groups. *International Journal of Sport Psychology*, **11**, 113–120.

Williams, J.M., Hoepner, B.J., Moody, D.L. and Ogilvie, B.C. (1970) Personality traits of champion level female fencers. *Research Quarterly*, **41**, 446–453.

Wojciechowski, Z. (1993) *Theory, Methods and Exercises in Fencing*. London: Amateur Fencing Association.

12
Measure, analyse and stagnate: towards a radical psychology of sport

Denis Salter

Introduction

This chapter was born out of a number of conversations with athletes, coaches, managers, and other psychologists. Some of the conversations occurred in academic settings while others happened late into the night at training camps or on long journeys to competitions. Time and time again I felt I had occasional glimpses of the magnitude and complexity of the psychological basis to the behaviour we know as sport. However, these glimpses left me feeling uncomfortable. What I was reading in the journals did not come close to capturing what I was being asked to work with as a psychologist.

The following is an attempt to illuminate some of what I feel is wrong with mainstream sports psychology in the UK. It is unashamedly conceptual in its outlook and offers no easy solutions. Instead I wish to illuminate issues for each practising sport psychologist to attempt to solve in a manner appropriate to the context within which they operate.

I would urge the reader to persevere as I fear that left unrectified British sports psychology is on the point of entering a conceptual and methodological cul-de-sac. I fear that as the position reveals itself the majority of British sports psychologists are adopting a naive realist position with regard to their work. Instead of questioning the unique demands of the sporting context, the profession appears to be content to ride on the coat tails of main-stream empirical psychology. Here, rather than innovate, sport psychologists appear to be content to fulfil their scholarly obligations by referencing the model of the physics laboratory and not the complexity of the world of sport. Indeed I fear that, left unrectified, sports psychology will conceptually stagnate in the very near future.

Instead of polarizing techniques with cognitive-behaviourism at one end and the psychodynamic at the other there is a pressing need to reconceptualize the basis to sports psychology. Neither approach captures the needs of the sporting context. There is a need to move away from the false certainty of 'hard data' and towards an approach that allows us to capture and work with the difficult to articulate, yet essential, aspects of sporting performance.

For the rest of this chapter I wish to closely examine the project that the majority of sport psychologists have embarked upon; I wish to argue that it is flawed and then to suggest that there is an alternative. Consequently I should like to describe what I consider to be the fundamental problems facing sport psychologists as we move towards the next millennium. My concerns embrace the concepts, methods and approach of sports psychology. In order to embrace such a wide ranging area and increase the applicability of my arguments I have pitched this discussion at a conceptual and reflective level. In the following discussions I sometimes adopt an urgent tone so as to inject appropriate passion into the interpretative principles I describe.

I have attempted to use language which is as plain as possible and have used a minimum of psychological terms that are not generally familiar. Literary references are absent from this chapter as I do not wish to urge readers to read more, but rather to look inward and examine their practice as sport psychologists. More importantly I have eschewed the convention of trying to prove my assertions by citing experiments, statistics and quotations from other authors. By breaking with tradition in not trying to prove myself right I have hoped to stimulate the reader by presenting my reflections with myself, colleagues and athletes.

Illuminating our conceptual blind spots

In order to illuminate our subject area we need to gain a new perspective. One means of seeing things differently is to create a metaphor. The process of metaphoric construction is central to all sense making processes. Essentially the use of metaphor entails placing a familiar and understood web of meaning over an unfamiliar entity in order to render it understandable. This in turn requires us to make an 'as if' statement. In order to render a situation understandable we pretend that the unfamiliar has the properties of the familiar.

In this case a computer in the form of a common or garden PC comes to mind. I am sure there might be others more suitable but this will do. Assume for a moment that this PC is ambulatory and surprise, surprise, it shows 'promise' such that there is the suggestion that with careful guidance it might just become an elite PC. Who knows, it might even be seen to posses something 'special' such that it might eventually represent other models from the same manufacturer in international competitions and become a super-computer. Let's leave the metaphor there a while and consider how we as psychologists might make sense of the PC's performance.

There are essentially three positions. The first concerns discussions of PC's hardware, the physical structures that make up PC. The second concerns PC's software, the internal intangibles that somehow governs what PC does. The third position, and this is often missed by those of a narrowly scientific disposition, is that of the interpreter of the performance. Obviously the first position can be recognized as roughly corresponding to that of physiology and psychobiology. Any extremes of performance are reduced to variations in the hardware. Position two corresponds to the concerns of social learning theory and cognitive psychology. Again any extremes of performance are considered to be explicable and understandable in terms of the software. The major thrust of sports psychology corresponds to either position one or two. In other words behaviour is considered to become intelligible if you have the correct data and know how to interpret them efficiently. However, by ignoring our role as interpreters we risk being left with a very partial analysis of PC's and any other performance. By endorsing the approach of narrowly defined science and the reductionism of positions one and two we miss important aspects of 'real' performance.

Approaches that eliminate threats to the scientific status of their conclusions must necessarily sacrifice a sense of 'real worldliness'. Indeed it is the hallmarks of scientific respectability (randomization, homogeneous samples, 'pure', manualized treatments and extensive measurement procedures) that, paradoxically, limit the applicability of the narrowly scientific approach to the sporting context. For example, randomization is held to be the best protection against systematic pre-treatment differences. However, athletes and psychologists are not randomly allocated to each other. Athletes more often than not seek out particular psychologists with particular reputations and approaches. Similarly, heterogeneity in the groups of athletes we investigate is perceived as a threat to the scientific status of sports psychology research. As a result stringent selection criteria are applied to subject populations in order to ensure that the subjects share some criteria of interest to the psychologist. In so doing the more authentic athletes with complex or multiple needs are excluded from evaluations.

Quite understandably for a profession trying to make its way in the world by establishing its scientific credentials, there is a preference in much sports psychology research for sacrificing external or ecological validity. In contrast, rather than attempt to generate table thumping assertions of ultimate truths, psychological research in the sporting setting should encourage an attitude of tentativeness and a respect for evidence.

The requirements of a radical psychology of sport

In order to develop a means of capturing aspects of 'realism' we need to consider the unique demands of the sporting context. Let us start by considering what is going on in the world of sport. The context in which we practise has tremendous implications for the way in which we work. Traditional sport psychologists appear to pay only passing attention to the influence of extra-individual variables. Here I am not just concerned with the intra-individual variables of social psychology, though these receive little enough attention at present. I am more concerned with the socio-political context in which sport occurs. I suspect that this may raise a few concerns amongst the more traditional psychologists as they appear to see themselves and their work being value free.

Perhaps I can best illustrate my concerns by relating a vignette from my own practice as a sport psychologist. For several years I have attempted to apply my psychological knowledge to the area of human behaviour known as sport. I worked at first with individual athletes and latterly with teams. However, it was my work with a female track athlete of some note that caused me to have major doubts about my role as a psychologist in sport.

The athlete in question had represented her country at an international level for several seasons and now was finding that she was unable to perform as well as she had in the past. She was injury free, the sport physiologists had done their stuff and could find no abnormalities, homage had been paid to deity known as Vo2 max and she had not been considered lacking. Similarly, high altitude training had done nothing to improve her performance. In short, she was stuck. As a last resort her coach referred her to me.

What I found was a bright young woman with an enviable combination of charm, intellect and ability. She had postponed her marriage to attend an Olympic games, taken a less demanding degree subject than she wished to study so that she could train and now plainly did not want to run any more. To this day I believe that this analysis did not require tremendous insights nor the eight years of training to allow me to be accredited. However, for me the application of psychology started when I gave the mobile phone clutching manager and coach my impressions. My streetwise friends tell me that the appropriate phrase to describe the extremely disturbed behaviour I observed is something to the effect of 'going ballistic'. It transpired that the athlete in question had several endorsement contracts with major sports goods manufacturers together with a full diary of promotions to attend for the coming year. Hanging up her shoes did not figure in *their* plans.

What transpired next could fill several volumes. Suffice it to say that both I and the athlete experienced the following in greater or lesser amounts: bewilderment, anxiety, depression, hostility, anger, aggression, hopelessness, role conflict and, to a certain extent, resolution. Indeed, I was sufficiently moved by my experiences in this context to question my continuation in the world of sports psychology.

Nevertheless, being what I considered to be a good psychologist, I persevered and attempted to make sense of my experiences. My experiences with this client forced me to broaden my horizons and widen my definition of what was relevant to the sporting setting. Through broadening the conceptual horizon we have to take seriously, and bring into the frame of sports psychology, the fact that sporting behaviour does not exist in a vacuum. As a result we need to make sense of the connectedness that sport provides within some of the oldest human concerns and interests.

This connectedness was illustrated by a further case. This concerned a track athlete who found that his performance deteriorated catastrophically whenever he had to run in particular stadia. As it transpired, this individual found it difficult to express himself verbally. His fear was a mystery to himself, he could not formulate his thoughts and feelings into words. However, he thought that the performance deficit was something to do with an awareness that he was being scrutinized by an unimaginable number of individuals, all of whom would find his behaviour lacking no matter what his performance was like in 'objective' terms. Beyond this he was stuck. In this case I feel that my traditional skills had little to offer in the way of go getting action interventions that seem to be filling the journals. I felt I functioned as a modern day translator, translating and interpreting his behaviour.

In adopting this mode we have to be creative in allowing our principal focus, the self awareness of the self aware subject, to be articulated. While this is a daunting task, this approach has had a long and distinguished history in both sociology and anthropology. Put most baldly, this approach asserts that human beings actively create their personal meanings and realities. Following from this, and again put very plainly, the goal of our interventions as psychologists is to facilitate the construction of new meanings. In other words, the individual is encouraged to reconstruct the meaning of affective experience by developing language that captures that which is experienced.

The need to recognize the importance of language

As you might imagine, this approach brings new complexities to the work of the sport psychologist. It places personal experience centre stage. In attempting to deal with personal experience we have to pay more attention to language, spoken and otherwise. The emphasis on the construction and development of increasingly more viable cognitive representations illuminates not only the central position of language, but also the process of metaphoric construction as the cornerstone of psychological development. Here language encompasses speech, pauses, body language, sub-vocalizations and the like. All of these, and in particular body language in the form of athletic behaviour, become part of the transcript where it is considered to be interactionally consequential. The recognition of the importance of language alerts us to the value-laden nature of our work and, more importantly, the strong politic of our involvement.

The political nature of the psychology of sport

Formalized, professional psychology is becoming increasingly deeply embedded in our culture. Witness the explosion of interest in counselling and the wave of psychological pundits ready to comment on all aspects of sporting life. Psychology, especially sports psychology, is not politically neutral. By adopting the mantle scientific respectability, sports psychology feigns political neutrality. However, nothing can be further from the case.

Sports psychology is deeply political. There is a politic shaping our ideas of what counts as normal and what is considered to be healthy functioning. In fact the very models we use ooze their political ancestry. It takes the likes of Foucault to point out that which appears neutral and part of the taken for granted assumptive framework is, in actuality, a culturally defined practice which had an origin at a point in time, and more importantly continues to exist through either explicit or implicit complicity.

Moreover, my presence as a 'psychologist' in any given situation, regardless of my intentions, regardless of what I say, almost regardless of whether I open my mouth or not, is political. My involvement launches me into a system of political relationships and relatedness. The politics exist at both micro and macro levels. The politics extend from the conspicuous task and role of the particular situation to connect me with roles in other political systems.

The reason I highlight the political dimension is the very fact that it is central to our work and yet ignored. The degree to which it is ignored perplexes me. This realization is not a startling new discovery; rather I feel it directs our attention to that which we neglect. I would go as far as to argue that it is the political and the moral level that we need to concern ourselves with most as we consider the future development of sports psychology.

The influence of the professionalization and commercialization of sport

Hand in hand with the rise of sports psychology has been increasing professionalization and commercialization of sport. The twin tendencies to professionalize and commercialize sport have resulted in a complex set of dynamics where the sport psychologist has a curious role. I would suggest that by encouraging an unswerving adherence to the empirical model, main-stream sports psychology has encouraged a myth. In its strongest form the myth is that the psychologist has direct access to athletes' mental processes. The myth of psychologist as expert, somehow knowing more about the athlete than they know themselves, is clearly ridiculous.

I would suggest that it is only the subject, the athlete, who can authenticate the data and so be the 'expert'. Is it the case that sports psychology is attempting to build and maintain what used to be called a good trade union differential. Are we seeking to deliberately mystify and obscure our work? Are we scared of being de-technologized and laid bare? At its most basic is sports psychology only really about care, comfort and clarification?

The costs of professionalizing and commercializing sport has meant marketing sport with an intensity that has never been seen before. The relentless marketing of sport has meant an awful lot of compromises. It has involved changing sport to pander to the needs of those paying the bills. This in turn has lead to a coarsening of the sport in order to describe it in a more user-friendly manner to the serried ranks of viewers.

Compromising the subtlety of the sport amounts to a form of playing to the gallery. This requires the formation of the all too common media stereotypes of the ultimate winner and ultimate loser, playing up nationalism and chauvinism, good guys and bad guys, heroes and villains. It means getting your face, or more accurately your sponsors logo, in the media. It means earning yourself, your sponsor and your athlete more money. The increasingly ferocious marketing of sport has polarized opinion such that extremes of praise and crushing blame are the norm. In sum, the increasing tendency to professionalize, commercialize and market sport has a direct impact on sports psychology.

More clearly than ever before, the delivery of sports psychology is political and commercially charged. In this cauldron the concept of a value-free sports psychology is more of a dream than it ever has been. Closer to home, the question of who we as sport psychologists are working for comes into sharp focus. We can no longer rely solely on our professional codes of conduct to guide us through the minefield of marketed sport. We need to face up to the fact that we never have been and never will be politically neutral. While at first it might be uncomfortable to recognize the political influences in sport I would argue that by admitting they exist we might allow them to find their rightful place and so, paradoxically, allow us to move on as a profession.

Why adopt a new approach?

So, what are the advantages of paying attention to the issues that I have illuminated so far? Adopting this approach draws our attention to the factors which directly impinge on the world of sport but do not fit nicely within the confines of science. By depicting the subject matter of sports psychology in broader terms than the limited criteria of experimental psychology we can move beyond some of the limitations of the current conceptual order and expand the conceptual repertoire of sports psychology. By altering our perspective and the terms which we bring to understanding our subject matter, we can alter our construction of it. This, in turn, allows ourselves, our colleagues and, above all, our clients to see things as they have not been seen before.

Through an attempt to examine these issues we are immediately aware that just about all of our models contain values and assumptions. These assumptions are generally so deeply embedded in the history of professional psychology that they are considered to be constants, the proverbial conceptual wallpaper. More importantly, this draws our attention to the way that these assumptions not only determine our approach but also our conception of self as a psychologist. Here, in examining our assumptive framework, we need to consider our values and beliefs as psychologists.

The integration of beliefs and meanings into our work might appear 'new' to the traditional sport psychologist, though this approach has an extensive lineage. The approach is usually described as the qualitative approach to understanding. In this paradigm theory is inductively derived from the phenomenon it represents. This is in contrast to the positivistic theories where one begins with a theory and proves it. Rather data collection, analysis and theory stand in a reciprocal relationship with each other. One begins with an area of study and what is relevant to that area is allowed to emerge only to be provisionally verified. In adopting this approach we become more concerned with the viability (the flexibility, generalizability, resilience and so on) rather than the empirical or rational validity of our explanations.

The concern with viability would require us to use non-mathematical forms of analysis. This would allow us to step back and critically analyse situations in order to recognize and communicate bias. This route to obtaining valid and reliable data requires a balance to be struck between theoretical and social sensitivities. Through striking this particular balance we would strive to remain at an analytical distance while at the same time drawing on past experience and theoretical knowledge. Following from this are a range of issues relating to what constitutes the data, the analytic and interpretative procedures, and the means of communicating results.

Data can come from a variety of sources, though this approach would probably include data which the empirically grounded approaches would reject as unimportant or unanalysable. The goal would be to collect pertinent data that would allow the informants to speak. That is, rather than collect data that fits a particular model, the aim would be to collect data in a spontaneous and meaningful way. While this form of data may not reflect the 'truth', the data would be generated via a concern with accurate description. This is not to say that reduction and ordering would not be occurring. Instead the process of selection and interpretation are meant to give a sense of what the observed world is really like. The researchers' interpretations are meant to represent a more detailed conceptualization of that reality. A direct implication of adopting this approach is the way certain common psychological terms take on a whole new set of connotations.

The importance of considering the reflexive nature of our work

Central to any research and intervention in this mode is the notion of reflexivity. This concept is central to all psychological theorizing and yet is largely ignored. Essentially the concept of reflexivity revolves around a recognition that the agency producing the account of the phenomena under investigation is not different from the agency producing the behaviour. That is, we as human beings share the same characteristics as those we study and seek to help. As a result we cannot accept the position where we claim a privileged perspective. We do not have the scientific equivalent of X-ray vision. We need to account for the biasing effects of attempting to gain the leverage and conceptual distance necessary to formulate our interventions. We do not just stumble across the data like finding a five pound note in the street. We actively create the data underpinning our formulations and as a result we need to ensure that our account takes account of, and makes explicit, the biases that are generated from our process of construction.

How would this approach be judged or evaluated?

Psychological interventions within this framework would require a new framework with which to evaluate their impact. This is not to say that this process is not scientific; rather, carefully designed interventions would, paradoxically, meet all the criteria for doing good science. That is the criteria of significance, compatibility between theory and observation, generalizability, reproducibility, precision, rigour and verification would be met. The important issue here is that interventions in this mode would require us to reconceptualize the criteria for acceptability as defined in the narrow positivistic fashion of experimental physical science.

Our interventions would need to be judged by means of the criterion of fit, understanding, generality and control in the inter-relationship between the theoretical base and the phenomenon under investigation. In other words, if the theory is well grounded and the intervention well done, the substantive area and the focus of the intervention should fit each other. We should not have to rely on the psychological equivalent of 'magic'. Similarly the formulation under-pinning the intervention should make sense to the psychologist and the athlete. By meeting these criteria the conceptualization of the intervention should provide a degree of control and direction with regard to the mode of action relating to the phenomenon under investigation. We should be able to predict in advance what is going to happen and provide a means of accounting for what we observe.

When I adopt the approach I have outlined so far and attempt to apply it to factors such as motivation, I more often than not find myself exploring issues in unfamiliar terms. Rather than restricting myself to exploring motivation in terms of factors such as reinforcement, equilibration or the conservation of psychic energy, I find my clients relating their experiences in terms such as 'the human spirit' or as a search for immortality. These factors appear worthy of exploration in their own right rather than be squeezed into the framework of science. An example of this phenomenon is provided first by considering the human spirit and then athletic behaviour as a means of maintaining immortality.

The need to explicitly recognize the human spirit

Any sport psychologist worthy of the name would be foolish to ignore the human spirit. There is a pressing need to remedy the excesses of the more positivistically based therapies with an awareness of the spiritual. There can be no doubt that it illuminates aspects of existence that would otherwise be seen as 'error variance' or the like. In considering the spiritual dimension I am not suggesting that we adopt a theological approach. The spiritual dimension relates to the powerful forces that connect our sense of self to our motivated behaviour. This factor has been largely ignored as it does not fit within the empirical framework. Indeed, I am struck by the fact that how, through simply pursuing fundamental questions relating to their sporting behaviour, I naturally gravitate towards examining the issues which athletes raise in terms of the human spirit. We can probably all report comments such as 'having the spirit knocked out of you in defeat', or how 'spirits' were lifted when you did well or excelled. The approach that I have outlined above makes factors such as the human spirit central to our work as sport psychologists.

The sport psychologist as a purveyor of immortality

Through being aware of the necessity of connecting psychological theory with a historical focus, I strive to help athletes understand their difficulties by examining the relationship of their personal beliefs or, more accurately, myths to their behaviour. In my experience myths have tremendous significance in the world of sport. As far as I can make out the function of these myths is to symbolize the relationship between individual actions and the larger enterprise. In this context, sporting performance has a direct psychic function. For the athlete the sporting performance provides a form of experiential transcendence. This is often so intense that the athlete is at once connected to the rest of humanity and at the same time alone and vulnerable swirling in what some writers have described as an oceanic feeling. This particular aspect of sporting performance appears to be central to athletes' motivation to compete.

While competing, athletes often report the feeling of timelessness and transcendence of the individual and yet an awareness of the impermanence of the experience. The impermanence manifests as questions such as whether the athlete can out-perform others, and for how long on how many occasions. Added to the intra-psychic doubts, the rapidly accelerating mass media revolution in sport has provided fertile soil for the athletes' awareness of impermanence to become manifest.

Thus one can conceptualize much of an athlete's career as attempts to either recapture or generate this sense of stability or immortality that accompanies elite performance. One can see just how much of the athlete's history can be understood as the struggle to achieve, maintain and reaffirm the striving for a sense of immortality under constantly changing psychological and physical conditions. By exploring the issues in these terms I feel I was able to work with the complexity of the athletes' experience rather than reducing it to fragmentary quanta of cognition or behaviour.

A conclusion and some thoughts on where to go next

This chapter has attempted to raise a number of issues relating to the conceptual and methodological status of British sports psychology. Sports psychology is a new discipline trying to emerge in a context with a number of competing influences. By seeking to establish its scientific credentials through religiously adhering to the axioms of empirical psychology, the emerging discipline is at risk of ignoring the most important aspects of our subject matter. While these concerns are not unique to the sporting context, I fear that sport has particular demands and we risk conceptual stagnation if we ignore them. I have attempted to highlight some of the issues relating to the current situation and the concerns of what I have called a radical psychology of sport. Unfortunately there are no 'off the shelf techniques' nor pat solutions; rather I would urge readers to consider their work afresh.

Perhaps I should close by urging readers not to become complacent but to augment the empirical approaches with some radical ideas. In my own work, number and statistics have their place alongside myth, belief and meaning.

Index